Grief in Contemporary Horror Cinema

LEXINGTON BOOKS HORROR STUDIES

Series Editors:

Lorna Piatti-Farnell, Auckland University of Technology

Carl Sederholm, Brigham Young University

Lexington Books Horror Studies is looking for original and interdisciplinary monographs or edited volumes that expand our understanding of horror as an important cultural phenomenon. We are particularly interested in critical approaches to horror that explore why horror is such a common part of culture, why it resonates with audiences so much, and what its popularity reveals about human cultures generally. To that end, the series will cover a wide range of periods, movements, and cultures that are pertinent to horror studies. We will gladly consider work on individual key figures (e.g. directors, authors, show runners, etc.), but the larger aim is to publish work that engages with the place of horror within cultures. Given this broad scope, we are interested in work that addresses a wide range of media, including film, literature, television, comics, pulp magazines, video games, or music. We are also interested in work that engages with the history of horror, including the history of horror-related scholarship.

Titles in the Series

Grief in Contemporary Horror Cinema: Screening Loss, edited by Erica Joan Dymond

Supranational Horrors: Italian and Spanish Horror Cinema since 1968, by Rui Oliveira

The Anthropocene and the Undead: Cultural Anxieties in the Contemporary Popular Imagination, edited by Simon Bacon

Gothic Mash-Ups: Hybridity, Appropriation, and Intertextuality in Gothic Storytelling, edited by Natalie Neill

Japanese Horror: New Critical Approaches to History, Narratives, and Aesthetics, edited by Fernando Gabriel Pagnoni Berns, Subashish Bhattacharjee, and Ananya Saha

Violence in the Films of Stephen King, edited by Michael J. Blouin and Tony Magistrale

Dark Forces at Work: Essays on Social Dynamics and Cinematic Horrors, edited by Cynthia J. Miller and A. Bowdoin Van Riper

Grief in Contemporary Horror Cinema

Screening Loss

Edited by Erica Joan Dymond

LEXINGTON BOOKS
Lanham • Boulder • New York • London

Published by Lexington Books
An imprint of The Rowman & Littlefield Publishing Group, Inc.
4501 Forbes Boulevard, Suite 200, Lanham, Maryland 20706
www.rowman.com

86-90 Paul Street, London EC2A 4NE

Copyright © 2023 by The Rowman & Littlefield Publishing Group, Inc.

All rights reserved. No part of this book may be reproduced in any form or by any electronic or mechanical means, including information storage and retrieval systems, without written permission from the publisher, except by a reviewer who may quote passages in a review.

British Library Cataloguing in Publication Information Available

Library of Congress Cataloging-in-Publication Data

Names: Dymond, Erica Joan, editor.
Title: Grief in contemporary horror cinema : screening loss / edited by Erica Joan Dymond.
Description: Lanham : Lexington Books, [2023] | Series: Lexington books horror studies | Includes bibliographical references and index.
Identifiers: LCCN 2022036870 (print) | LCCN 2022036871 (ebook) | ISBN 9781793633934 (cloth) | 9781793633958 (pbk) | ISBN 9781793633941 (ebook)
Subjects: LCSH: Horror films—History and criticism. | Grief in motion pictures. | Bereavement in motion pictures.
Classification: LCC PN1995.9.H6 G75 2023 (print) | LCC PN1995.9.H6 (ebook) | DDC 791.43/6164—dc23/eng/20220912
LC record available at https://lccn.loc.gov/2022036870
LC ebook record available at https://lccn.loc.gov/2022036871

♾️ The paper used in this publication meets the minimum requirements of American National Standard for Information Sciences—Permanence of Paper for Printed Library Materials, ANSI/NISO Z39.48-1992.

Contents

List of Figures	vii
Acknowledgments	ix
Introduction: The Horror Is Living *Erica Joan Dymond*	xi

PART I: LOSS AND THE CHILD: GRIEF AND ENDANGERED YOUTH   1

Chapter 1: Horror at the Crossroads: Mapping the Child's Grief in *Pan's Labyrinth* (2006)   3
Lindsey Scott

Chapter 2: "We Can Survive This": An Examination of Loss and Grief in Juan Antonio Bayona's *El orfanato* (*The Orphanage*) (2007)   19
Erica Joan Dymond

Chapter 3: Elevating Grief: Ari Aster's *Hereditary* (2018) and the A24 Horror Film   49
Andrew Grossman and Todd K. Platts

PART II: LOSS AND GENDER: GRIEF AND MOTHERHOOD/WOMANHOOD   69

Chapter 4: To Make You Feel My Love: Jennifer Kent's *The Babadook* (2014), Motherhood, and Loss   71
Rebecca L. Willoughby

Chapter 5: The Myth of the Natural Woman: Horror and Grief in
Ari Aster's *Midsommar* (2019) 87
Aspen Taylor Ballas

PART III: LOSS AND NATIONAL IDENTITY: GRIEF AND HISTORY 105

Chapter 6: O Father, Where Art Thou?: Grief and Cannibal Culture in Jorge Michel Grau's *Somos lo que hay* (*We Are What We Are*) (2010) 107
Megan DeVirgilis

Chapter 7: Sadness Is Rebellion: The Ontopolitics of Queer Loss in *The Life and Death of a Porno Gang* (2009) 127
Andrija Filipović

Chapter 8: The Grieving Dead: Haunting and the Haunted in the Spierig Brothers' *Winchester* (2018) 145
Racheal Harris

PART IV: LOSS AND THE KNOWN WORLD: GRIEF AND ANNIHILATION 167

Chapter 9: "No One Will Miss It": Lars Von Trier's *Antichrist* (2009) and *Melancholia* (2011) and the World-Without-Us 169
Michael Brown

Index 197

About the Contributors 209

List of Figures

Figure 1.1: Ofelia meets a fairy in the woods. Ivana Baquero (as Ofelia). *El laberinto del fauno* (*Pan's Labyrinth*) (2006). Screen Capture.   9

Figure 2.1: "'S' is for Simón." Roger Príncep (as Simón). *El orfanato* (*The Orphanage*) (2007). Screen Capture.   24

Figure 2.2: Close-up of wedding rings. *El orfanato* (*The Orphanage*) (2007). Screen Capture.   33

Figure 4.1: Amelia shows Samuel a monster-free closet. Kent's framing illustrates Amelia's feelings of entrapment in the mother-son dyad as she appears hemmed in by blackness on either side, Samuel clutching her waist. Left: Noah Wiseman (as Samuel Vanek). Right: Essie Davis (as Amelia Vanek). *The Babadook* (2014). Screen Capture.   75

Figure 4.2: Amelia experiences the loss of her husband once more in an expressive close-up, revealing the depth of her grief. The full-front angle of the shot gives additional emphasis to the intensity of these repressed feelings now coming to the surface. Essie Davis (as Amelia Vanek). *The Babadook* (2014). Screen Capture.   82

Figure 5.1: Amidst a panic attack, Dani seeks refuge in an outhouse. Devoid of light and electricity, Dani strikes a match, revealing her own reflection in the mirror alongside a haunting apparition of her deceased sister over her right shoulder. Left front: Florence Pugh (as Dani). Right back: Klaudia Csányi (as Terri). *Midsommar* (2019). Screen Capture.   96

Figure 5.2: A procession unfolds to celebrate Dani (Florence Pugh), who has just been crowned the May Queen. In the background, a superimposed face of Dani's deceased sister (left, top corner), Terri, is faintly visible in the trees and bushes. Extending from Terri's mouth area and to the right are brown and light green leaves that are distinguishable from the rest of the forest, creating detail and depth that resembles the long tube that Terri used to siphon gas into her mask while carrying out her suicide. *Midsommar* (2019). Screen Capture.   101

Figure 8.1: Dr. Eric Price (Jason Clarke) with the keepsake bullet. *Winchester* (2018). Screen Capture.   156

Figure 9.1: "I'm trudging through a grey woolly yarn. It's clinging to my legs. It's really heavy to drag along." Kirsten Dunst (as Justine). *Melancholia* (2011). Screen Capture.   186

Figure 9.2: Peering over the horizon of extinction. Left: Cameron Spurr (as Leo). Center: Kirsten Dunst (as Justine). Right: Charlotte Gainsbourg (as Claire). *Melancholia* (2011). Screen Capture.   191

Acknowledgments

I would like to thank my parents, Eric D. Dymond and Joan A. Dymond, who rented me two films every Friday night from the time I was a child until rentals stop existing . . . and for watching them with me. The same applies to my brother, Jason B. Dymond, who has watched many an A24 film with me (even though he secretly doesn't like horror). I extend a thank-you to Roland M. Nguyen who watched the films in this book with me (even though he not-so-secretly doesn't like horror).

I offer my sincerest gratitude to Roday Y Rodar and Mediaset Spain who gifted me the cover photo to this book. I am profoundly, unspeakably humbled by this. A particular thank-you to both Joaquín Padró and Ghislain Barrois, who made all of this possible.

It should be noted that without the constant guidance of Lexington Books editor Judith Lakamper, none of this would be possible. Thank you, Judith, for your tremendous compassion, your remarkable diligence, and your endless patience.

Finally, I would like to thank Jan Selving for her early work on this book. You are a wonderful friend and colleague.

Introduction

The Horror Is Living

Erica Joan Dymond

> "Horror often resides in the psychological ravages of extreme sorrow."
>
> —Richard Armstrong

Globally, horror cinema has become more nuanced over the past twenty years. Once consumed in large gulps by teenage "boys," these films are now experienced in curated bites by mature adults. Jump scares have been replaced with atmospheric tension. Screaming violin strings have transformed into plaintive orchestral scores. And the encroaching threat of death has turned into the pain of living. In fact, much of this new wave of horror focuses on the aftermath of loss. In "Home Is Where the Horror Is," *The New York Times*' Jason Zinoman discusses this trend: "While horror has always reflected the social and political concerns of its day, if you had to pinpoint a unifying theme that distinguishes this renaissance, it's the ominous danger of overwhelming grief" (2018). From indie to mainstream, the concept of loss has moved to the fore of horror.

Indie and art films like Robert Eggers' *The Witch* (2016), Trey Edward Shults' *It Comes at Night* (2017), and Yorgos Lanthimos' *The Killing of a Sacred Deer* (2017) present as genre-straddling juggernauts. An amalgamation of horror, psychological thriller, and drama, these pieces demand a great deal from their audience, pulling them through profound grief. They engage viewers as much on an emotional level as they do a visceral one. Now, it may seem that spectators would prefer to avoid such emotionally exhausting works; however, many find these films as a legitimate source of catharsis.

As a child, *The New Yorker* contributor Eren Orbey lost his father during a violent home invasion. In his piece (seemingly inspired by his viewing of Jennifer Kent's *The Babadook*), Orbey explains: "In my own experience, horror movies provide not an example for actions but an outlet for empathy, a chance to see characters contend with a kind of fear that my own peers could not fathom" (2016). It was, in fact, Jennifer Kent's *The Babadook* (2014) that made this trend of "mourning horror films" explicit. Kent's work features a wife struggling with the loss of her husband. Bereavement leads Amelia to neglect herself, her child, and her career. While this is fairly typical for any dramatic film about loss, the degree to which Amelia fails to cope with grief relegates it to horror. Bordering on psychosis, unchecked grief becomes the catalyst for the film's violence and for its "manifestation" of Mr. Babadook. Kent's work catalogs the pain of loss in a way that that makes Amelia's guilt, anger, and anguish visible in the form of this menacing figure. Moreover, the film's cinematography entrenches viewers in claustrophobic sorrow. The desaturated color palette, dim lighting, looming shadows, vacant scenery, and minimalist soundtrack all create a strong sense of despondency. They reflect Amelia's personal hell and bring viewers right there beside her. Upon its release, reputable journals and magazines eagerly tackled the use of grief in *The Babadook*. For instance, *The Atlantic*'s Lenika Cruz writes that "the film has a solid grasp on the mutable, but ever-present pain of loss" (2014). Horror films, for the foreseeable future, have gained a sort of validity. They are shown as having the power to express what once seemed to be inexpressible.

This trend shows no signs of abating. Grief is the lynchpin of new horror films such as Ari Aster's *Hereditary* (2018), Ari Aster's *Midsommar* (2019), as well as Kevin Kolsch and Dennis Widmyer's revisioning of *Pet Sematary* (2019). Most importantly, directors are conscious of this trend and the manner in which it engages the audience. In an interview with *Vanity Fair*'s Emma Stefansky, Ari Aster says of *Hereditary*,

> I wanted to make a film that served as a serious meditation on grief and trauma. It begins as a family tragedy, and then continues down that path, but gradually curdles into a full-bore nightmare—in the same way that life can really feel like a nightmare, like everything is falling apart. (2018)

In the case of *Hereditary*, the death of a child provokes unmitigated anger, guilt, and resentment. Viewers watch as family members emotionally separate and then cocoon themselves in pain. Like *The Babadook*, this unhealthy approach to grieving conjures the supernatural. However, unlike Kent's work, the supernatural in *Hereditary* is not the result of psychosis or left to speculation. It is purely demonic. One by one, family members fall victim to misery. Whereas *The Babadook* concludes with a scene of healing (Amelia learns how to navigate loss and begins to celebrate her life with her child), *Hereditary* ends in death and chaos. In this new world of horror, there is room for both hope and despair. One can recover from loss—or be consumed by it.

These last twenty years have also seen "mourning horror films" with an unprecedented degree of ambiguity. In many of these works, the overwhelming crush of grief seems to provide passage for the supernatural; however, these manifestations may well be in the imagination of the protagonist. In some cases, it is difficult (if not deliberately impossible) to delineate what is actual from what is a delusion. In films such as Guillermo del Toro's *Pan's Labyrinth* (*El laberinto del fauno*) (2006) and Juan Antonio Bayona's *The Orphanage* (*El orfanato*) (2007) reality is significantly, purposefully blurred. This reflects the surrealness of loss. That viewers cannot decipher what is real aligns them with the sufferer, placing them in that liminal space often occupied by the bereaved.

Not restricted to the loss of a loved one, this new wave of horror addresses complex ideas of grief. Films such as Tomas Alfredson's *Let the Right One In* (*Låt den rätte komma in*) (2008) as well as Andrés Muschietti's *It Chapter One* (2017) and *It Chapter Two* (2019) closely examine loss of innocence and the lifelong mourning that can accompany such trauma. Meanwhile, works like Alejandro Amenábar's *The Others* (2001), David Lowery's *A Ghost Story* (2017), and Michael and Peter Spierig's *Winchester* (2018) dig deeply into the grief of the departed themselves. Moving more broadly, works like David M. Rosenthal's *Jacob's Ladder* (2019) and Mladen Đorđević's *The Life and Death of a Porno Gang* (*Zivot i smrt porno bande*) (2009) mourn entire communities. And, Lars von Trier's *Melancholia* expands to show an entire world cast in grief. All of these works underscore that grief can extend beyond the loss of a loved one and still be experienced as unfathomably profound.

Often stylized, these sophisticated works have become a global phenomenon. They receive full reviews in prestigious newspapers. They are premiered at exclusive film festivals. And, they are given complete consideration by those in academia. Usurping the coveted space once held by films predicated on blood and gore, horror films about loss speak to a world reeling from grief. Whether expressing the intimate grief experienced by a small family or the collective grief of an entire nation, these films offer an opportunity for unity, catharsis, and—sometimes—healing.

LOSS AND THE CHILD: GRIEF AND ENDANGERED YOUTH

The first part of this collection examines films involving loss and children. In chapter 1, Lindsey Scott explores the generic hybridity of Guillermo del

Toro's *Pan's Labrinth* (*El laberinto del fauno*) to discuss representations of the child's grief. As Ofelia struggles with the untimely loss of her father and attempts to cope with his cruel replacement, she retreats into a fantastical Underground Realm where she must recover her lost identity as Princess Moanna. In this chapter, Scott considers how del Toro's film breaks new ground in the horror genre by harnessing the transformative power of childhood to explore multiple layers of loss and grief. In her assessment of how this film is reflective of the national grief felt throughout post–Civil War Spain, Scott moves a stratum deeper, stepping outside of the text to address the responses of both child and adult viewers. As Scott asserts, the lullaby sung over Ofelia's body at the film's conclusion might be just as much for viewers as it is for the child. In its movements and entanglements, *Pan's Labyrinth* reflects changing attitudes towards grief at the turn of the century, exploring through the lens of horror the value of continuing relationships with the deceased.

The collection then moves to chapter 2, "'We Can Survive This': An Examination of Loss and Grief in Juan Antonio Bayona's *El orfanato* (*The Orphanage*)." Much like how Scott approaches del Toro's work as a layered event in the previous chapter, Erica Joan Dymond looks at the world within the film as well as without. In the world within the film, Bayona depicts a couple consumed by the loss of a child. The disparate grieving methods that each spouse employs prohibits connection. As one spouse slides into abject grief, the film reveals yet another tragedy: the suicide of the child's mother. Here, the director details this descent in chilling detail. However, Bayona also offers an abundance of compassion to his viewers. In the world outside of the film, the director carefully dilutes the work's brutality in an effort to spare the audience undue trauma. Through ample clues and the coding of more challenging moments, Bayona ensures that the audience's grief is never so acute that they disengage from the film. It is a brilliant balancing act that earned the director and his film countless awards and accolades.

In chapter 3, "Elevating Grief: Ari Aster's *Hereditary* and the A24 Horror Film," Andrew Grossman and Todd K. Platts explore how the death of a child opens the door to terror and destruction. In this chapter, Grossman and Platts first catalog the history of A24's watershed horror films, deeming these works as using both dread and grief to create a more multifaceted viewer experience. The hotly contested concept of "elevated horror" is carefully unpacked by the writers. The chapter then moves on to a close examination of A24's commercially and critically successful *Hereditary*. A work told in two parts, Ari Aster's *Hereditary* transitions from a more clinical study of abject grief to a fairly traditional possession film. Trying to reconcile this whiplash shift becomes a complex project. Here, Grossman and Platts use religion and psychology as a lens through which to examine Aster's work. The response of the grieving mother as well as the guilt-stricken grieving brother receive full attention.

LOSS AND GENDER: GRIEF AND MOTHERHOOD/WOMANHOOD

The second part of this collection examines the ways in which gender affects grieving. In chapter 4, "To Make You Feel My Love: Jennifer Kent's *The Babadook*, Motherhood, and Loss," Rebecca L. Willoughby considers issues of grief as it applies to motherhood and self-care. In the film, a tragic car accident robs the protagonist, Amelia, of her husband. She is left to cope with that loss while trying to raise her clingy, defiant son. Deprived of time to address her own pain and her own needs, these overwhelming feelings of loss exceed the borders of her own being and manifest as the horrific Mr. Babadook. Willoughby explores the unfair and destructive expectations society places on mothers—even those enmeshed in grief. And, most importantly, this chapter shows how Kent's film depicts managing pain. Mr. Babadook will always exist, but he can be kept at bay by acknowledging and accepting emotional trauma.

In chapter 5, "The Myth of the Natural Woman: Horror and Grief in Ari Aster's *Midsommar*," Aspen Taylor Ballas analyzes loss as it applies to both gender and culture. Following the murder/suicide of her parents and sister, Dani seeks solace in her boyfriend Christian. However, this tragedy has foiled Christian's plan to break up with Dani. Merely performing the role of consoler until he can end the relationship in a socially acceptable manner, Christian offers little help. Dani is alone in her grief until a fated trip finds her in a remote Swedish village where her pain is embraced—but the consequences are dire. In this chapter, Ballas explores how Dani is surrounded by screens and people who should offer her comfort, but she only experiences isolation. In an American setting, Dani's crushing grief is viewed as a burden by the men surrounding her, all anthropology students. While they treat her politely, the men view her (legitimate) struggle as inconvenient. Amidst these shrewd male scholars, Dani stands out as the quintessential woman who is defined by her (again, legitimate) emotions. Ballas contrasts this to Dani's reception in Sweden. In the village of Hårga, Dani's pain is embraced and becomes part of a collective sorrow. And, it is here that the analytical, cold view of the male scholars is challenged. Though this reversal is gratifying to viewers, it soon turns into something aberrant. As Dani's male companions are ritualistically slaughtered, she rises to the rank of May Queen. While Dani's grief is not a burden to this village, it does fuel something both grotesque and horrifying.

LOSS AND NATIONAL IDENTITY: GRIEF AND HISTORY

The third part of this collection looks at how loss can reflect a nation. In chapter 6, "O Father, Where Art Thou?: Grief and Cannibal Culture in Jorge Michel Grau's *Somos lo que hay* (*We Are What We Are*)," Megan DeVirgilis explicates grief through the lens of gender and sexuality as it is perceived in Mexican culture, and more specifically within the framework of the Mexican nuclear family. After the loss of their patriarch, a family of cannibals in Mexico City struggles to reestablish a power dynamic. As a result, the family descends into chaos and self-destruction. Here, DeVirgilis examines the conservative concept of machismo and how this affects the family's attempt at regaining balance. Steeped in history and influencing everyday life, machismo has increasingly been challenged in modern Mexican horror cinema. In this sense, while *Somos lo que hay* is founded on grief, it uses this as a vehicle to explore a society verging on change. In the film, the once-closeted, gay son finds freedom in his grief. And a daughter who could never be at the forefront of the family because of her gender and age gains recognition. DeVirgilis arranges all of this under the lens of colonization offering a profoundly complex portrait of grief influenced by centuries of history.

The collection then moves on to chapter 7, "Sadness Is Rebellion: The Ontopolitics of Queer Loss in Mladen Đorđević's *Život i smrt porno bande* (*The Life and Death of a Porno Gang*)." In this chapter, Andrija Filipović examines the history of the LGBTQIA+ community's reception in conservative Serbia and how Mladen Đorđević's film, one of extreme loss, reflects those tensions. In the film, a group of social misfits create a traveling burlesque show. On the way, those on the margins of society are embraced into the group. However, as a result of the transgressive nature of their performances, the troupe draws the ire of villagers and authorities alike. Ultimately, all members of the gang succumb to a country that is at best unsupportive of and at worst resistant to their existence. Throughout his work, Filipović analyzes Serbia's fraught political history as it compounds the challenges presented to the LGBTQIA+ community. Here, the author excavates strata of loss that become so compounded that "queer pessimism" seems the only option—that grief and death are all that logically remain. All of this is applied to Đorđević's film, showing that the bleak conclusion to his film was the only possible ending.

In chapter 8, "The Grieving Dead: Haunting and the Haunted in the Spierig Brothers' *Winchester*," Racheal Harris examines the consequences of gun culture in America. Loosely inspired by the life of Sarah Winchester—heiress to the Winchester Repeating Arms fortune—the film depicts Sarah's attempts to atone for the deaths of those lost to gun violence. For each victim, she creates a room in her home and strives to reach into the beyond to provide that spirit with reconciliation. When Sarah's behavior attracts the attention of the Winchester board members, a physician is sent to assess her mental fitness. While at the Winchester mansion, Dr. Eric Price copes with his own feelings of loss, ultimately reaching a peaceful resolution—and finding Sarah of sound mind. In addition to looking at gun violence, Harris closely explores the history of mediumship as well as its relationship to gender. The chapter explains how women were a revered authority in this field in a time when many were striving for *any* degree of recognition. After exploring these layers of history, Harris skillfully ties this film and its message to our modern-day struggles, offering both caution and hope.

LOSS AND THE KNOWN WORLD: GRIEF AND ANNIHILATION

In this final part, Michael Brown's "'No One Will Miss It': Lars Von Trier's *Antichrist* and *Melancholia* and the World-Without-Us" explores a world that defies the perception of being benevolent. Nature, in *Antichrist*, actively exacerbates the grief of a couple who have lost their child in a horrific accident. Seeking solace in an isolated cabin, the couple finds that instead of providing consolation, nature offers aberrant images and disquieting sounds. It is, by all means, antagonistic, pushing the couple towards destruction. In *Melancholia*, a rogue planet is set on a collision course with Earth. It is an extinction event and the Earth—as well as the universe—seems entirely indifferent. Here, no one will grieve the loss of humankind. Brown's chapter begins with the personal grief portrayed in *Antichrist* and then moves the cataclysmic collision of planets in *Melancholia*. In this work, Brown challenges romantic views of nature and the idea of human exceptionalism by employing Eugene Thacker's concept of "world-without-us." Through this lens, von Trier's film becomes a stark reminder that nature does not mourn with us—or mourn for us.

BIBLIOGRAPHY

Armstrong, Richard. 2012. *Mourning Films: A Critical Study of Loss and Grieving in Cinema*. Jefferson, NC: McFarland.
Cruz, Lenika. 2014. "What the Hellish *Babadook* Has to Say About Childhood Grief." *The Atlantic*. December 10, 2014. https://www.theatlantic.com/entertainment/archive/2014/12/what-the-hellish-babadook-has-to-say-about-childhood-grief/383528/.

Orbey, Eren. 2016. "Mourning through Horror Movies." *The New Yorker*. November 22, 2016. https://www.newyorker.com/books/page-turner/mourning-through-horror-movies.

Stefansky, Emma. 2018. "That Horrific *Hereditary* Scene Is Director Ari Aster's Favorite." *Vanity Fair*. June 8, 2018. https://www.vanityfair.com/hollywood/2018/06/hereditary-toni-collette-horror-movie-ari-aster-director-interview.

Zinoman, Jason. 2018. "Home Is Where the Horror Is." *The New York Times*. June 7, 2018. https://www.nytimes.com/2018/06/07/movies/hereditary-horror-movies.html.

PART I

Loss and the Child

Grief and Endangered Youth

Chapter 1

Horror at the Crossroads

Mapping the Child's Grief in Pan's Labyrinth *(2006)*

Lindsey Scott

Guillermo del Toro's *Pan's Labyrinth* (*El laberinto del fauno*, 2006) tells the story of Ofelia (Ivana Baquero), an eleven-year-old girl who navigates the parallel worlds of Franco's post–Civil War Spain and a fantastical Underground Realm to recover her lost identity as Princess Moanna. With its child protagonist, explicit violence, and unusual generic hybridity, the film has long been acknowledged as difficult to categorize against the markers of classical cinema (Orme 2010, 224). Del Toro's approach disrupts the boundaries between fairy tale and horror, human and monster, childhood and adulthood, life and death, and in doing so, produces a work described, amongst other things, as an "adult fairy tale" (Spector 2009, 81) and "hypertextual metafiction" mobilized for sociopolitical critique (Kotecki 2010, 237). Scholars such as Andrea Sabbadini view the film's complexities as its major strength: "Ultimately, this is just a del Toro movie—a true auteur's own original and impressive contribution to world cinema" (2014, 48). As such, *Pan's Labyrinth* can be celebrated for the entanglements of its parallel worlds, which "enter into a conflictual state with each other, then meet and finally merge" (Sabbadini 2014, 48). These entanglements are of central interest to this chapter, for they invite us to re-examine reductive readings of horror which prioritize immediate viewer responses over the genre's capacity to explore a deeper range of human emotion: in particular, our own understandings of grief.

Like other horror texts, del Toro's film includes representations of death, violence, and trauma, but its entanglements connect audiences to their responses to such encounters: namely, individual and shared expressions of grief. According to Bob Wright, the expression of grief is "a universal response by which people adapt to a significant loss" (2007, vii). Ofelia's experiences in both worlds are shaped by her feelings of loss following the death of her father, as well as those relating to the later loss of her mother (Ariadna Gil) who dies in childbirth towards the end of the film. For the entirety of the narrative, Ofelia refuses to call her mother's new husband, Captain Vidal (Sergi López), her father, instead holding on to the fairy tales of her childhood, which connect her to the loving parent she has lost. "It's just a word," her mother tells her as they journey towards their new home, but Ofelia understands, like Hamlet before her, that something is rotten in the captain's mill [00:04:55]. Adopting the name "Father" means an indoctrination into the patriarchal and Fascist order which Captain Vidal represents. By refusing to give voice to it, Ofelia maintains her bond with her lost parent and demonstrates her alignment with the Republicans who actively rebel against the national identity so violently thrust upon them. By giving voice to Ofelia's imaginative world of fairy tales and monsters, del Toro also rebels against the conventional forms of fictional horror, utilizing the transformative power of childhood to explore loss and preserve meaningful relationships with the dead.

If, like the prince of Denmark, Ofelia exists in a state of grieving, she is also herself a lost object of grief. The dying girl at the start of the film is being mourned by a parental figure the audience cannot see: a woman, who murmurs a soft lullaby as the bleeding Ofelia draws her final breaths. What follows in voiceover is the story of a princess who ran away from the Underground Realm to escape to the human world. It is reported that the princess dies, but the narrator ends by saying that her father will wait for her "until the world stopped turning" [00:02:31]. Thus, *Pan's Labyrinth* begins by presenting grief through a kaleidoscope of shifting perspectives: the grief that is long felt by the parent; the grief that is newly felt by the adult nursing the child; and the grief that will soon be felt by viewers, once del Toro's film has "stopped turning." In this moment, *Pan's Labyrinth* suggests a healing process, for the blood that has been spilled is shown to be returning to Ofelia's body. Like Ofelia's *Book of Crossroads*, viewers cannot be sure if what they are witnessing is "a version of events, a prediction of the future or a rewriting of the past," (Ellis and Sánchez-Arce 2011, 178) for the *Book of Crossroads* is also an account of grief, focalized through the lens of horror. As blood spills across its pages, Ofelia and the film's spectator will confront loss through the myriad connections between past, present, and future.

This chapter explores the relationship between horror and grief in *Pan's Labyrinth*, concentrating on its multifaceted representations which center around the child's experiences of death and loss. Following an assessment of the film's symbolic use of the child as a representative of adult loss and trauma, the chapter re-examines Ofelia through wider shifts in sociological and psychological thought, which demonstrate changing attitudes towards grief at the turn of the century and highlight the importance of children and adults maintaining "interactive relationships with the deceased" (Normand et al. 1996, 91). According to Roger Clark and Keith McDonald, the film "utilises key codes and conventions of children's literature as a means of encountering the trauma of Fascism" (2010, 52). Running parallel to this argument, this chapter proposes that del Toro's film utilizes the conventions of horror as a means of encountering the non-linear movements and emotional complexities of individual grief.

THE BOOK OF CROSSROADS: ADULT HORRORS, CHILD PROTAGONISTS

Discussing the child protagonist in *Pan's Labyrinth*, del Toro imagines the transition between childhood and adulthood as a type of crossroads that all humans must encounter: "her age is one when we put away our toys, we put away our fairy tales, and we put away our souls, to become just another adult" (cited in Sabbadini 2014, 49). The loss being described here relates specifically to the loss of childhood, an inevitable "crossroads we have all grown through," which, for del Toro, is "a profoundly melancholic one in all our lives" (cited in Sabbadini 2014, 49). Addressing the relationship between childhood, loss, and time, Fiona Noble observes that the significance of the child's death in *Pan's Labyrinth* is both local and global, representative of "the many children who died at the hands of the Franco regime," while also functioning metaphorically as "a potent symbol for the perceived loss that accompanies the transition from childhood into adolescence" (2017, 440). On both levels, any sense of loss within the film, along with its capacity to explore feelings of grief, appears to be tied to the emotions and experiences of adults. Ofelia, although herself a child, is a construct like any other child in horror. Whether that child is presented as innocent or monstrous, victim or threat, hope or destruction, gift or curse, such binaries tend to typify representations across the genre, which are founded upon the fears, wants, and desires of adults. At the same time, horror demands an appropriate level of maturity from its audiences, shaped by a rating system where age still dictates viewer suitability. Childhood, then, despite its symbolic power within the genre, is a time that adults must "put away" to enter the fictional world of horror.

However, as Noble's own reading of *Pan's Labyrinth* goes on to demonstrate, the conventional notion of rejecting childhood to gain entry to the social world of adulthood and the fictional world of horror is something del Toro's film ardently resists on multiple levels. Ofelia rejects the linear progression into the "real" world of adulthood, represented firstly by her continued love of fairy tales, and secondly by her arrival at the captain's mill. Instead of following her mother, who is ushered inside the walls of Vidal's encampment as a wheelchair-bound invalid, Ofelia enters the outdoor space of the Labyrinth, an ancient realm of many different pathways associated with non-linearity, possibility, and imagination. Importantly, Ofelia remains in the physical form of a child for the duration of the film, despite its sprawling narrative across different ontological and temporal spaces. She becomes immortal in her life as Princess Moanna, while her adult equivalent in the human world, Mercedes (Maribel Verdú), will mourn her passing and surely age and die. The ancient mythological Faun (Doug Jones), Ofelia's immersive agent in the realm of the fantastic, also begins to look younger as the film moves towards its conclusion, a reversal which suggests the boundaries between childhood and adulthood are as fluid and malleable as those between past and present, fantasy and reality, life and death (Balanzategui 2015, 85). The crossroads del Toro imagines thus remains an open possibility for viewers of his film. Childhood is not "put away" to access the world of horror. Instead, it plays a fundamental part in its creation.

As a director, del Toro frequently aligns his creative vision with child protagonists and his personal experiences of being a child, an entanglement beyond the film's diegesis which returns audiences to the crossroads of childhood and adulthood. As a result, *Pan's Labyrinth* gives voice to the experiences of the child on multiple levels, a powerful invocation which saw many young people watching and embracing this film, even as others criticized its marketing and generic hybridity for inviting children to inadvertently gain access to such horrors. For film scholar Rikke Schubart, encountering *Pan's Labyrinth* was itself a traumatic experience, as the film had been mistaken for a fantasy suitable for family viewing: "My children, eleven and eight at the time, would later blame me for childhood trauma, and rightly so, because this explosion of violence into what we expected to be a marvellous film felt like an assault" (2018, 59). By contrast, John Perlich, addressing the lack of suitable fictional role models for his young daughters, proposed that while "few would find the cinematic tale of this heroine as appropriate viewing for children, the story provides a window into the type of narrative that warrants our consideration" (2010, 102). For del Toro, the violence and horror within *Pan's Labyrinth* was neither intended to exclude nor directly target young audiences. As Jessica Balanzategui explains, del Toro "often creates his films with a child audience in mind" and "expressed profound disappointment that *Pan's Labyrinth* received an R rating and not PG-13" (2015, 90). In noting the shift from an adult-centric perspective, Balanzategui argues that the child protagonists in del Toro's work are "empowered to shape a *new* discourse, which stands in contrast to the staid, inflexible grasping of logic and reason which characterizes the adult character's response to traumatic experience" (2015, 79 original emphasis). What remains to be explored in such insightful discussions is the ways in which the child, as well as the adult, may experience grief in relation to the horror genre. If the narrative development of *Pan's Labyrinth* rejects linear progression, then such rejection may also convey the impact grief can have on a child's self-development, as well as alluding to the notion that grief is an ongoing process in which any individual, child or adult, will have changing responses over time. The text's narrative runs in a type of loop, beginning and ending with the moment of Ofelia's death and effectively suspending this moment in time for the duration of the film, until Ofelia's white flower appears on the barren tree. Past, present, and future continue to merge and overlap alongside different stages of loss in the grieving process. This is one of the film's most significant achievements. Del Toro's narrative deals in trauma, but its movements and entanglements are also a study in grief.

Mapping Loss:
Discovering Meaning in the Grieving Process

At the beginning of del Toro's film, viewers' emotional investment and attachment to Ofelia's character is immediate for several reasons. Firstly, she is a child suffering from severe injury. Secondly, the pain caused by her injury is captured on her face in close-up, signaling her emotional centrality to the film's narrative. Thirdly, the proximity of her death is both shocking and instant. There is no explanation for it, no preparation, and such treatment encapsulates how the audience's "inability to control loss causes feelings of helplessness and despair" (Wright 2007, vii). Del Toro's film tackles these feelings directly, as viewers are rendered powerless in its opening moments, unable to comprehend or intervene to save the dying child. However, its complex unravelling invites viewers to recognize and address these feelings, offering various strategies for reflection and transformation, which may then be applied to their own experiences and recollections of grief.

As the film journeys back in time, the story of Ofelia's life in the human world begins. The presentation of her near death is realigned with the story of Princess Moanna and her grieving father, whose suffering in the Underground Realm, recounted in voiceover, spans an untold number of years. The princess died a long time ago after escaping to the human world and her father still waits for her soul to return, "perhaps in another body, another place, another time" [00:02:22]. At this point, the film shifts to its central body of action, as the narrator's tale ends and viewers join Ofelia sitting in the back of a car, reading her book of fairy tales. Her journey is captured first in long shot, as a procession of black cars moves slowly through the ruined town of

Belchite, famously destroyed in the Spanish Civil War and left untouched as "a monument to all of the prevailing success of Nationalist forces" (Brown 2015, 64). The mood of the scene is appropriately somber. Del Toro's camera passes over the remains of human bones left unburied in the ghost town, while Ofelia and her mother appear dressed in dark coats, Ofelia also wearing a black hat and black shoes, as though in mourning.

Grief, as Wright explains, describes "the reactions a person experiences while in a state of bereavement" (2007, 9). Throughout the course of the film, Ofelia is in a state of bereavement, adapting to the loss of her father. According to Wright, children "express very strong feelings about loss," and Ofelia's behavior at the start of the film suggests "sadness, stillness and a quiet withdrawn response" (2007, 2). For the first two minutes of screen time, she moves slowly, looks forlorn, and does not speak. She listens as her mother chides her for still reading fairy tales and attempts to turn her face towards the window until her mother gently but firmly pulls it back. Ofelia's feelings about the loss of her father are implied through her mother's actions and the insistence that she give up fairy tales because she is too old for them. On the surface, this request associates inferiority with the imaginative time of childhood: Ofelia must leave these "nonsense" stories behind if she is to grow up and become a successful adult [00:02:55]. However, mapped against the setting of Belchite, a frozen relic of wartime destruction, Carmen's request carries with it a denial of Ofelia's right to grieve. Under the Francoist regime, "Republican sympathizers were forbidden to mourn their dead," and Carmen's new marriage to Captain Vidal suggests that she is willing to internalize such beliefs (Brown 2015, 59). As Alexandra West observes, the adults in *Pan's Labyrinth* are "unable to be the guides the children need" (2015, 144), a problem which not only points to the ongoing suffering of a fractured nation under Fascist rule, but to the very real and continued difficulty that many children "grow up without ever being allowed to give expression to their feelings of loss" (Wright 2015, 2). As Ofelia wanders from her mother's side into the woods, she discovers a relic from an ancient time, resembling the head of a tombstone. As she picks up its broken eye and restores it to its rightful place, her encounters with the Underground Realm begin. At this point, Ofelia's feelings of grief are given vivid and imaginative expression in del Toro's film; not compromised or marginalized against the "real" world of Franco's Spain, but provided with an equally powerful diegetic space to "co-exist" (Derry 2009, 324). As a magical creature springs from the stone's open mouth, Ofelia speaks her first words of the film to her mother: "I saw a fairy" [00:04:39].

It is telling that Ofelia, in journeying through Belchite into the green world of the forest should see a fairy at a tombstone rather than a ghost. Unlike Hamlet, Ofelia's grief is associated with signifiers of nature, life, and growth.

Horror at the Crossroads 9

Figure 1.1 Ofelia meets a fairy in the woods. Ivana Baquero (as Ofelia). El laberinto del fauno.
Source: *Pan's Labyrinth* (2006)

If her book of fairy tales "contains the spirit of Ofelia's father," then the fairy she sees at the tombstone also signals her continued connection to her lost parent (Brown 2015, 68). Fittingly, this connection is not instigated by a spectral being asking for revenge or remembrance. Instead, it is insect-like, at one with its natural surroundings and buzzing through the air with life. Ofelia's mother, however, does not wish to see or hear about the fairy. She reprimands her daughter for dirtying her shoes, then insists that when Ofelia greets the captain, she must call him "Father." As Carmen gives this instruction, she guides her daughter away, but del Toro's camera still lingers in the woods. At this point, the fairy returns to the foreground of the shot and secretly observes Ofelia's departure. As the cars begin to move at speed, the fairy follows, suggesting that Ofelia's feelings over death and loss will continue to find expression in the movements of del Toro's film.

Throughout these early scenes, del Toro presents a world of ruptured time, which corresponds with definitions of the early stages in the grieving process. The denial of "natural" progression and the passing of linear time, coupled with the grieving father's promise to wait forever after the suspension of Ofelia's death can be attributed to the human process of denial, defined in early theoretical responses as "shock, disbelief and an inability to accept the death" (Wright 2007, 10). Following viewers' own feelings of shock and disbelief, due to an inability to accept the impending death of a child, *Pan's Labyrinth* then shifts to the space of the "real" world, which, although still fractured, depicts nature and suggests the beginnings of loss acceptance, so that "the working phase of normal grieving begins" (Wright 2007, 10). According to Wright, this phase can include being "disinterested in daily affairs" and experiencing "feelings of loss and loneliness" as well as "a strong desire to be alone" (2007, 10). Viewers witness this when Ofelia stands apart at the captain's encampment, ignoring the many servants and soldiers assembled for their arrival. At first, she is motionless, clinging to her beloved books, but then she spots the fairy again and drops them, her solemn black cap falling to the ground as she runs after it into the Labyrinth. In John Bowlby's early grief phase of disorganization, withdrawal and social isolation can occur alongside "signs of regression, that is, a return to an earlier, more primitive form of behaviour" (Wright 2007, 11). Ofelia's journey to the oldest part of the mill, the Labyrinth, suggests this and is coupled with her rejection of the hectic adult world. Mercedes tells Ofelia that the Labyrinth's stone walls are ancient and that she should avoid going further inside, or risk getting lost. It is at this moment of potentially being "lost" that Ofelia tells Mercedes that Captain Vidal is not her father, because her father was a tailor who died in the war. Entrance to the Labyrinth thus gives voice to the child's grief and becomes a space where private thoughts and feelings can be realized and transformed through the power of Ofelia's imagination.

In Freud's conceptualization of melancholia, ambivalent feelings can lead to self-reproachment, or, as Wright suggests, feeling "hurt, neglected and wounded, resulting in the false belief that he [or she] is going to be punished" (2007, 10). These feelings can be traced through Ofelia's ambivalent relationship with the Faun, the setting of the tasks, and the reprimand and punishment that occurs when Ofelia disobeys the magical creature and eats from the Pale Man's table. In Bowlby's third phase of restructuring, "new interests and attachments" are formed, and viewers see this in Ofelia's new attachment, not to the fantastical creatures of the Labyrinth, but to her baby brother, following the death of her mother (Wright 2007, 11). If the world of the Labyrinth represents the middle stage of Ofelia's encounter with grief, then her rejection of the Faun's instruction to sacrifice her brother encapsulates the next important phase and its movement towards individual recovery. Rather than "looking for the lost one or for signs that he may still be available," Ofelia's task and purpose changes: instead of losing herself to despair after the death of her mother, she gears her actions towards departing from the Mill and saving her brother's life (Wright 2007, 11).

It is during the bleak period after Carmen's death that change becomes crucial if Ofelia is to save herself and her brother. It seems, therefore, that her journey in working through feelings of loss and grief assists her in coping with this next painful separation: "If the person has failed to confront loss in the past it may re-emerge, making present problems worse" (Wright 2007, 14). In the recovery stage, "old ways of thinking are left behind" so that the individual is released from the past and can "begin living again" (2007, 11). For Ofelia, this is true in the sense that her own death marks the beginning of her life as Princess Moanna with her family in the Underground Realm. For viewers, Ofelia's rejection of "reality," linear time, and adulthood has exploded the old ways of thinking, and living again, with the ability to imagine a different future, becomes a very real possibility.

However, *Pan's Labyrinth*'s outlook and narrative trajectory corresponds most strongly with shifting paradigms of grief at the close of the twentieth century. As Phyllis R. Silverman and Dennis Klass explain: "The post-Freud paradigm for understanding grief has maintained the idea that the primary goal of grieving is to cut the bond with the deceased so that new attachments can be formed" (1996, 7). However, in their influential study, they observe how Freud's own personal experiences of loss did not match his theoretic model of grief (1996, 6), while valuable insight gained through other phenomena often "fails to be passed on and incorporated into the next generation of research and theory" (1996, 7). Studies that challenge the dominant model of grief from the twentieth century offer a highly useful approach for interpreting del Toro's film. Grief is not about severing a bond with a lost one, although this has often been upheld as the desired goal, as "continued attachment to the deceased was called unresolved grief" (1996, 4). Instead, Ofelia ensures a continuous bond with her father, and her return to the Underground Realm is presented not as an act of regression, but as a continuation of this bond in the movement of the film. Similarly, del Toro ensures a continuous bond between Ofelia and the film's viewers, as they now know "where to look" for her in the human world, actively encouraged to see the flower on the tree and to remember rather than forget [01.47.22]. Over separation, the film privileges continuous bonds with the deceased, reinforced by the permanence of *Pan's Labyrinth* itself as a cinematic work of art. Rather than centering on loss or giving way to feelings of despair, the film moves towards a sense of hope in its entanglements, and in doing so, offers viewers a powerful form of transformation. Perhaps most unexpectedly, monsters play a crucial role in this transformative process.

TRANSFORMED BY MONSTERS: HORROR, TRAUMA, AND RECOVERY

For children, the grieving process can be particularly difficult, due to adult desires to protect or exclude them from the horrifying reality of death. In Western families, "children are often excluded from the events surrounding a death," as adults may want to keep them "innocent and unspoiled" (Wright 2007, 23). Adults may also feel that contact with death would "contaminate" them with the stark reality of life, in the same way as sex "contaminates" them and removes their innocence (Wright 2007, 23). However, adult desires to prevent or postpone the child's experiences also "delays their growing understanding of life" (Wright 2007, 23). Significantly, this desire relates to adult fears regarding children's exposure to forms of fictional horror. Although in del Toro's vision, *Pan's Labyrinth* should not necessarily exclude child viewers, many adults feel a deep concern over its more mature content. As Balanzategui explains, "due to the frightening elements and gory imagery of his films, they usually attract 'adults only' ratings" (2015, 90). Schubart argues that *Pan's Labyrinth* is "not aimed at the young and innocent, but at adult audiences in need of a new and 'innocent' perspective" (2018, 59). Evy Varsamopoulou similarly addresses the film's power to invite adult viewers to engage with the story "from the perspective of the child viewer in order to reanimate the power of imaginative perception" (2019, 247). However, the taboo treatment of death in children's literature and popular culture has shifted in recent decades, along with the presence of horror and other "mature" themes in children's media. In merging elements of children's literature and fairy tale with graphic horror images of monsters, violence, and death, del Toro confronts the motives behind such exclusions and, in turn, redefines horror through the tropes of children's literature, leaving his own legacy on the genre's evolution and its subsequent value for both young and adult audiences (Scott 2022, n.p.).

The darkness Ofelia confronts in the magical realm is often perceived as a coping mechanism for the cruelties she suffers in the adult world, rather than as confirmation of the vitality of horror within the child's imagination and their own experiences of grief. According to Jessica McCort, "Ofelia's fantasy world is horrific for a reason; it allows her to manage the fear she experiences in the Captain's mill" (2016, 15). Such readings, although positive in their focus on the child's emotions, can threaten to reproduce hierarchies of the all-powerful parent versus the helpless child, the "real" world of adulthood versus the "fantasy" world of childhood. Like other critics, McCort agrees that *Pan's Labyrinth* is "not meant for children," yet del Toro's film still earns a place in her critical introduction on horror in children's literature and culture (2016, 15). In her brief analysis of the text, she concludes that "in the external real world, [Ofelia] has no control whatsoever," whereas in her fantasy world, "she can outwit or vanquish monsters that are veiled symbols of some limb of the Captain's power" (McCort 2016, 15). Here, divisions between child and adult, fantasy and reality, seem to work against the entanglements of del Toro's film, assuming the child's powerlessness in the external world and thus aligning with adult desires to protect children from real experiences of death and loss.

According to Wright, children "need to know as many details about the death as they are mentally equipped to process," and the level of questions they ask will depend on the needs of the individual child (2007, 24).

However, many children are still "left to themselves rather than encouraged to reveal their grief" when they might also "need help to discover their own responses" (Wright 2007, 24). *Pan's Labyrinth* suggests many important advances in this area, as it tells the story of an inquisitive child experiencing her own individual responses, which include, rather than exclude, violence and horror. With grief comes the expression of the child's fear and distress. The horror landscape of del Toro's film makes these feelings immediate and palpable. Ofelia's encounters in the Labyrinth permit her to express a range of emotions, with an invitation for her to make her own choices, signified by the blank pages of the *Book of Crossroads*. As West explains, "del Toro's personal view of life and death comes from transcendence. Letting go or trying to let go of the fear that can freeze a person" (2015, 132). In del Toro's films, the child is often able "to see the 'monster' and therefore is able to see the world much clearer than those who deny their existence" (2015, 132). This clarity of vision provides Ofelia with an opportunity to explore and work through her own fears, an important element in the grieving process.

The environment Ofelia must inhabit following the marriage of her mother to Captain Vidal is one of violence, cruelty, and oppression. In families where "feelings have to be hidden or controlled," individuals may find it more difficult to "move usefully through the process of grieving" (Wright 2007, 24). In the captain's mill, it quickly becomes apparent that stories and emotions must be hidden and controlled. Vidal silences his wife at the dinner table in front of the other guests when she tries to recount with feeling the story of how they met. This silencing also controls Carmen's ability to move through her own grieving process, as telling a story about her new relationship implies a coping mechanism for coming to terms with the loss of her first husband. Ofelia's fairy tales, too, have no place in the captain's mill, and Carmen tells this brutally to her daughter after Vidal discovers the mandrake root under the bed, which was intended to heal Carmen. After the mandrake root burns in the fire, Carmen's sickness worsens. When she appears standing before Ofelia with her nightdress covered in blood, the uncanny image recalls the film's opening sequence with Ofelia bleeding. This traumatic link serves as a further rupturing of time and a painful reminder for viewers of the unpredictability of experiencing loss in grief.

Ofelia's Underground Realm is often dark, suggesting not a mirror image of the darkness she must confront in the adult world, but rather, an invitation for adults to accept the complex feelings that children also possess in their experiences of grief: "It helps children if an adult can sensitively explore their deepest fears and imaginings" (Wright 2007, 24). In creating the world of the Labyrinth, this is exactly what del Toro's film does. In her first task, Ofelia must encounter a monstrous toad living under a tree. While the toad grows fat, the tree dies, as the monster is draining its life force. This may be interpreted in terms of the war and the impact of fascism, draining the life force of Spain. However, it can also be read as an individual sufferer succumbing to death and loss. The monster in this task prevents the tree from growing, thus suspending the healing process. In finding the key and fulfilling her task, Ofelia unlocks the potential for life and loss beyond pain, and proceeds to the next task.

The Pale Man, located in the Faun's second challenge, poses a greater threat, as here, Ofelia is confronted by a devouring monster who is nourished by death itself. By killing children, the monster sustains its own existence, but its wasted appearance betrays the futility of its feeding. In front of the Pale Man is a banquet of food which he does not look at or touch, an indication of the disregard for life through nourishment. There has been much speculation about Ofelia's eating from the table, but by taking the fruit, she displays her own humanity and her choice of life over death. By refusing to sacrifice her brother at the Faun's demand in the third task, Ofelia proves that she will not be consumed by death or loss, as her one wish is to protect him. As Charles Derry explains: "For Del Toro, fauns are neither good nor bad, but a representation of nature, which is amoral, containing elements of creation and destruction" (2009, 327). Ofelia's ability to face her own fear and choose life is contrasted with Vidal's inability to face personal trauma and grieve for his own lost father. Instead, Vidal remembers the moment of his father's death, frozen in time, and cannot move beyond it. Suffering from this festering wound, he inflicts wounds on others as a way of coping with individual loss and instils fear to achieve his desired sense of power. In the Labyrinth, as Vidal searches for his lost son—his only hope for immortality—he cannot see the healing monster, the mythological Faun, standing beside Ofelia. By the end of the film, the message seems clear: unlike Vidal, viewers of *Pan's Labyrinth* will see the Faun and Ofelia's flower on the tree, if they are open to grief and healing.

TIME TO GRIEVE:
REALIZATION AND LOSS

Grief, like del Toro's film, cannot be experienced or resolved in any simple or linear way. According to Wright, "rather than saying the grief is resolved the person works—or struggles—towards living with the loss" (Wright 2007, 13). Children and adults need to experience grieving if they are to manage their own sense of loss. Del Toro's film makes this process possible by creating a powerful artistic space for the realization of grief. The film's bitter-sweet ending carries with it a lasting emotional impact of loss, with Ofelia's death in the human world ensuring that there is no false attempt at closure or denial. Instead, loss is mingled with feelings of joy, reunion, and hope. For the bereaved, "loss becomes part of their life experience and they enter a new phase of life" (Wright, 2007, 26). Del Toro's dual ending, merging Ofelia's death in the human world with her subsequent rebirth in the Underground Realm, invites audiences to accept loss as part of a new phase of life. The film's nonlinear movements also invite audiences to experience the process of grieving *before* Ofelia's actual death has occurred. Thus, the film's closure suggests an ongoing process through the ending of a human life and the beginning of a new existence.

Feelings of grief "can occur over a lifetime," and *Pan's Labyrinth* embodies this by extending Ofelia's dying moments over the entire length of the film (Rosenblatt 1996, 45). The complex narrative shifts align with the notion that grief is "an amalgam of differing feeling/thought blends" which can change "for any specific person bereaved for a specific loss" (Rosenblatt 1996, 45). Del Toro's film centers on the death of a child without ever neglecting a sense of the shifting, nonlinear, and deeply personal experiences of individual grief. The film also approaches a significant death beyond the assumption that all loss experienced will occur at this particular time. Instead, there is "a sequence, perhaps extending over one's lifetime, of new losses or new realizations of loss" (1996, 50). This is presented through Ofelia's own journey, while it is simultaneously absent from Vidal's. Ofelia experiences many losses throughout the film: the loss of her home, a way of life, the fairy, her mother, and her infant brother when Vidal seizes him. For Vidal, the watch belonging to his deceased father has been stopped at the precise moment of death, while the progression of time remains necessary for patrilineality and the continuation of the Fascist order. But there is no time to reflect on loss. Vidal shows that he will not even stop to mourn his own wife as he instructs the doctor to "save the child" and let her die if a choice must be made at the birth [01:03:14]. For men like Captain Vidal, no time exists to grieve.

With the first significant loss in an individual's life, such as the loss of Ofelia's father, there occurs "a realization of one's own mortality and of the human incapacity to stop death or to reverse it" (Rosenblatt 1996, 51). Del Toro presents this desire in the opening moments of his film, as viewers witness the camera turning counterclockwise as it approaches Ofelia's eye, and then the blood flowing in reverse as it returns to Ofelia's body. Finally, through its dual ending, which returns viewers to Ofelia's dying moments and sees her restored to the Underground Realm, the film reveals its challenge to the grief work process: to "come to terms with a loss while honoring and perhaps even holding on to the meanings, memories, investments, and identities connected to the deceased" (Rosenblatt 1996, 53). Thus, Ofelia appears with her family in the Underground Realm, a transformation which ensures these connections are honored "in such a way that the past is validated" (Rosenblatt

1996, 53). As Rosenblatt argues, "one of the most significant reminders of previous loss is a new loss," and this is the case for the film's protagonist and its viewers (1996, 54). As new losses connect Ofelia to the death of her father, they also return viewers to the moment of Ofelia's death, which, despite the film's suggestion of reversal, cannot be erased or avoided.

However, the desire to do so remains within the shifts of the film's non-linear fabric. Its dual ending, with Ofelia's death at the edge of the Labyrinth alongside her eternal life being granted in the Underground Realm, shows there is more to recurrent grief than sorrow: it can also be "a link with the best of life, an affirmation of light and joy" (Rosenblatt 1996, 55). Thus, while *Pan's Labyrinth* invites Spain to remember its turbulent past and to grieve for those lost, the film's ending also demonstrates that "the American cultural notion about finishing grief in a defined period of time is not as incongruent with the idea of recurrent grieving as it seems" (Rosenblatt 1996, 55). Rather, the movement of the film, along with changing attitudes towards grief at the turn of the century, follows "a postmodern sensibility in which the diversity of realities is acknowledged" (Rosenblatt 1996, 56). As Rosenblatt explains: "In a postmodern approach, assertions about grief must be understood as framed in a specific perspective and relative to that perspective" (1996, 56). Here, the film's use of the child's point of view enables viewers to understand grief as relative to perspective, while also inviting them to reflect on the ways that children, as well as adults, may experience loss and grief.

If viewers perceive in del Toro's work a complex entanglement of feelings of loss, fear, hope and recovery, then perhaps it is the truest definition to say that *Pan's Labyrinth* is a film about grief. As Wright explains, grief is often thought of "as a negative experience, but in fact, it is the process by which people are healed and which helps them to emerge from a significant loss" (2007, 9). However, because people often struggle to recognize the value of grief, they may "attempt to avoid the process altogether," while others may help them to avoid any sense of pain (Wright 2007, 9). Significantly, critical responses to horror and its place in del Toro's film can also expose an attempt to avoid this process, instead desiring the happy ending to be "real," or its entanglements to be fully explained. For Schubart, the loss of the film's heroine was profoundly felt: "I was devastated when Ofelia died [. . .] Why should she die? And why were there two endings?" (2018, 60). The consistent use of fairytale tropes meant that this viewer soon forgot about Ofelia's death and instead expected the conventional "happy ending" for her story. But the "default rules of horror invade the fairy tale," and for Schubart, this invasion was the film's "true horror" (2018, 60). Alternatively, for Brown, del Toro's Spanish Civil War films "deal with unresolved grief and the importance of remembrance" (2015, 72). Like the bereavement scholars at the turn of the century, *Pan's Labyrinth* "lays to rest the notion that grief ends, or should end," (Rosenblatt 1996, 57) and in doing so, expands the territory of the horror genre to explore individual experiences of loss. Mercedes hums a lullaby in Ofelia's dying moments, but the song carries across the film's diegetic and non-diegetic sound, providing the audience with ongoing companionship and solace. Loss has been confronted repeatedly throughout, meaning that when Ofelia does pass, viewers can be prepared for the separation and uplifted by the suggestion of her immortality. *Pan's Labyrinth*, then, although darker than some viewers may have anticipated, offers a greater sense of comfort, because children as well as adults, like Ofelia, are given time to grieve.

BIBLIOGRAPHY

Balanzategui, Jessica. 2015. "The Child Transformed by Monsters: The Monstrous Beauty of Childhood Trauma." In *The Supernatural Cinema of Guillermo del Toro: Critical Essays*, edited by John W. Morehead, 76–92. Jefferson, NC: McFarland.
Brown, Karin. 2015. "Time Out of Joint: Traumatic Hauntings in the Spanish Civil War Films." In *The Supernatural Cinema of Guillermo del Toro: Critical Essays*, edited by John W. Morehead, 58–75. Jefferson, NC: McFarland.
Buckley, Chloé Germaine. 2019. *Twenty-First-Century Children's Gothic*. Edinburgh: Edinburgh University Press.
Clark, Roger, and Keith McDonald. 2010. "'A Constant Transit of Finding': Fantasy as Realisation in *Pan's Labyrinth*." In *Children's Literature in Education* 41 (1): 52–63.
Del Toro, Guillermo. 2006. *Pan's Labyrinth (El laberinto del fauno)*. DVD. Spain: Warner Bros.
Derry, Charles. 2009. *Dark Dreams 2.0: A Psychological History of the Modern Horror Film From the 1950s to the 21st Century*. Jefferson, NC: McFarland.
Ellis, Jonathan, and Ana M. Sánchez-Arce. 2011. "'The Unquiet Dead': Memories of the Spanish Civil War in Guillermo del Toro's Cinema." In *Millennial Cinema: Memory in Global Film*, edited by Amresh Sinha and Terence McSweeney, 173–91. New York: Wallflower Press.
Freud, Sigmund. 1917. *Mourning and Melancholia*, vol. XIV. London: Hogarth.
Kotecki, Kristine. 2010. "Approximating the Hypertextual, Replicating the Metafictional: Textual and Sociopolitical Authority in Guillermo del Toro's *Pan's Labyrinth*." *Marvels & Tales: Journal of Fairy-Tale Studies* 24 (2): 235–54.
McCort, Jessica. R. 2016. "Introduction." In *Reading in the Dark: Horror in Children's Literature and Culture*, edited by Jessica R. McCort, 3–36. Jackson: Mississippi University Press.
Noble, Fiona. 2017. "'Once Upon a Time': Childhood Temporalities in Late- and Post-Franco Spanish Cinema." *Journal of Children and Media* 11 (4): 436–50.
Normand, Claude L., Phyllis R. Silverman, and Steven L. Nickman. 1996. "Bereaved Children's Changing Relationships with the Deceased." In *Continuing Bonds: New*

Understandings of Grief, edited by Dennis Klass, Phyllis R. Silverman, and Steven L. Nickman, 87–111. London and New York: Routledge.

Orme, Jennifer. 2010. "Narrative Desire and Disobedience in *Pan's Labyrinth*." *Marvels & Tales* 24 (2): 219–34.

Perlich, John. 2010. "Rethinking the Monomyth: *Pan's Labyrinth* and the Face of a New Hero(ine)." In *Millennial Mythmaking: Essays on the Power of Science Fiction and Fantasy Literature, Films and Games*, edited by John Perlich and David Whitt, 100–128. Jefferson, NC: McFarland.

Rosenblatt, Paul C. 1996. "Grief That Does Not End." In *Continuing Bonds: New Understandings of Grief*, edited by Dennis Klass, Phyllis R. Silverman, and Steven L. Nickman, 45–58. London and New York: Routledge.

Sabbadini, Andrea. 2014. *Moving Images: Psychoanalytic Reflections on Film*. London: Routledge.

Schubart, Rikke. 2018. *Mastering Fear: Women, Emotions, and Contemporary Horror*. New York: Bloomsbury Academic.

Scott, Lindsey. 2022. "Through a Darker Looking Glass: Alice's Adventures in Horrorland." In *Alice in Wonderland in Film and Popular Culture*, edited by Antonio Sanna, n.p. London: Palgrave Macmillan.

Silverman, Phyllis R., and Dennis Klass. 1996. "Introduction: What's the Problem?" In *Continuing Bonds: New Understandings of Grief*, edited by Dennis Klass, Phyllis R. Silverman, and Steven L. Nickman, 3–37. London and New York: Routledge.

Spector, Barry. 2009. "Review: Sacrifice of the Children in *Pan's Labyrinth*." *Jung Journal: Culture and Psyche* 3 (3): 81–86.

Varsamopoulou, Evy. 2019. "Entering the Labyrinth of Ethics in Guillermo del Toro's *El laberinto del fauno*." In *The Palgrave Handbook of Children's Film and Television*, edited by Casie Hermansson and Janet Zepernick, 246–60. London: Palgrave Macmillan.

West, Alexandra. 2015. "Where the Wild Things Are: Monsters and Children." In *The Supernatural Cinema of Guillermo del Toro: Critical Essays*, edited by John W. Morehead, 130–45. Jefferson, NY: McFarland.

Wright, Bob. 2007. *Loss and Grief*. New updated edition. London: M&K Publishing.

Chapter 2

"We Can Survive This"

An Examination of Loss and Grief in Juan Antonio Bayona's El orfanato (The Orphanage) (2007)

Erica Joan Dymond

BEAUTIFUL PAIN RATHER THAN TORTURE PORN

The early 2000s dripped with blood. On-screen violence had reached a nearly unpresented degree of pervasiveness and realism. The trend was so inescapable that *New York* magazine's David Edelstein felt compelled to give it a name, "torture porn" (2006). For Edelstein, torture porn was any film containing persistent sadistic brutality, spanning from obvious works like Rob Zombie's horror-thriller *The Devil's Rejects* (2005) to award-winning pieces like Mel Gibson's biblical epic *The Passion of the Christ* (2004). In the United States, the *Saw* (2004–2021) and *Hostel* (2005–2011) franchises were box-office toppers. And, at prestigious international film festivals, productions like Takashi Miike's *Ichi the Killer* (2001), Gaspar Noé's *Irréversible* (2002), and Alexandre Aja's *Haute Tension* (2003) were welcomed, screened, and winning accolades. Torture porn was both lucrative and gaining legitimization.

As many filmmakers—of all caliber and recognition—were engaged in an outrageous and profitable game of one-upmanship, Juan Antonio Bayona elected to create a decidedly gentler film. In fact, *El orfanato*'s MPAA rating—an R for "some disturbing content"—is somewhat misleading for its time ("*The Orphanage*: Parent's Guide" n.d.). The notoriously conservative

Common Sense Media reports, "Parents need to know that even though the R-rating is too harsh, brief but grotesque visuals let us know the filmmakers could do worse if they wanted to" (Cassady 2022). Rendering a similar assessment, famed film critic Roger Ebert asserts,

> *The Orphanage* has every opportunity to descend into routine shock and horror, or even into the pits with the slasher pictures, but it only pulls the trigger a couple of times. The rest is all waiting, anticipating, dreading. We need the genuine jolt that comes about midway, to let us see what the movie is capable of. (2007)

Acknowledged in the reviews of both writers, *El orfanato* has the potential to be a cruel gorefest with on-screen visuals created to rival the other works of its time. The premise could have been exploited to drag viewers through the nadir of torture porn. However, as *The New York Times*' John Anderson states, the film "doesn't have to resort to jump-scare tactics to generate thrills or great bloody oceans to maintain a crowd's attention" (2007). In a cinematic era defined by unmitigated carnage, Bayona distinguished his work by implying violence rather than showing it. This worked to tremendous effect, earning the film forty-three award nominations and thirty-two wins ("*The Orphanage*: Awards" n.d.).

Ahead of its time and seen much more frequently in mid-to-late 2010 films like Jennifer Kent's *The Babadook* (2014), Yorgos Lanthimos' *The Killing of a Sacred Deer* (2017), and Emma Tammi's *The Wind* (2018), the foundation for *El orfanato* is the concussive psychological impact of bereavement. The film is a meditation on how abject grief can erode relationships and corrupt the mind. The strength of this piece resides not in its body count or creative on-screen deaths but in its ability to communicate a compelling narrative about loss. In the press kit for *El orfanato*, Guillermo del Toro—the film's producer and presenter—notes that "it is one of the best crafted, most beautiful stories about the profound pain caused by loss that I have seen" (*El orfanato: Press Kit* 2007). What warrants consideration here is the notion that a film predicated on pain could be considered "beautiful." This virtually impossible feat is accomplished by something that nearly seemed old-fashioned in the early 2000s: Bayona cares about the sensibilities of his viewers as much as telling a riveting tale. Essentially, the world outside of the film means as much to this director as the world within. In one world, Bayona uses a compassionate form of filmmaking to abate viewer-trauma, mitigating shock and pain. In the other, Bayona allows the ravages of loss to unspool a close-knit family, offering a cautionary tale about the destructive power of unchecked grief. It is this expertly executed tightrope act that elevates Bayona's film about bereavement to art.

A pillow in a field of running chainsaws, *El orfanato* delivers a layered narrative about loss. By unpacking the work's gentle treatment of its audience as well as its frank depiction of grief, an understanding emerges of how a film about beautiful pain "received a ten-minute ovation" at the Cannes festival (Blake and Bailey 2013, 147) and became "the second biggest Spanish film of all time" (Smith 2012, 61).

THE WORLD OUTSIDE OF THE FILM: LOSS AND THE VIEWERS

In her film review for *USA Today*, Claudia Puig notes that *El orfanato* "is infused by a palpable sense of mounting dread" (2008, 9d). Similarly, in his review for *The Boston Globe*, Ty Burr declares, "From the opening moments in which wallpaper is ripped away to reveal the credits lurking below, the movie administers dread in fiendishly measured doses" (2008). And, at the same time, David Ansen's review for *Newsweek* explains how the film creates "shivers of dread" (2007). In all of these statements, one word resounds—"dread." Juan Antonio Bayona and Sergio G. Sánchez respectively create this pervasive sense of foreboding through deft cinematography and scriptwriting. Not merely atmospheric, this dread announces the trajectory of the film, better preparing viewers for tremendous loss. And, while this ubiquitous sense of doom is employed to caution the audience of disaster, a variety of other techniques also apprises viewers of an unfavorable dénouement. Fantasy sequences, detail-obscuring angles, and protective time skips (that avoid showing graphic but easily inferred information) all soften the more devastating aspects of the film. While this does create some ethical concerns, it also allows for a measure of grace, permitting *El orfanato* to reside in the realm of beloved dark fantasy rather than notorious family tragedy.

Bayona primes his viewers for loss early in *El orfanato*. In the first scene following the title sequence, the director alludes to Laura and Simón's imminent demise as well as their conversion to phantasms who establish residency in the Gothic beachside mansion. The scene opens in complete darkness. Simón (Roger Príncep) is heard repeatedly crying, "Mamá!" [00:04:27–00:04:30]. The first scream is distant, echoing. The second "Mamá!" is closer and louder but still resonating dreamily. And, as the final "Mamá!" gains sharp clarity, the black screen instantly disappears, indicating Laura's entrance into consciousness. This technique thoroughly and quickly aligns viewers with Laura (Belén Rueda)—they share Laura's sleep with her. Now, as the black screen snaps away, a framed window appears. It features a nighttime vista. This vista is then broken when Laura sits up, entering the composition. She is entirely covered with a bedsheet. Less than a beat passes before she struggles to remove the sheet from her head and processes her wakefulness. This introduction to (adult) Laura becomes startlingly relevant when she leaves her bed to check on Simón. Here, she opens the double doors to her son's bedroom and simply says, "Simón" [00:05:08]. A cut shows a shallow focus of the child's room. Similar to Laura hearing Simón's voice, upon hearing his mother's voice, Simón sits up—entering the frame with a bedsheet over his head. Superficially, this visual echo indicates the closeness of mother and son. Both sleep in the same unusual manner. However, the subtext suggests "bedsheet ghosts" and alludes to the mother and son's looming deaths as well as their spectral future.

In *Performing the Unstageable: Success, Imagination, Failure*, Karen Quigley examines the history of the "bedsheet ghost." The author describes how "historically, the bedsheet ghost has represented a range of meanings, stereotypes and behaviours, corresponding to its continuing liminality in culture and society" (2020, 171). Quigley notes how the image of a bedsheet ghost in nineteenth-century England would cause people to be "immobilize[d] with terror" and even offers the anecdote of "people dying of fright (or terror-related fevers or attacks) . . . when friends or family members donned a white sheet and dressed up as a ghost in order to scare them" (2020, 173). However, she proceeds to explain that as this iconic figure moves through time, it becomes "gently lampoon[ed] . . . in stories as diverse as *Father Ted*, *E.T.*, *Scrubs*, and *Beetlejuice*" (2020, 178). And, as the author explores the transformation of the bedsheet ghost in the films of the last two decades, she adds that "the bedsheet ghost appears, in the twenty-first century, to signal sadness and ridicule rather than fear" (2020, 178). These images from *El orfanato* support Quigley's findings since the vision of Laura and Simón clad in bedsheets is not intended to frighten viewers but to gently inform them of impending calamity. Likewise, the cozy pattern of the sheets—goldenrod stripes for Laura and powder-blue gingham for Simón—do not connote the sense of horror that a stark white sheet would. Instead, the homey patterns (much like those Quigley discusses in reference to Tim Burton's *Beetlejuice* [1988]) underscore this film as something of a domestic drama (2020, 178). Ultimately, the intent of the bedsheet trope in Bayona's film is not to cause distress in the audience but to prepare them.[1]

Of course, Bayona's forewarning of tragedy extends beyond mere bedsheets. In the subsequent scene, viewers are directed toward seeing Simón as unwell. The scene opens with Laura bounding down the stairs of her new home. As she rolls up her sleeves and prepares to help the movers, Carlos (Fernando Cayo) catches her attention. A subjective shot shows Laura approach her husband as he plays the piano. Savvy viewers take inventory of this moment. The study is entirely paneled in a dark wood. Likewise, the drapes, piano, and furniture are all equally as dark in hue. While daylight illuminates the oversized windows, Carlos remains cast in shadow. In the entire room, there is precisely one point of visual interest: the backlit glass of orange juice positioned on the right side of the piano lid. The importance of this object is emphasized by the balance of this composition. Carlos occupies the left side of the frame while this single, small glass bolsters the entire right side of the frame. The visual "weight" of this glass cannot be overstated. It is a neon sign imploring viewers to take note. Even if the glass goes unnoticed, Bayona ensures its conspicuousness through a cut to the right side of the piano. The glass now resides in the foreground as Laura joins Carlos on the bench. Its polka-dot design stands out as garish (in a decidedly posh home), lightly pulling focus and creating a layer of visual dissonance in an otherwise (literally) harmonious moment between the husband and wife. There is a mild hum of "something" being amiss. At this juncture, Simón speeds into the frame and stops directly in front of the glass. He sports an eye-catching red and white cape, a blue diver's cap, and clear goggles. There are echoes of these colors in the glass, and now there is little doubt to whom it belongs. Without question, and thus insinuating this next action as part of the family's everyday life, Simón takes a pill from the plate situated on the piano lid. All action stops. Laura and Carlos pause their duet, hands hovering above the keys. This moment consumes the totality of their focus. The parents' eyes remain fixed on Simón as the child places the pill in his mouth, grabs the polka-dot glass, and completes the ritual. With no further information, the routine and yet grave nature of this moment informs viewers that this pill is critical to Simón's wellbeing. He becomes a vulnerable child who requires close observation and care. Though Simón runs off screen at the end of this scene, the camera returns to the right side of the piano, the orange glowing glass still in the foreground—screaming a warning that viewers cannot miss, preparing them for disaster.

Just as the props and cinematography of the aforementioned scene communicate doom to viewers, costuming and scriptwriting do likewise. Here, the child is ostensibly dressed as a superhero but ultimately revealed as the one in need of protection. In addition to the cape, cap, and goggles, Simón sports a pale-yellow T-shirt that has a crudely drawn shield with a flamboyant "S" emblazoned in the middle. Admittedly obsessed with the character of Superman, Bayona expertly employs this fanboy reference (Dawson 2007).[2] Outwardly, this costume seems to position Simón as a heroic figure. However, much in the sense that the polka-dot glass (and the small pill beside it) announces the child's vulnerability, this "S" soon reveals Simón as all too mortal. Having just swallowed the pill and still holding the glass, the child points to the "S" on his chest and boasts, "'S' is for Simón!" [00:08:13]. In this single line, the costuming is shown as misdirection: the child refers to himself not with the prefix of "Super" (e.g., "Supermán!" or "Supersimón!"), but simply "Simón." This is both disarming and grounding. The whimsy created by the ensemble is silenced. Even when wearing a costume that explicitly permits identification with extraordinary strength and exceptional talents, in this moment, Simón remains himself: a precious but evidently ill child. This frankness cautions viewers that there will be no last-minute rescues, no incredible saves, and no impossibly satisfying resolution.

While Bayona continues to cultivate affection for Simón, he simultaneously readies viewers for the inevitable. A scene with Laura's childhood caretaker pushes the audience to see the child's existence as precarious. Here, a much older, less recognizable Benigna (Montserrat Carulla) visits the Gothic mansion in the guise of a social worker. She arrives in a downpour which not-so-subtly forecasts the grim nature of the interaction. As Benigna and Laura converse over a warm drink, the discussion turns increasingly confrontational. Thunder is heard punctuating their words. The pathetic fallacy is in full effect. While no specifics are granted, Benigna reveals Simón as physically ill. Benigna's mention of "new treatments" and "an experimental program" underscores the gravity of his condition [00:15:03]. Viewers are left a moment to reconcile the appearance of this cherub-faced child with the magnitude of this conversation. However, after Benigna is ushered from the home, Laura carefully examines the alleged social worker's notes. An insert shot discloses a change of address and as Laura flips to the next page, Simón's status as HIV positive is seen in bold font. It is a shock to even cosmopolitan viewers who understand that this disease has become much more manageable in prosperous countries such as Spain (Trickey et al. 2017). In addition to the low rumbles of thunder heard throughout this scene, the enormity of this information is punctuated by a single, sustained piano note followed by a plaintive oboe and then tense strings. After Laura locks the file

Figure 2.1 "'S' is for Simón." Roger Príncep (as Simón). El orfanato.
Source: The Orphanage (2007)

in a vault (indicating her perception of this diagnosis as dire), a cut brings her to the doorway of her son's room. She solemnly peers through a crack in the double doors. Simón's happy play is offset by her intense stare. Never does her gaze soften. Viewers are left with little doubt that Simón's ties to the corporal are tenuous.

Bayona crafts the scene previous to Simón's disappearance as blatantly ominous. After the child discovers he is HIV positive, his parents attempt to open a dialogue with their son. This scene begins with a close-up of a tray nervously set on a coffee table. Residing in the background, a white ceramic plate offers toast and jam while the contents of a ceramic bowl and mug remain unknown. Featured in the foreground, atop a white ceramic plate, are the previously seen polka-dot glass (again filled with orange juice) and a petite silver plate bearing the child's HIV medication. There is no practicality in this. The pills could reside next to the toast and jam and the glass could be stationed anywhere on the tray itself. Not only would this make carrying the tray easier, but it would normalize Simón's regimen. Segregating these items emphasizes them, declaring Simón as fragile. The camera then tilts up from the tray to Carlos and Laura. Throughout this scene, the couple is featured in a two shot, presenting a loving and unified front. However, their words and body language do little to soothe the child—or viewers. Laura begins by saying, "You can ask us anything" [00:26:42]. A reverse shot shows Simón seated in a large, tufted, wing-back chair. The style of the chair makes him seem small and vulnerable. As Carlos speculates how Simón discovered his HIV positive status, an insert shot shows a close-up of the pills from the child's perspective. A slow zoom indicates his fixation. Finally, Simón asks about the medication, "What if I don't take them?" and his father (a physician) answers, "Nothing would happen" [00:27:04–00:27:08]. But the arrangement of the tray belies his words. And Laura's body language serves a similar purpose. While Carlos maintains eye contact and a receptive posture (his arms are unfolded, he leans forward and hunches just a bit to be on his child's level), Laura squirms. Throughout, she folds and unfolds her arms and hands, takes deep breaths, twitches her nose, looks away, stares at the floor, and purses her lips. In essence, her behavior betrays Carlos' statement. Understanding his father is diluting the truth, Simón bluntly inquires, "If I don't take them, how soon would I die?" to which his father provides an honest response, "It would take many days, many weeks" [00:27:10–00:27:15]. The child's mortality leaps to the fore. However, less than a beat passes before Carlos earnestly adds, "Don't worry, we'll take care of you. You won't get sick or die. Okay?" [00:27:16]. Of this moment, Charles St-Georges asserts, "Fiction is deployed here to assure the child death and sickness are not going to happen to him" (2018, 130). While Carlos' expression is warm, the "Okay?" hangs in the air, forever answered. Nothing is "okay." A reverse shot shows

Simón's eyes shift from his father to his mother. Here, Laura remains silent but drops her hands from her face to appear more open and more in accord with her husband; nonetheless, her discomfort and fear are evident. A cut to black and a beat of silence create a chilling effect for viewers. In the next scene, Simón disappears.

As the search for Simón becomes a protracted event, engaged viewers attuned to Bayona's "clue-strewing" film understand that the child is, most likely, dead (Schwartzbaum 2008). They have been provided ample evidence to indicate this (though it is physical trauma, not illness, that kills the child). Nonetheless, even the shrewdest, most discerning viewers may still struggle with the film's tragic conclusion. Therefore, Bayona blunts the otherwise cruel conclusion. In the same way that the director employs "dread" to forewarn viewers of Simón's loss, he uses a variety of cinematic techniques from this point forward to guide his audience toward a gentler landing.

When Laura discovers Tomás' "casita," Bayona amply equips the audience for this most challenging of scenes. Beginning with what initially appears as a subjective shot, Laura's descent into the mansion's basement is dauntingly claustrophobic. A tight square of light illuminates the first dozen steep stairs but then darkness engulfs the remaining space. As Laura disappears down this "rabbit hole," a cut brings viewers to a wide shot. The camera is stationed at the back of basement, allowing for a full side view of Laura's descent. Though an expansive shot, the bottom of the lengthy staircase does not—at first—fit within the frame. For a brief second, there is a surreal quality to Laura's journey down the seemingly interminable stairs. As the camera tracks to the left and tilts to reveals the final steps, Laura flips on the lights. The basement repeatedly blinks into existence, as though waking after a long sleep. In the background (and unbeknownst to Laura), ghost children appear and disappear with the lights' flicker. After the electricity stabilizes, a warm hue illuminates Tomás' elaborate workspace. Viewers see detailed pencil sketches of birds and deer, a mixed-media representation of a beetle, and color illustrations of anthropomorphic mice. And now, the walls of the basement gain clarity. On the concrete is a massive mural of the landscape outside the mansion's door. The lighthouse, the beach, the fish: all are represented, but all are fixed in time.[3] This entire series of events creates a distinctly fantastical feeling. Bayona is visually encouraging the audience to question the veracity of what they are seeing. Therefore, as Laura moves to the curtained sleeping cubby, viewers are already dubious. There are too many indications of a reality that is ruptured. And, for a brief interim, the audience will be forced to see Laura through a more objective lens.

As this scene continues, a cut positions viewers behind the closed curtain of the cubby. In an area entirely concealed from Laura, they watch through the gauzy fabric as she furtively approaches. For the audience, the sensation is uncanny: they occupy space unknown to Laura—one that is the source of her investigation. As she draws closer to the curtain, discordant sustained strings become incrementally amplified. Then, when her hand touches the curtain, another set of strings enters, higher in pitch and growing increasingly loud. In a different film, the cues presented here would indicate Laura as the monster slowly closing-in on the hapless victim. And, in a hyperbolic way, this is true since it is she who inadvertently trapped Simón in the basement.[4] In this moment, viewers experience an acute separation from Laura, witnessing her derangement . . . experiencing her, for an instant, as oddly menacing. All of this jolts the audience into a more critical mindset, presenting them with an opportunity to reconsider their assessment of Laura before the curtain is drawn. Therefore, when the next cut brings viewers to a fully shrouded Simón who then turns and removes a maroon blanket from his face, the moment reads as a lie. The vibrancy of this child's physical appearance, his mild reaction upon seeing his mother after being trapped in a basement for months, his Kubrick-esque request for Laura to "stay and play with us" . . . all aspects of this moment indicate that this less than the truth [01:29:37]. Laura's elation at finding her child is not shared by viewers. In fact, the vision of this perfect child makes the scene all the more taut with suspense.

As Laura prepares to leave the subterranean room, she hears the benevolent voices and playful thumps of the supposed ghost children. In an act of protection, Laura re-shrouds Simón—a troubling gesture seeming to indicate his status as not among the living—and moves towards the stairs with Simón in her arms. Unnerved by the sounds, she begins to turn clockwise, scanning her surroundings. The turning escalates into spinning as she becomes increasingly defensive of her newly located son. If viewers have not realized the improbability of this moment, Bayona will now force a visceral reaction.

As Laura spins in a clockwise motion, the camera begins to move around her in a counterclockwise direction. While this arc shot starts slowly, it reaches a frenetic, nearly unsustainable pace. In spirit and purpose, this moment appears as an homage to the technically renowned "First Dance" scene from Brian DePalma's *Carrie* (1976).[5] Film scholar Ron Backer describes the result of DePalma's iconic shot: "Tommy and Carrie spin and spin to the music, faster and faster, with the camera doing 360° turns in the opposite direction as if Tommy and Carrie are in their own personal land of make-believe" (2015, 346). Certainly, this transfers to Bayona's film. Laura *is* in a "personal land of make-believe," one in which Simón is alive. However, James Bernardoni offers a less "magical" description of this shot as "create[ing] an unpleasant, vertiginous effect . . . create[ing] a dizzying, almost sickening effect" (1991, 97). Bernardoni's assessment of this shot in *Carrie* seems to effortlessly apply to this moment in *El orfanato*. If any viewers have resisted the ample signals Bayona provides to indicate this moment as mere wish-fulfillment, the director literally overwhelms them with physical unease. The bodily discomfort created by this shot prepares those unwilling audience members for the film's sobering truth.

Before the reveal of Simón's body, one final aspect of viewer preparation occurs. In an effort to quiet the alleged ghost children, Laura implores her son to close his eyes as she shuts her own. The film cuts to an extreme close-up of Laura's clinched eyes. As the shot tightens, the music crescendos. Then, as the warmth rapidly drains from the film, the orchestra falls silent. The children's voices are muted. All signs of life are stripped from the scene. A cut to a medium shot shows a dimly lit basement. An ominous green hue drapes the scene, revealing everything since Laura descended the "rabbit hole" as illusory. She allows the maroon blanket in which she is holding Simón to unfurl, showing no child inside. Only a few feet away lies the reality. At this critical juncture, Bayona has done everything possible to prepare the audience for the worst outcome.

In the same sense that the film takes pains to alert viewers of impending doom, it also strives to soften that loss. Viewers know Simón as a beautiful child. His full face, large eyes, rosy cheeks, and luminous curls are emblematic of youth in bloom. He is sweet and precocious, intelligent and adventurous. Bayona makes it effortless for viewers to care about this child. Therefore, if the film is to retain its tone as a dark fairy tale (rather than unadulterated horror), the reveal of Simón's body must be executed with caution. While Bayona often uses Laura's perspective to evoke sympathy for her character, the next sequence of shots will momentarily withhold that perspective to mitigate the trauma to viewers. Here, Laura kneels before what she correctly suspects to be Simón's body. A low-angle shot exposes both Laura's trepidation and resolve. A reverse shot shows a close-up of the child's masked head. As Laura tugs at the mask, a cut brings viewers behind the child's body, denying the audience Laura's point of view. Here, viewers are shielded, allowed to process this moment much more slowly. The barely perceptible curls that tumble from the mask suggest that this is Simón. And Laura's devastated reaction validates these fears. The audience's sorrow is intensified by Laura's agonizing screams. By witnessing Laura's reaction, viewers understand the need to psychologically brace themselves. Only after proof of the body's identity and beholding Laura's anguish are viewers permitted to see child's face via a subjective shot. This shot is mercifully obscured in darkness, but Simón's hollow eyes and desiccated face are more than enough for viewers to understand that he has been dead for an extended period. However, by remaining partially in shadow, this shot allows heartbreak to supersede revulsion. The moment delivers a sad confirmation—rather than a savage shock—that allows viewers to sympathize with Laura and continue this journey rather than disengage or resent the film.

In the subsequent scene, Laura carries Simón's corpse from the basement to the orphans' room. He is enshrouded in the maroon blanket from the fantasy sequence. Viewers cannot help but to recall that only moments ago, he was shown "alive" in this very blanket. A cut then brings viewers to a poignant shot of Laura sitting in a window seat, rocking her child. A close-up shows her forcing Simón's HIV medication into his rigid mouth. These are the pills he needs to be well. And, in a parallel thought, Laura takes a bottle of sleeping pills from her pocket and forces herself to swallow them. There seems to be an insinuation that these are the pills that will make her "well"—through death. Viewers are now beholding reality. Simón's lifeless body, Laura's choking and gagging on the pills, her loss of consciousness, her head and shoulders slumping forward . . . all are, in fact, *too* real. Laura's death closely reflects the fact that bereaved mothers are susceptible to early death both via natural and unnatural causes. In 2003, a Danish study published in *The Lancet* reports: "We observed a significantly increased overall mortality in bereaved mothers . . . Bereaved mothers were more likely to die from natural and unnatural causes, respectively, than were mothers whose child had not died . . . Bereaved mothers were at an increased risk of death from unnatural causes throughout follow-up, but especially during the first 3 years" (Li et al. 2003, 365).

The researchers added that "sudden or violent deaths cause more stress than other types of death. Accordingly, we noted that the unexpected death . . . of a child resulted in higher relative maternal mortality rates than did the expected death of a child" (Li et al. 2003, 366). As viewers witness Laura's suicide, the real world seems too present, too painful. And, once again, through skillful cinematography, Bayona releases the audience from this pain (but not without some unintended, controversial consequences).

Rather than remaining in reality with Laura's body, the film shifts perspective. Bayona now cuts to the exterior of the Gothic mansion, removing viewers from the gruesome actuality of this scene. In the foreground, a merry-go-round creaks and starts to spin. The suggestion is that the audience is re-entering an illusory world. A series of cuts then returns viewers into the home. First, there is a shot of the ground-floor staircase. Next, a cut seems to walk viewers to the second floor. The following three cuts glide viewers through the various hallways and end at the door leading into the orphans' room. A final cut brings viewers back to Laura's body. These cuts are not random. They logically and sequentially move viewers from the exterior of the mansion directly through the home to Laura. It seems akin to a classic sit-com "reset"—the establishing shot followed by an interior shot that reveals that *somehow*, though *some* cinematic wizardry, the situation has changed in the brief interim.[6] And, indeed, the situation *has* changed.

El orfanato opens in Laura's sleeping world and closes in her dying mind. When the camera returns to Laura, her slumped body is roused. She makes a wish for the return of Simón and the contents of the maroon blanket become imbued with life. In a clear echo of the basement fantasy scene, Laura stands with the maroon blanket. Instead of an empty cover unfurling, the film cuts to a shot of the bedroom floor as a close-up shows a tiny pair of Converse touch the ground. Indicative of this renewed vivaciousness, the toes dramatically wiggle in the shoes. Laura removes the shroud from the child's head and viewers behold Simón as though he were alive again. The high-angle shot emphasizes his diminutive stature, large eyes, and loose curls. The desiccated body of only a few seconds ago becomes a dissolving nightmare for viewers. It is a classic "feel-good" moment as Laura gathers the phantasmagoric orphans about her, sharing a bedtime story with the implication that this is now her chosen eternity. A match cut then turns the lighthouse spotlight into the rising sun of morning. And, while it may now be daytime, it is many, many days after Laura locates Simón. A time skip brings viewers to a monument that reads, "In memory of Laura and Simón and of the orphans Martín, Rita, Alicia, Guillermo, Víctor, and Tomás" [01:40:14]. In the gap in celluloid, Carlos commissioned this memorial and had it erected. Likewise, enough time has elapsed that he can kneel in front of it while maintaining his composure. The final scene shows Carlos inside the Gothic mansion, finding the Saint Anthony medal in the orphans' room. As he plucks it from the floor, the double doors swing open like arms preparing for an embrace. Not without hesitancy, scholar Ann Davies observes, "He [Carlos] is apparently reunited with his family" (2011, 82). Evidently, this time skip protects the viewers from the horrific truth of this loss and allows for nothing but bittersweet tears. But protection is a tricky "thing" . . .

Alfred Hitchcock coined the term "icebox trade" (also referred to as "icebox factor," "icebox talk," "icebox syndrome," "icebox question," etc.). In an interview with journalist Charles Thomas Samuels, Hitchcock was asked why *Psycho* (1960) included the psychiatrist's evaluation of Norman Bates. Hitchcock replied, "Because the audience needed it. Otherwise, they'd have a lot of questions. You'd run afoul of the icebox trade" (1972, 247). When the interviewer requested an explanation of "icebox trade," Hitchcock responded:

> The people who get home after seeing a movie, go to the icebox, and take out cold chicken. While they're chewing on it, they discuss the picture. In the morning, the wife meets the neighbor next door. She says to her, "How was the picture?" and the wife says, "It was alright but we discovered a number of flaws in it." (Samuels 1972, 247)

With regards to Bayona's *El orfanato*, the icebox trade would not focus on literal flaws, but the "deception" created by the protective time skip and how that gap in the celluloid affects the viewers' interpretation of the film.

Here, the icebox trade begins. Viewers are allotted room to speculate that it is Carlos who will return to the Gothic mansion for Laura. And in this protective time skip, he will find his wife dead, having committed suicide. Within the context of film, viewers are given no reason to believe there would be a note to explain Laura's actions since she commits suicide in haste. In fact, it would seem the Saint Anthony medal is intended to serve this purpose. Of course, thoughtful viewers realize that the solace this pendant is intended to deliver is nullified by the fact that Carlos only locates it many months after Laura's suicide. Carlos' grieving process is well underway when he spies the necklace wedged between two floorboards. Though finding the medal upon his return to the mansion creates a satisfying conclusion to the film, viewers are forced to envision the heartbreak that rules Carlos in the interim. In addition to discovering Laura's corpse, Carlos will also find his son in an advanced state of decomposition. Carlos' entire family—to the best of the audience's knowledge—has been decimated. In this protective time skip, viewers are shielded from the profound guilt this the grisly tableau would provoke—ultimately, it *is* Carlos who left Laura alone in the house. Viewers are shielded from the hard work that brings Carlos to the point of commissioning a monument and revisiting the mansion. In the academic text *The Two Cines con Niño*, Erin K. Hogan notes of *El orfanato* that "happy endings are not possible for most Gothic heroes and heroines in the here and now" with the insinuation that the "happy ending" will be found in the hereafter (2018, 125). However, this "happy ending" is an illusion intended to provide closure for viewers. It disregards the pain that Laura creates. Importantly, when describing his own film, Bayona states that "it's a fairy tale for grown-ups. No happily-ever-after" (Anderson 2007). Nonetheless, viewers are at peace with the film because their last vision of Laura is of a beautiful, nurturing mother surrounded by gentle children who need and adore her. Viewers are at peace because their last vision of Simón is of a rosy-cheeked child. Carlos was not so fortunate. His last vision of his loved ones is in various states of death. The ethics of this conclusion have proven as a point of contention for critics. For instance, Tim Kroenert of the long-running *Eureka Street* magazine states:

> This is a highly effective but imperfect film. It saves its greatest imperfection until last. Unwilling to leave his audience with the harrowing outcome of the film's climactic movement, Bayona instead tacks on an uplifting final note. The film's ending is discordant and suggests dubious means for finding peace amid grief. (2008, 28)

Here, the critic expresses fear that in the director's desire to protect viewers, there exists the potential to (mis)read the film as romanticizing suicide. This is a valid concern. By the director concealing the literal and collateral damage of Laura's choice, viewers do not (actually) witness the incalculable trauma and pain she has created. Nonetheless, Maria Delgado of *Sight & Sound* asks for patience, writing: "Yes, one can quibble over an unnecessary prologue, a drawn-out séance and a sentimental final sequence, but these are minor flaws in a poignant film that looks to the past and the world beyond to illuminate the realities of the present" (2006, 45). Equally as ambivalent about the film's conclusion, one reviewer for the *San Antonio Current* also comes to the film's defense by bluntly expressing:

> There's a moment near the end where the Bayona and Co. very nearly leave us with what had the capacity to be one of the most merciless endings in horror history (I still haven't decided if [I would have] been imbued with respect or simply appalled), but then soften matters substantially—and manage, somehow, to turn immediately sweet, giving us instead what must be the most heartwarming tale ever about Peter Pan, suicide, and spectral special-needs orphans. ("Believe: 'El Orfanato' is the Most Solid Straight-Up Thriller in Years" 2008)

In all of this commentary, there seems an acknowledgement that Bayona's goal was to tell viewers a captivating story rather than to make a film with an infamous ending. His goal was to protect viewers from the pain of this extraordinary loss. He executed a measure of grace, leaving viewers with a beautiful film about pain.[7]

In *El orfanato,* viewers witness the destruction of a charming little family. The audience watches them play the piano, explore the beach, discuss literature . . . and be torn asunder. It could have been structured as a gut-punch, played for full effect. Instead, Bayona forewarns viewers of impending doom with an abundance of clues. Therefore, rather than have the death of a child be a core-shaking shock, it becomes a sad inevitability. And, when he must challenge the audience's pain tolerance, the director mercifully obscures and/or codes the sharpest edges. As a result, the suicide of a mother averts becoming a harrowing scene crafted for water-cooler discussions and turns into a powerful element of the overall storytelling. In *El orfanato,* Bayona's mitigation of the audience's distress is critical to the enjoyment—perhaps, even acceptance—of a film with an unfavorable outcome. Viewers still feel the loss of these characters but are better able to process it and remain engaged in the story. Having no interest in torturing his audience, Bayona holds (even gently pats) the audience's hand while offering them a sometimes challenging but always engaging narrative about the (sometimes deadly) nature of grief.

THE WORLD WITHIN THE FILM: LOSS, MARRIAGE, AND FATAL GRIEF

The audience first meets the fully conscious version of Carlos while he is playing the piano. As Laura approaches, he gazes up at her with big, soft eyes. Carlos' affection for his wife is clear. He does not need to make room on the bench: that space is already reserved for her. Without a single word, Laura joins Carlos, making the solo piece a duet. A cut shows a close-up of the couple's hands as they play. Their gold wedding bands provide the sole point of visual interest, underscoring Laura and Carlos as formally pair bonded. These rings—and the love instilled in them—become a critical symbol throughout the film, used repeatedly to reveal the state of the marriage. As the scene continues, the camera then tilts up to the couple's happy faces. Laura giggles and Carlos continues to smile warmly. The tenderness seen in their expressions emphasizes their fondness for each other. In the literal and the figurative, they make beautiful music together. As the two continue to play, they discuss their son's overactive imagination. Their ability to perform a duet and simultaneously hold a serious conversation emphasizes their capacity for cooperation. It also foregrounds the ease in which Laura and Carlos talk about more challenging topics. The couple's healthy, playful, and affectionate relationship is captured in this moment. And it is from this idyllic starting point that viewers witness the brutal separation of this pair following their son's disappearance. The music, the side-by-side rings, the smiles and giggles, the effortless cooperation, even the will to live—all disappear with Simón.

In *El orfanato*, viewers see the quiet separation of Laura and Carlos—physically and emotionally—after the loss of their son. Both become withdrawn. They are often shown grieving in separate spaces and in disparate

Figure 2.2 Close-up of wedding rings. El orfanato.
Source: The Orphanage (2007)

ways. In such a moment of profound anguish, communication and empathy between spouses is paramount. A recent study published in *OMEGA: Journal of Death and Dying* asserts one crucial point:

> Good interaction in the couple was put forward as the most important factor for finding new closeness following the death. A sine qua non for succeeding, parents stated, was to use time with one another and talk about the loss, and having respect and understanding for different reactions. In addition, joint activities were emphasized. By "reading" how the other partner was faring and adapting one's own way of being accordingly, showing respect and sensitivity to one's partner's needs, and being supportive when that was needed, new closeness could be found. (Dyregrov and Dyregrov 2015, 15)

But in *El orfanato*, the manner in which each spouse processes loss is often prohibitive to the other. The couple simply—through no fault of their own—fail to connect on an effective level.

Carlos' processing of loss is largely depicted as dynamic, often referred to as "instrumental grief" (Doka and Martin 2010, 8). He studies maps in his office, gathers information via the phone, seeks the help of the police, and so forth. Essentially, he remains busy. Conversely, Laura's grief is shown as expressing itself in emotion, often referred to as "intuitive grief" (Doka and Martin 2010, 8). She lies in bed, gazes out windows, sits on the stairs outside her home, and so on. In contrast to Carlos, she frequently appears as a static figure (though her mind is processing thoughts and emotions). Both forms of grieving are considered normal and healthy. However, while Carlos' method of grieving is grounded in the rational, Laura's approach increasingly turns to the metaphysical. Her attending lectures on doppelgängers, allowing a medium into their family home, and even trying to personally communicate with the dead show her desperation and create the vast canyon disallowing their mutual mourning. None of this has gone unnoticed by critics. In an online article for *Culture Snob*, Jeff Ignatius states, "While there is marital tension between Laura and Carlos because of her [Laura's] insistence that Simón is still alive, his [Carlos'] patience with her over such a long period of time strains credulity in light of his spiritual skepticism" (2008). Nonetheless, *Sight & Sound*'s Maria Delgado perceives the situation differently, stating that "Laura gradually withdraws into the inner recesses of the house as she rejects the voice of reason represented by her kindly but ineffectual husband" (2008, 44). While both assessments note the schism in the couple's grief, there is no agreement as to which character is "correct." Whereas one critic views Laura's approach as intolerable, another finds Carlos' approach as unhelpful. Perhaps producer/presenter Guillermo del Toro provides the most interesting yet "self-serving" response in saying, "I really love that in her

[Laura's] character. I really love that she has that drive regardless of her husband, regardless of society, regardless of any semblance of sanity or rationality" (Nasson 2007). In this statement, del Toro praises Laura for her tenacity in being led by her intuition, but he also underscores that she has rejected the caring advice of her husband (as well as a variety of other helpful authorities) and has plummeted into psychologically perilous territory (as evidenced by her suicide). For del Toro, Laura's approach to grieving has the hallmarks of a captivating story—but it is also one that results in isolation, despair, madness, and death.

The vast differences in Laura and Carlos' grief begin to appear at the thirty-eight-minute mark of the film. It is here that viewers sense Laura begin to slip from healthy, emotion-based grief to something much more dangerous—one that del Toro says can potentially be read as "the psychological decaying process of Laura" (Gingold 2019). In this scene, Laura awakens from a dream and enters the hallway in her wheelchair. She hears booming noises and as she presses her ear to the wall, the sound of shattering wood explodes from somewhere inside the house. Viewers rationally understand this is when Simón accidentally breaks the basement railing and falls to his death. However, Laura suspects a supernatural explanation. She screams for Carlos as she rolls into Simón's room. There, she finds a doll concealed in the child's bedsheets and looks to her husband with pained puzzlement, trying to discern its meaning. However, for Carlos, there is nothing to decipher. It is not a clue to his son's disappearance: it is merely a doll. He stares at Laura with a mixture of concern and amazement. What follows are two thematically similar, sequential pairs of scenes that demonstrate how Laura and Carlos each process grief differently—and imply Laura's continued deterioration.

The next full scene moves Carlos from Simón's bedroom into a brightly lit classroom that he has transformed into a command center. He is using the telephone. Though he is standing, the camera resides at hip level. This opening moment explicitly showcases his wedding ring [00:39:55]. Here, there is an echo of the piano scene. Viewers recall another ring, on another hand, but grieving in a different space (presumably, also alone). Laura's absence is immediately felt. The voice of a reporter from either a radio or television can be heard in the background. It reveals that a "seven-year-old boy disappeared from his home six months ago" [00:39:59]. Only speaking the word, "Okay," Carlos hangs up the phone [00:39:52]. Viewers can glean that the call provides information since Carlos grabs a pushpin and then moves to a wall that hosts a large map, newspaper articles, two "missing person" flyers, and Post-it notes. The camera glides around Carlos' desk, following him. As a result of the dynamic quality of this moment, the audience feels Carlos' active involvement in locating his lost son. An insert shot then details Carlos removing a Post-it note and adding a pushpin. However, while viewers try to process this wealth of knowledge, Laura's voice enters. As the audio for next scene bleeds into this one, Laura overpowers the news report. Here, the film privileges her emotions over Carlos' investigation—this is, after all and quite literally, her story.[8] But, more importantly, Bayona emphasizes how her pain has become so acute that it cannot be contained—going so far as to invade into another scene. In a bleak tone, she states, "My son disappeared six months ago. His name is Simón" [00:40:10]. Before Carlos' scene fully transitions into Laura's, a medium wide shot of Carlos shows him stepping back and analyzing his pinboard. His laptop, the television, the news report, the newspaper articles, all show how his pain motivates him to seek assistance in traditional, rational ways. In the twenty-three seconds that Carlos' is allotted here, viewers are permitted a small window into this father's grief. It is controlled, methodical and investigative, conducted in right angles and thumb tacks. It is the definition of instrumental grief.

Designed to be compared, this subsequent scene with Laura and the previous one with Carlos share striking similarities as well as variances. Like the preceding scene, this one opens at hip level, showcasing Laura's wedding ring. There is an immediate sense of loss—again—in witnessing this ring without its mate. And, whereas Carlos' hand rested on the telephone in the last scene, Laura's ringed hand clutches at a tissue. Again, the implication of instrumental versus intuitive grief is very much at work here. This disparity is also emphasized by Bayona's directing. In the previous scene, Carlos physically moves into a position that allows viewers to see him. However, in this moment, the camera must tilt up from Laura's hand to her face since she remains stationary for the totality of the scene. As the scene continues, viewers soon understand that Laura is participating in a bereavement group. In a tightly framed single shot backgrounded by darkness, Laura shares her efforts to locate Simón. A reverse shot shows attentive listeners. Approximately thirteen seconds of discussion elapse before viewers suspect Carlos' presence—he is briefly shown from behind in a group shot [00:40:13–00:40:27]. Approximately another fourteen seconds elapse before his presence is confirmed in an equally as tightly framed single shot [00:40:28–00:40:41]. In reality, Laura and Carlos are seated side by side. Certainly, Bayona could have opened with a two shot of Laura and Carlos—perhaps showing their hands resting on the schoolroom desks, rings visible to communicate their solidarity. However, the context of this scene precludes such closeness. While Carlos is in attendance with Laura and genuine in his support, this group is not for him. In this entire scene, he never speaks. Only Laura shares. And what she shares will both expand the chasm between the married couple as well as press on the boundaries of psychological acceptability—even for a newly bereaved parent.

As Laura continues her "share" in this scene, she pauses. Her hand shakes. Her eyes dart about the room. She takes a breath and exhales. A small, sad smile appears as though Laura understands the absurdity of what she is about to say before adding, "My son had imaginary friends with whom he played" [00:40:41]. This leap into the supernatural triggers a rapid series of cuts. Before Laura can finish this sentence, a cut brings viewers to a single shot of Carlos. Once looking at the members of the group, he now turns toward Laura. His face remains soft but blank. Another cut shows a single shot of Laura looking in Carlos' direction. Her face remains equally as soft. There is no judgement in these glances between spouses but it is plain that Laura is alone in her belief. The next cut presents a single shot of Carlos turning toward the group's facilitator for guidance. His expression is concerned but open to guidance. Then, a cut shows the group leader judiciously motion for Carlos to hold his thoughts. And the next cut displays Laura turning from Carlos and back to the group as she explains that she feels these imaginary friends are in her home—with the assumption being that the phantasms are the key to Simón's return. While all of this vigorous camerawork and editing creates a more visually dynamic and dramatic scene, it also implies distance. This bereavement group is situated in a small classroom. Even with only eleven people in this space, it feels a confined. Physically, Laura and Carlos may be inches from each other, but they are worlds apart in their grief and beliefs.

In this scene, the first (and only) two shot of Laura and Carlos happens as one mother describes having seen the ghost of her daughter. She relates that the encounter was peaceful and adds, "I think it was her way of telling me, 'I'm fine, I'm safe. Don't suffer for me'" [00:41:48–00:41:58]. Here, a cut brings viewers to a two shot of Laura and Carlos, both in thought and both united in empathy for this woman. This shot offers momentary hope that the couple can bond through and beyond their pain. However, after nearly all of the parents report a similar spectral encounter with their loved ones, Laura becomes indignant. The framing returns to a tight single shot. She rolls her eyes and is shown insisting her son "is not dead" but merely kidnapped by ghosts [00:42:32]. And, again, a cut brings viewers to Carlos, already turned toward Laura with a profoundly concerned expression [00:40:37–00:40:39]. Carlos' alarm is accentuated by the score. In this moment, the strings swell and then quiet as he opens his mouth for a breath and then exhales. A cut to Laura shows her pledging to get her child back and as she continues, another cut features Carlos' face as she says, "I'm not crazy . . . believe me" [00:42:46]. Carlos, who has been watching the facilitator, breaks eye contact and gazes down with a slight pursing of his lips. This is the only point in the entire discussion that Carlos expresses any dissention. However, at no point does Carlos verbally interrupt Laura. And, at no point does he seem anything less than respectful. However, as Laura strives to set herself apart from the other grieving parents, asserting her situation is somehow special, his frustration becomes evident. Given that this is Laura's scene, a final cut returns viewers to her as she casts her eyes to the floor and says, "I know what I'm saying" [00:42:51]. Laura has slipped from intuitive grief into self-destruction: alienating herself from these grieving parents, closing discussion with the facilitator, and rendering her husband silent. As Carlos reaches out to more and more people, gathering a stockpile of information and contacts, Laura is seen disregarding the supportive voices she simply does not want to hear. For certain, del Toro's assessment of Laura as stubbornly pressing forward "regardless of her husband, regardless of society, regardless of any semblance of sanity or rationality" seems accurate but, most assuredly, detrimental.

A scene transition ushers viewers from the bereavement group to a medium shot of Laura gazing out a window in the Gothic mansion. Though she is mostly facing away from the camera, her fluttering eyelashes indicate that she is observing the rainstorm just beyond the glass, engaged in thought. In this static shot, the only other movement is the rain falling outside and Laura's breathing. The window appears as a sliver of glowing space on the screen with a crush of blackness on the right and left, emphasizing Laura's isolation. The natural sound of rain permeates this brief interlude, telegraphing the nature of Laura's anguished mind.

And, not uncoincidentally, the snippet of Laura looking out the window transitions to a close-up of Carlos' pinboard. The camera travels over a mass of pushpins and Post-it flags. The abundance of pins—many more than previously shown—communicates a time skip from last the viewers saw the board. A cut brings the audience to a medium full shot. Like with Laura in the last scene, Carlos remains turned away from the camera, thinking. The map has been dramatically expanded, now consuming the wall. Polaroids, a police sketch of Benigna, and larger Post-it notes obscure parts of the map. This shot communicates the tremendous time and work Carlos has invested in locating his child. Almost unfairly, it is quantifiable (and yet, as viewers discover, essentially futile). In the foreground, Carlos' laptop is seen open adjacent to the telephone. Instead of rain, viewers again hear information from either a television or radio. Carlos brushes his hand across the wall of notes. His jagged breath is heard under the mournful score. Undeniably, his suffering is immense. And, while Carlos is physically alone in this moment, he is in perpetual active contact with the outside world, accepting of its help. Therefore, instead of the wide pillars of black screen that encase Laura in the previous scene, Carlos' workspace is well lit and open. The framing is loose. Rather than being constricted in a box of darkness, Carlos ends the scene by walking off screen. When next viewers see this workspace, it will be with Laura in it, bringing with her a crush of black screen.

At this point in the film, it would be easy (i.e., conventional) to exclusively show Carlos' grief as instrumental/masculine and Laura's as intuitive/feminine. It would be easy to allow viewers to assume that each spouse's expression of pain differs so greatly that no bridge can be built—too easy. Offering his audience a more complex film, Bayona includes a gut-wrenching bookend to the initial piano scene. This complementary scene opens with a close-up of the piano's fallboard. In it, Carlos' hands and ring are perfectly reflected. A gradual pan to the left allows for both the reflection and the reality to appear on screen simultaneously. The pan continues until the reflection is pushed out of the frame and only Carlos' actual hands and ring are featured [00:48:27–00:48:34]. This is done in a single, slow sweep of the camera that lasts mere seconds. However, that this is the entry point for the scene—and all the audience is permitted to view—stresses its importance. In this illusion of a second ring, there a reminder of its mate and a suggestion that it may be reunited since Laura is soon revealed as covertly watching her husband from the doorway. But much like the illusion of the ring in the fallboard, a reunion is just that. Laura observes but cannot act. She is confined by a thick wall of blackness on both her right and left. The door's threshold becomes a visual representation of the debilitating grief that is destroying her. A cut then brings viewers to a medium close-up of Carlos from behind. In the dark and somewhat hunched to the side, Carlos can he heard softly crying. He slowly strikes the same piano key. A single note hauntingly resonates throughout this scene. Here, Bayona is blatantly asking viewers to compare this moment to the one earlier. The side-by-side rings, the music, the laughs are all reduced to isolation and tears as a cold metronome counts out endless minutes of pain. Echoing the movement of the camera from the fallboard to Carlos' hands, the camera now slowly pans left, moving from the right side of the piano to the midpoint. The glowing glass of orange juice that once sat on the piano lid and symbolized Laura and Carlos' active efforts to maintain their child's health has been replaced two framed photographs: one of Laura and one of Simón. All that remains of their former life are frozen memories. That Laura's photo resides next to Simón's seems to imply that she, in many ways, is already lost.

In this scene, it is most essential to note is that Laura's grief is so incapacitating that she cannot engage her husband regardless of how his pain is manifested. This inability is emphasized by the camera that repeated sweeps over Carlos. Even when Carlos is shown stationary and overwhelmed by grief, the framing is still loose and camera remains active. However, in a moment of outward composure, Laura is shown as a fixed figure in a doorway. She cannot engage her husband even when Carlos' grief is expressed as the same unbearable sorrow. As stated by Sohyun Lee, "The whole story of *El orfanato* consists of Laura's physical pain and moral suffering at the loss of her child, and her distress cannot be transferred to anybody else nor can it be shared with her husband" (2017, 55–66). This will prove deadly.

In the film's dénouement, the interaction between Laura and Carlos is fraught with frustration. Viewers helplessly watch as husband and wife—too far apart in their grief—begin to separate. This commences after a contentious moment following the séance scene. Carlos' patience is exhausted when a "medium" informs Laura that those "closest to death" are best able to communicate with the departed [01:03:33]. Angry at this irresponsible comment (Laura will, in fact, use sleeping pills both to get "close to death" in an effort to commune with the alleged ghost children and later kill herself), Carlos dismisses the ghost hunters from the couple's home. However, as the medium's vehicle prepares to leave, Laura dashes toward it—dashes toward death. A cut features Carlos standing in the mansion's doorway, and then rack focus is used to concentrate on the conversation between the two women. Even while out of focus, Carlos' presence can still be seen, but never does he interfere. After the medium tells Laura that "only you know how far you are willing to go to find your son," Carlos abruptly turns and moves inside the home [01:04:57–01:05:05]. When the medium adds a cryptic message, Laura looks back at Carlos, seeking his response; however, Carlos is gone. To Carlos, the woman is a dangerous opportunist (whose advice, ultimately, pushes Laura to her demise). And, that Laura failed to notice Carlos' departure emphasizes her distorted priorities: her desperation is so profound that she holds a medium's double-speak in higher regard than her own husband. This is a critical moment for Carlos. He has reached his limit of torment. A cut brings viewers to his pinboard. He is disassembling it.

A series of rapid cuts showcase items being removed from the pinboard and reveals that while his exterior is placid, Carlos is in turmoil. Laura now enters Carlos' workspace for the first time in the film. This room has always been presented as a loosely framed oasis of sunlight. However, Laura brings with her a literal darkness that seems to be a reflection of her toxic, deteriorating mental health. With a combination of trepidation and guilt, she approaches Carlos. She tugs at the sleeves of her sweater, nervously shifts her weight, and asks, "What are you doing?" [01:05:38]. However, she undoubtedly understands that after this *Poltergeist*-inspired horror show, Carlos has relented in his search for Simón, unwilling to expose himself to what cruel absurdities may come next. Gently setting his papers aside, he faces Laura and says, "We can't stay here any longer. We should go, at least for a while" [01:05:49]. Here, Carlos expresses the desire for them both—together—to take a reprieve from this constant onslaught of pain. He is invested in seeing Laura and himself healthy again—he is invested in them being "we" again. However, as Laura resists (wanting further time with the alleged ghost children), viewers witness the rending of their relationship. Vehemently, Carlos pleads, "I am neither willing nor able to take this. Please, Laura, let's leave this house . . . We can survive this" [01:06:49–01:07:04]. Visibly distressed, Carlos articulates that he cannot continue to live in this liminal space between life and death. He is explicitly reaching out to Laura, imploring her to leave the house with him, as a couple. He never tells Laura that she is lost in her grief, but states only what he knows to be true—*he* has reached *his* threshold. And, while Carlos is referring to his marriage when he states that they can "survive" the loss of their child, this statement functions as a form of foreshadowing. Viewers see Laura moving toward self-destruction. Here, it seems that a forking path lies ahead: one path leads toward life and one towards death. Carlos wants Laura to take the path of life with him; however, Laura has different plans. In contrast to Carlos' statements which refer to he and Laura as a couple, Laura cries, "I just want to be with Simón, don't you understand? If you want to go, I can't stop you. I just want to see him Carlos . . . that's all I want" [01:07:07–01:07:14]. Foremost, Carlos does not "want to go," he "needs to go." Laura, blinded by her own despair, minimizes Carlos' pain. Moreover, contrary to Carlos' use of "we" and "us" (i.e., "let's"), Laura's use of "you" and "I" shows her separation from her husband. At this point, she folds her arms against Carlos and collapses against his chest. Carlos, shown as distraught, simply holds Laura. A cut transitions viewers from a medium shot to a medium full shot where Carlos can be seen fully embracing his wife, tilting his head to set his cheek tenderly against hers. He gently sways side to side. Nonetheless, viewers also note that though Laura initiates physical contact with her husband, she does not reciprocate this embrace. There is no one to hold Carlos even though this conversation is specifically about *his* grief, about *his* mental health being endangered. The last image of this scene is from a doorway. Thick blocks of black screen stand on both sides of the frame. That visual crush that defines Laura's grief, that darkness that follows her, is now surrounding them both as Carlos silently capitulates to Laura's desire to stay in the home.

Even after articulating that he needs to leave, Carlos stays in the home until Laura finds the bodies of her childhood playmates in the shed. As Laura insists that she is engaged in a paranormal game that she does not know how to play, Carlos says, "I've packed. I don't want us to stay here. I won't live here . . . and you're not staying alone" [01:16:24–01:16:34]. In the first half of this statement, Carlos' expression is resolute. To alleviate his suffering, he must remove himself from this situation. And, as he asserts that Laura cannot remain alone, his features considerably soften. There is pain as well as sympathy in his expression. When Laura replies, "Two days. Alone. Please, I need this. Please," his anguish is unmistakable, verging on tears [01:16:47]. Carlos has asked for togetherness and Laura has asked to be alone. He has surpassed his plainly articulated limit and can no longer live in this waking-nightmare.

His leaving Laura is nothing less than an act of self-preservation. And, for Laura, this separation is her deepest desire.

As Laura walks Carlos to the car, viewers see that she is carrying her husband's overnight bag in an effort to efficiently remove him from the home. Her eyes dart about suspiciously. When Carlos opens the driver's side door, he pauses. He takes a breath and turns to Laura. But before Carlos can utter one word, Laura deliberately places her hand on his face and kisses him, disallowing further conversation. Encouraging his departure, she adds a reassuring stroke of his cheek. At this point, Carlos gets in the car and partially rolls down the window. Again, viewers take inventory of this moment. Carlos gazes at her with naked fear and concern. However, in the window's reflection, viewers can see Laura smiling at him. She does everything in her power to foster his comfortable exit—and to discourage an untimely return. As Andrew Hock Soon Ng astutely observes, "Her request for a [two]-day respite alone, accordingly, is merely a ruse to dismiss him so that, in the event she cannot restore Simón back to herself, she will be free to go to him" (2015, 176). With hesitance, Carlos separates from Laura in the only car viewers see in the horseshoe driveway of the far-removed home. Just as Laura wanted. Her grief has, essentially, turned fatal. As noted by Michael Walker in *Modern Ghost Melodramas: What Lies Beneath*, "Like a number of other protagonists in these [types of] films, Laura can be seen under the sway of the death drive" (2017, 369). This is the last time Carlos will see Laura alive.

As the film concludes, Laura's pain is at an end; however, Bayona shows that Carlos' grief continues. The penultimate scene features a close-up of a mirrored monument devoted to Laura, Simón, and the orphans. In the reflection, Carlos is seen leaving his car and approaching the memorial. Initially, this seems to suggest healthy closure. Nonetheless, as Carlos draws closer, his reflection becomes distorted and carnivalesque, implying unresolved emotions. Emphasizing a feeling of loneliness, there is no score—all that can be heard is the haunting sound of Carlos' footfalls and an occasional bird call. The camera pulls back, and Carlos kneels into the frame. He is shown as pensive. His exterior is composed. But, the large brown leaves that fall around him communicate an interior still coping with loss. Also indicating his ongoing struggle are two red roses that he sets before the monument. While eight names are inscribed on the plaque, Carlos only brings two roses—presumably for Laura and Simón. He could have offered a bouquet of eight roses in deference to his wife's love of her childhood friends (and Tomás). He could have even brought a bouquet of eight roses, separated them into two and six (to acknowledge the death of his family members as well as Laura's friends), and then set one bouquet in the permanent vase on the left and one on the right. The monument is designed for such use. However, that the six children remain unacknowledged by Carlos in this moment shows some resistance (though he surely commissioned the memorial to have the orphans' names on it). This action seems to suggest that Carlos suffers still. Bayona shows that even time cannot always ease the profound feelings of loss. Nonetheless, the costuming choice here allows for a tender ending.

When Simón is first introduced, he is in bed wearing an oversized, maroon, knit sweater [00:05:15–00:06:59]. That the child is sleeping in a knit sweater and that it is much too large for his petite frame attracts attention. It reads as belonging to one of his parents. Seeming a cozy source of comfort, this sweater reappears on Simón throughout his remaining time in the film: when coloring a picture [00:15:50–00:16:17], when waking up in Laura's bed [00:19:45–00:20:07], and then when reading *Peter Pan* [00:21:04–00:22:09]. Following Simón's disappearance, Laura is seen wearing the sweater throughout *her* remaining time in the film. She sleeps in the sweater [00:37:52–00:39:24], pleads for two days alone in the sweater [01:14:59–01:16:58], and walks Carlos to the car for the last time in the sweater [01:16:58–01:17:54]. It is fair to see this sweater as providing Laura with a degree of solace since her son so frequently wore it. And, as Carlos sets the roses on the memorial, this same sweater is clearly seen [01:40:10–01:40:44]. A transition to the interior of the Gothic mansion shows Carlos gazing out an open window in the orphan's room. The home has been relieved of possessions and leaves litter the floor. Physically, and as promised, Carlos has moved on. A cut to a medium shot allows the sweater to take center stage. Until this final sequence, Carlos is exclusively seen in blue form-flattering leisurewear and business attire; therefore, this shapeless maroon sweater easily invites notice and reminds the audience of its lineage. He is not seen stroking it, smelling it, clutching at it, or even gesturing toward its meaning (as Laura does with a number of artifacts). Instead, the sweater is simply used to bring him closer to his wife and son. This sentimental display seems a light nod toward Carlos embracing his emotions. The inspirational score that enters and swells delivers hope before a cut to a black screen . . . and a roll of credits.

A cautionary tale about the ravages of grief, Bayona's film shows a tight-knit family succumbing to loss. Failing to connect in their pain, Laura and Carlos mourn separately. For Carlos, instrumental grief allows him to direct his feelings in a seemingly productive and dynamic manner. Conversely, for Laura, intuitive grief allows her to access and manage her emotions in a thoughtful manner. Both approaches are valid and healthy. However, as Laura begins to self-isolate, she turns to less rational forms of coping. Her attempts at communing with "the beyond" transform into a full-tilt sprint toward death. Ultimately, Laura enters a perilous realm where she can no longer be reached or reach out to others. Laura's abject grief becomes a visible darkness that seems to accompany her on screen. By literally depicting Laura's toxic grief, Bayona underscores why Carlos must separate from his wife—which is precisely what Laura desires. While Laura was unable to overcome loss (and, perhaps, guilt), Bayona leaves his viewers with hope that Carlos will surmount his pain. As John Kerr states, while Bayona shows Laura's eternity in so-called Neverland, the film's final seconds indicate Carlos "will continue to live in the adult world" (2019, 243).

CONCLUSION:
COMPASSION WINS THE DAY

In a time where films about chainsaw-brandishing, scalpel-wielding, machete-swinging degenerates were a box-office draw, *El orfanato* offered a gentler, more complex tale. There are no comfortable binaries—no Erin versus Leatherface—but there is compassion. Understanding the potential for his film to be read as traumatizing, Bayona ensures his audience the softest landing possible, cushioning the crash pad with generous clues and coded violence. Even with much of the film's more graphic aspects implied, viewers understand all that happens—even in the time skips. This merciful approach allows Bayona to address taboo topics like child loss and maternal suicide in a way that averts the label of exploitation. His frank presentation of grief coupled with his vast cinematic talents separates this piece from the "crushingly literal-minded" films of this era (Ansen 2007). Perhaps this is why *El orfanato* won seven, prestigious Goya Awards (distributed by the Spanish Academy of Motion Picture Arts and Sciences) "including Best Young Director and Best Screenplay" (Juan-Navarro 2018, 292). Compassion, indeed, wins the day.

BIBLIOGRAPHY

Anderson, John. 2007. "Subtly Terrifying, Just Like Real Life." *The New York Times*. December 30, 2007. https://www.nytimes.com/2007/12/30/movies/30ande.html.
Ansen, David. 2007. "A Visit to 'The Orphanage.'" *Newsweek*. December 24, 2007. https://www.newsweek.com/visit-orphanage-94341.
Backer, Ron. 2015. *Classic Horror Films and the Literature That Inspired Them*. Jefferson, NC: McFarland.
Bayona, J. A. 2020. "Happy 80th Birthday, Brian De Palma!" *Twitter*. September 11, 2020. https://twitter.com/filmbayona/status/1304394748182945793.
"Believe: 'El Orfanato' is the Most Solid Straight-Up Thriller in Years." 2008. *San Antonio Current*. January 9, 2008. https://www.sacurrent.com/arts/believe-el-orfanato-is-the-most-solid-straight-up-thriller-in-years-2321391.
Bernardoni, James. 1991. *The New Hollywood: What the Movies Did with the New Freedoms of the Seventies*. Jefferson, NC: McFarland.

Blake, Marc, and Sara Bailey. 2013. *Writing the Horror Movie*. London: Bloomsbury.
Burr, Ty. 2008. "In 'Orphanage,' A Masterful Mix of Dread and Suspense." *The Boston Globe*. January 11, 2008.http://archive.boston.com/ae/movies/articles/2008/01/11/in_orphanage_a_masterful_mix_of_dread_and_suspense/.
Cassady, Charles Jr. 2022. "The Orphanage." *Common Sense Media*. Last updated March 31, 2022. https://www.commonsensemedia.org/movie-reviews/the-orphanage.
Davies, Ann. 2011. "The Final Girl and the Monstrous Mother of *El orfanato*." In *Spain on Screen: Developments in Contemporary Spanish Cinema*, edited by Ann Davies, 79–92. London: Palgrave Macmillan.
Dawson, Nick. 2007. "Juan Antonio Bayona, *The Orphanage*." *Filmmaker Magazine*. December 28, 2007. https://filmmakermagazine.com/1296-juan-antonio-bayona-the-orphanage/.
Delgado, Maria. 2008. "The Young and The Damned." *Sight & Sound* 18 (4): 44–5.
Del Toro, Guillermo, Juan Antonio Bayona, and Sergio G. Sánchez. 2007. *El Orfanato: Una Película de J. A. Bayona: La Película y sus Creadores*. Madrid: Telecinco Cinema.
Doka, Kenneth J., and Terry L. Martin. 2010. *Grieving Beyond Gender: Understanding the Ways Men and Women Mourn*. Revised Edition. New York: Routledge.
Dyregrov, Atle, and Kari Dyregrov. 2015. "Parents' Perception of Their Relationship Following the Loss of a Child." *OMEGA—Journal of Death and Dying* 76 (1): 1–18.
Ebert, Roger. 2007. "Did the son disappear into the fears of the mother?" *RogerEbert.com*. December 27, 2007. https://www.rogerebert.com/reviews/the-orphanage-2007.
Edelstein, David. 2006. "Now Playing at Your Local Multiplex: Torture Porn." *New York*. January 26, 2006. https://nymag.com/movies/features/15622/.
Family Guy. Season 12, episode 15. "Secondhand Spoke." Directed by Julius Wu, Dominic Bianchi, and James Purdum, aired March 30, 2014, on FOX.
Gingold, Michael. 2019. "Interview: Screenwriter Sergio G. Sánchez on Giving Birth to *The Orphanage* and Collaborating with Guillermo Del Toro." *Fangoria*. December 20, 2019. https://www.fangoria.com/original/interview-screenwriter-sergio-g-s%C3%A1nchez-on-giving-birth-to-the-orphanage-and-collaborating-with-guillermo-del-toro/.
Hogan, Erin K. 2018. *The Two Cines con Niño: Genre and the Child Protagonist in over Fifty Years of Spanish Film (1955–2010)*. Edinburgh: Edinburgh University Press.
Ignatius, Jeff. 2008. "Children Shouldn't Play with Dead Things." *Culture Snob*. May 12, 2008. https://www.culturesnob.net/2008/05/the-orphanage/.
Juan-Navarro, Santiago. 2018. *El Orfanato*. In *The Encyclopedia of Contemporary Spanish Films*, edited by Salvador Jiménez Murguía and Alex Pinar, 292–94. Lanham, MD: Rowman & Littlefield.
Kerr, John. 2019. "Children Redefining Adult Reality in Maternal Gothic Films." In *Representing Agency in Popular Culture Children and Youth on Page, Screen, and*

In Between, edited by Ingrid E. Castro and Jessica Clark, 231–54. Lanham, MD: Lexington.

Kroenert, Tim. 2008. "Spanish Chiller Evokes Ghosts of Grief." *Eureka Street* 18 (11): May 29, 2008. https://www.eurekastreet.com.au/article/spanish-chiller-evokes-ghosts-of-grief.

Lee, Sohyun. 2017. "Monstrous (Re)productions: Mothering Patriarchy on the Spanish Horror Screen." In *Tracing the Borders of Spanish Horror Cinema and Television*, edited by Jorge Mari, 53–66. New York: Routledge.

Li, Jiong. Dorthe Hansen Precht, Preben Bo Mortenson, and Jørn Olsen. 2003. "Mortality in Parents after Death of a Child in Denmark: A Nationwide Follow-up Study." *The Lancet* 361 (9355): 363–67.

Merin, Jennifer. 2007. "Guillermo del Toro—Interview re 'The Orphanage' and Female Creativity." *AWFJ*. December 18, 2007. https://awfj.org/blog/2007/12/18/guillermo-del-toro-discusses-the-orphanage-and-female-creativity-with-jennifer-merin/.

Nasson, Tim. 2007. "Guillermo Del Toro *The Orphanage* Interview." *Wild About Movies*. December 15, 2007. https://www.wildaboutmovies.com/interviews/guillermo-del-toro-the-orphanage-interview/.

Ng, Andrew Hock Soon. 2015. *Women and Domestic Space in Contemporary Gothic Narratives: The House as Subject*. New York: Palgrave Macmillan.

El Orfanato: Press Kit. 2007. Barcelona: Rodar y Rodar.

"*The Orphanage*: Awards." n.d. *IMDB*. https://www.imdb.com/title/tt0464141/awards/?ref_=tt_awd

"*The Orphanage*: Parent's Guide." n.d. *IMDB*. https://www.imdb.com/title/tt0464141/parentalguide#certificates

Puig, Claudia. 2008. "If You Love Being Scared to Death, Visit 'The Orphanage.'" *USA Today*. January 4, 2008, 9d.

Quigley, Karen. 2020. *Performing the Unimaginable: Success, Imagination, Failure*. London: Methuen.

Samuels, Charles Thomas. 1972. *Encountering Directors*. New York: Putnum.

Smith, Paul Julian. 2012. *Spanish Practices: Literature, Cinema, Television*. Oxon: Legenda.

St-Georges, Charles. 2018. *Haunted Families and Temporal Normativity in Hispanic Horror Film: Troubling Timelines*. Lanham, MD: Lexington Books.

Schwarzbaum, Lisa. 2008. "*The Orphanage*." *Entertainment Weekly*. January 9, 2008. https://ew.com/article/2008/01/09/orphanage-2/.

Trickey, Adam, Margaret T. May, Jörg Janne Vehreschild, Niels Obel, . . . and Matthew Williams. 2017. "Survival of HIV-positive patients starting antiretroviral therapy between 1996 and 2013: A collaborative analysis of cohort studies." *The Lancet HIV* 4 (8): 1–9.

Vo, Alex. 2008. "J.A. Bayona and Sergio Sánchez on *The Orphanage*: The RT Interview." *Rotten Tomatoes*. January 9, 2008. https://editorial.rottentomatoes.com/article/ja-bayona-and-sergio-sanchez-on-the-orphanage-the-rt-interview/.

Walker, Michael. 2017. *Modern Ghost Melodramas: What Lies Beneath*. Amsterdam: Amsterdam University Press.

NOTES

1. In this same scene, savvy viewers will also notice Laura's unusual attempt to tuck Simón back into bed. Three times she attempts to place the bedsheet over Simón's head. The optics are of a mother attempting to get her child back to sleep, but there seems an allusion to Laura's culpability in Simón's death.

2. In the promotional book created for *El orfanato*, Bayona is seen wearing a T-shirt with a classic Superman logo in several full-page color photos of him on the set of the film, connecting the director's love of the superhero to the film (del Toro et al. 2007, 12, 16, 53, 114). And, in a *Fangoria* interview with Bayona, the director digresses from *El orfanato* and openly discusses his Superman obsession (Dawson 2007).

3. There is a dark irony here. Laura once thought she lost Simón on the beach. As she lies broken in the rising tide, her leg shattered, she believes she sees her child near the cave. And, while Simón was not on that beach, he *was* trapped in this basement replica.

4. Many critics view Laura through the lens of Barbara Creed's "monstrous mother." For instance, in "The Final Girl and the Monstrous Mother of *El orfanato*," Ann Davies describes the moment where Laura finds her child's body: "Laura, in the end, confronts her own self and the horror of what she herself has done: in addition, she also confronts, not a monster that is diametrically opposed to her but a concept of monstrous motherhood, one which penetrates the boundaries between mother and child, to which she herself participates" (2011, 90–1).

5. Bayona's admiration of Brian DePalma not only translates in his cinematography but has been verbalized by the director himself. On Bayona's verified Twitter page, he wished DePalma a happy birthday, writing, "Happy 80th Birthday, Brian De Palma! What is your favorite De Palma movie? #BrianDePalma" (2020).

6. Famed farceur Seth MacFarlane frequently mocks this trope in his artistry. In fact, in an episode of *Family Guy* titled "Secondhand Spoke" (S12: E15), Peter Griffin's physical person is shown as suffering the ravages of tobacco use. In a meta-moment, Peter tries to cure himself by requesting an establishing shot, "Try cutting to the outside of the house over some music, that usually works" [00:20:49]. Here, the establishing-shot-as-reset is mocked as trite (whereas in Bayona's film it is a needed technique to re-enter the illusory world).

7. In 2009, Sergio G. Sánchez submitted to an interview with *Fangoria* magazine's Michael Gingold. Here, the interviewer expressed concern that the pending American remake would prove problematic: "At least one plot element involving Simón, and the movie's uncompromising ending, would likely give more conservative American filmmakers—and filmgoers—pause" (2019). To which Sánchez replied, "I'm terrified about the test screenings . . . That's the good thing about doing movies in Spain—you don't have those previews, and you don't have to shoot three different endings just in case" (2019). That the interviewer found the conclusion "uncompromising" is startling. It is so gently padded that many still categorize the film as a fairytale. And, in Sánchez's response is a chilling preview of how diluted an American adaptation could become. Films such as Jee-woon Kim's *Janghwa, Hongryeon* (2003) and Tomas Alfredson's *Låt den rätte komma* (2008) both provide examples of acclaimed

(but complicated) international films that were gutted by American directors catering to American sensibilities. Perhaps it was with this in mind that the film's producer/presenter, the renowned Guillermo del Toro, mused in an interview with *AWFJ*'s Jennifer Merin: "If this movie had taken the mainstream route, the mother would have arrived at the cellar in time to give the kid mouth to mouth and he would happily cling to her and they'd run into the forest as the house explodes in a ball of flames" (2007). Here, del Toro reminds sage viewers that if they wish to argue with Bayona's softened conclusion—designed to protect the grieving audience but still deliver a potent story about loss—perhaps they best consider the alternative.

8. In an interview for *Rotten Tomatoes*, J. A. Bayona and Sergio G. Sánchez discuss point-of-view shots. Here, Sánchez reveals that "Antonio [Bayona] was very convinced [on] a single point of view. That the audience knew what Laura knew so that you could identify with her. So whenever the story drifted away, he just chose to leave it out of the film" (Vo 2008). Herein resides why much of Carlos' grieving happens off screen. However, what little viewers see of Carlos' pain underscores how he processes the literal loss of his son much differently than Laura.

Chapter 3

Elevating Grief

Ari Aster's Hereditary *(2018) and the A24 Horror Film*

Andrew Grossman and *Todd K. Platts*

Netting global box office returns of $81.2 million on a $10 million budget, Ari Aster's *Hereditary* (2018) stands as not only one of A24's most lucrative films but as a vanguard for an apparently "new" breed of horror film, alternatively named "elevated horror" and "post-horror" among other problematic labels ("*Hereditary* (2018)" n.d.).[1] Though the debate over the nature of—and even the existence of—"elevated," "post-," "smart," and "art" horror is ongoing, this chapter elides the argument and employs the term "elevated/post-horror" throughout. While some scholars and critics see the terms as mutually exclusive, many use "elevated" and "post-" synonymously. It is beyond the scope of this chapter to enter into this dialogue. In the business and trade press, A24 and elevated/post-horror have received significant attention unmatched in extant academic literature. This oversight is significant, as industry journalists have labeled A24 "Hollywood's leading tastemaker brand" (Barnes 2018) and "the most interesting, creative, and reliable film company of the 21st century" (Baron 2017). Meanwhile, elevated/post-horror has been the subject of much contention among critics.[2] Though several scholars have documented the presumed tonal shift in cinematic horror, much remains to be written.[3] This chapter primarily links one of elevated/post-horror's central themes, grief, to the shrewd brand identity of a specific film company, A24. A24's strategy is referred to here as "elevating grief."

In documenting this strategy, this chapter first defines "elevated/post-horror" and then provides a brief history of A24 and its horror films. From there, this chapter offers a brief synopsis of the film before focusing on its deployment of grief. Given the complexity of grief in psychological and philosophical literature, the present discussion parses out several ontological orientations toward the concept as they relate to Aster's film. *Hereditary* offers an ideal case study for the examination of grief in contemporary horror cinema: it is A24's most profitable and arguably best horror film (in the eyes of critics) (Nordine 2022), is routinely included as a "primary/core text" (Church *Post-Horror* 2021, 14), and is perhaps "the best example of post-horror cinema about mourning, trauma, and maternal influence" (Church *Post Horror* 2021, 86). Before proceeding, it is worth noting that the employment of "elevated grief" is not without controversy. As the forthcoming analysis demonstrates, the strategy and its execution are more a matter of publicity than a reflection of reality.

ELEVATED/POST-HORROR

"Elevated/post-horror" is a term that refers to genre films that construct emotionally and psychologically demanding and disturbing narratives. According to David Church, elevated/post-horror films, " . . . evince minimalism over maximalism, largely eschewing jump scares, frenetic editing, and energetic and/or handheld cinematography in favor of cold and distanced shot framing, longer-than-average shot durations, slow camera movements, and stately narrative pacing" (*Post-Horror* 2021, 11).

Elevated horror significantly departs from the standard commercial paradigms of the genre in a way that "'artfully' inverts or undermines its salient features" (Falvey 2021, 64). The employment of languid pacing and brooding atmosphere, of course, is not a new development in the narratives of Western horror cinema.[4] Precedents can be found in the deliberately paced, cryptic, and cerebral horrors of Val Lewton's *Cat People* (1942) and *I Walked with a Zombie* (1943), Ingmar Bergman's *Hour of the Wolf* (1968), Andrei Tarkovsky's *Stalker* (1979), and Stanley Kubrick's *The Shining* (1980). Such examples, however, are the products of auteurs dabbling in genre conventions. A24 films represent not auteurist experiments but an umbrella movement, encompassing multiple producers and directors who are intent on rescuing horror from the doldrums of exploitation filmmaking.

Beyond narrative atmosphere, family trauma and grief are common themes in elevated/post-horror films, according to Christopher Sharrett (who uses *Hereditary* as his first example) (Sharrett 2021, 27). Viewed in this light, elevated/post-horror films serve as visual essays focusing on "family dramas about grief, mourning, and monstrous reproduction" (Church *Post-Horror* 2021, 13). Numerous elevated/post-horror films feature the tragic death of a family member early in the narrative to spark an emotionally fraught family drama before supernatural elements intrude, as seen in David Lowery's *A Ghost Story* (2017), Trey Edward Shults' *It Comes at Night* (2017), and Ari Aster's *Midsommar* (2019), among other A24 horror films (Church *Post-Horror* 2021, 68). Critics and audiences alike have acknowledged the highbrow pretenses of elevated/post-horror, though opinion is predictably split along lines of taste and class. A24's films have accumulated strong critical acclaim, while dissatisfied audiences have regarded the films as "boring, confusing, not scary, and utterly unsatisfying" (Church *Post-Horror* 2021, 11). While *Hereditary* was nearly universally praised amongst film critics, it received a D+ from audiences on *CinemaScore* (Gleiberman 2018). *Variety* reporter Owen Gleiberman, who positively appraised the film, claimed audiences saw it as "slow, odd, goofy, arty, inexplicable" (2018).

Significantly, Aster has admitted to directing a film that mixes highbrow and commercial aesthetics: "I wanted to make a film that was simultaneously restrained and also driven by maximalist attitudes of going as far as you can with the toys" (Chen 2018). Rather than draw inspiration from any particular auteur, *Hereditary* (vaguely) expands the early twenty-first century trend toward "slow" cinema. It is spare, often quiet, almost clinically objective, and marked by traumatic incidents without devolving into sentimentality. The solemnity of the film's style is itself grief stricken. Importantly, the film is defiantly humorless, surely a reaction against the comic relief endemic to the puerile monster movies of prior generations.

A24 AND THE A24 HORROR FILM

More than any other production company, A24 is indelibly linked to elevated/post-horror.[5] A24 began operations in 2012 under independent film veterans Daniel Katz, David Fenkel, and John Hodges with the goal of releasing "eight to ten titles annually," dividing its focus on distributing completed films and "financing and producing its own content" (McNary 2012). Though A24 initially acquired completed films for distribution, it quickly became recognized as one of the industry's most daring and cutting-edge companies—a "distributor auteur," to paraphrase David Ehrlich (2015). Not conscripted to horror, the company has also distributed crime (e.g., Harmony Korine's *Spring Breakers* [2013], J. C. Chandor's *A Most Violent Year* [2014]), sci-fi (Alex Garland's *Ex Machina* [2015]), drama (e.g., Lenny Abrahamson's *Room* [2015], Barry Jenkins' *Moonlight* [2016]), and comedy films (e.g., Lynn Shelton's *Laggies* [2014], Kyle Newman's *Barely Lethal* [2015]) as part of its bid to become the "most" successful arthouse studio (Barnes 2018). Included amongst their horror output are Jonathan Glazer's *Under the Skin* (2014),

Jeremy Saulnier's *Green Room* (2016), Robert Eggers' *The Witch* (2016), Oz Perkins' *The Blackcoat's Daughter* (2017), Trey Edward Shults' *It Comes at Night* (2017), David Lowery's *A Ghost Story* (2017), Yorgos Lanthimos' *The Killing of a Sacred Deer* (2017), Gaspar Noé's *Climax* (2019), Claire Denis' *High Life* (2019), Peter Strickland's *In Fabric* (2019), Ari Aster's *Midsommar* (2019), and Robert Eggers' *The Lighthouse* (2019)—nearly all of which have contributed to critical discussions of elevated/post-horror (Falvey 2021, 67). Though a thorough assessment of the critical reception of A24's horror films is beyond the purview of the chapter, it bears noting that many reviews of A24's horror films highlight grief as a common narrative element.

A24 emerged amidst a dramatic sea of change in the North American film industry. Up to 2009, the major studios employed specialty divisions to plumb the incredibly lucrative DVD market, which collapsed during the 2008–2009 financial recession and the transition from DVD to streaming in the ancillary market(s), where potential return on investment initially lagged (Platts 2021, 112–13). As large studios cut back on modestly budgeted films, including horror (Platts and Clasen 2017), smaller companies witnessed their profit margins shrink (Gottlieb 2018). A24 joined the film business with the innovative approach of appealing directly to consumers through social media, including the development of algorithms to target potential ticket buyers (Barnes 2018). A24 took on the films passed over by larger producers and distributors. In the words of David Ehrlich, "A24 has established itself as the film industry's most forward-thinking company by releasing the kind of midsized, stylish, quality films that seemed on the verge of going extinct, transforming them into a collective theatrical experience" (2015). In short order, A24 built a reputation as an upstart company willing to back subversive and atypical films, the types of films once associated with conglomerate indie divisions like Focus Features, Screen Gems, and Searchlight Pictures (Baron 2017). In 2015, the company entered the realm of production after more than doubling its credit line through Bank of America, J.P. Morgan, and SunTrust. In a press release, A24 claimed the extended credit would allow it to "build upon its core film-distribution business, as well as to expand its film development/production and television business" (Lieberman 2016).

Hereditary stands as one of the first films that A24 produced under its expanded credit. The film, however, was in development for years before A24's involvement. Director Aster made a name for himself by directing short films featuring deeply broken and dysfunctional families, such as *The Strange Thing about the Johnsons* (2011) and *Munchausen* (2013). After garnering critical acclaim, Aster started scripting *Hereditary* in 2013. Initially, Danny DeVito's Jersey 2nd Avenue company showed interest in the film, even arranging for a table read of the script (Kohn 2018), which was completed in late 2016 ("*Hereditary*" n.d.). At the table read, Jersey 2nd Avenue passed on the film because it "ran long and sounded expensive" (Kohn 2018). At some point before then, Aster met with A24's head of acquisitions and production, Noah Sacco, where interest in working with Aster was expressed but not immediately pursued because A24 was not financing any films at the time (Rao 2019). In the meantime, *Hereditary*'s script passed through several hands, eventually settling on the desks of Kevin Frakes and Lars Knudsen, the latter of whom brought *The Witch* (2015) to A24. A24 backed *Hereditary*, in part, because it meshed with other horror films released by the company and was attached to a producer who delivered one of their most successful films.

As A24 established its brand identity, it became noted for a distinctive type of horror film, one at the forefront of elevated/post-horror. Steve Rose, one of the first critics to note an ideational change in horror that he claimed focused on existential dread, singled out A24's role in this shift: "if anyone's pushing horror into new realms, it's them" (Rose 2017). Laura Bradley similarly wrote that A24's horror output is "more darkly contemplative and immersive than scary" (Bradley 2019). According to Nicholas Barber, A24, along with Blumhouse Productions, trafficked in "idea-based rather than gore-based horror" (2018). Kate Gardner, though critical of the term "elevated/post-horror," credited A24 with releasing "slow-burn stories that focus more on thematic terror rather than jump scares" (2019). Despite the fervor of commentators castigating the notion of elevated/post-horror, A24's marketing leans into the label, a tendency noticed by Jacob Knight, who accuses the company of making "a rather recognizable habit out of somewhat misrepresenting movies with an idiosyncratic '*art house*' bent in their marketing from the label's beginning" (emphasis in the original) (2018). Consistent with this observation, an A24 promotional trailer for *Hereditary* informed would-be viewers that the film was not only scary but featured "Oscar-worthy" and "awards-caliber" acting, elements rarely associated with horror (A24 2018).

SYNOPSIS

Hereditary begins with Annie (Toni Collette) eulogizing her estranged mother, a domineering matriarch who, though never seen, exerts a malevolent presence throughout the narrative, first psychologically and then supernaturally. The funeral is presented as a perfunctory ritual—the film even cuts away before a reticent Annie begins to eulogize, suggesting not only a fractured relationship with her mother but the futility of conventional grieving rites. Returning home, she finds among her mother's possessions a handwritten note, secreted within a book on demonology, that suggests Annie will somehow be reunited with her mother. The family's compulsive, apparently autistic young daughter, Charlie (Milly Shapiro), was the favorite of her grandmother, who nevertheless wished Charlie were a boy. The teenage son, Peter (Alex Wolff), is similarly uncommunicative and withdrawn, lost in the bourgeois banality to which American culture condemns its adolescents. Peter's possible future is signified only by an obligatory SAT class and his glance at a computer webpage, "Popular Career Interests," which features stock photographs of artificially happy models. Annie's husband Steve (Gabriel Byrne) acts as a frustrated voice of reason whenever Annie stumbles too close to the abyss, but reason cannot hinder the demonic forces at work. Indeed, throughout the film Steve is weak and passive, ultimately no match for the maternal evils at work.

At first, viewers suspect that the family's profound depression stems from Annie's late mother, who lorded over the family with an iron fist. Eventually, they learn of a second explanation: Annie, prone to somnambulism, unconsciously tried to immolate her children while they slept. A plastic artist, Annie attempts to bury her grief and unresolved anger by constructing an elaborate dollhouse that recreates her own home, including the room her mother used for hospice care. As the film continues, she returns to add new details to the dollhouse that reflect changes in the family. As she attempts to symbolically reconstruct her chaotic environment, Annie towers godlike over the tiny dolls that represent family members to whom she cannot relate in reality. Begrudgingly, Annie attends a group therapy session to "work through" her unresolved anger. In the film's first significant dialogue sequence, she claims her mother suffered from dissociative identity disorder and suspects her family is genetically predisposed to schizophrenia. This predisposition perhaps explains Annie's pyromaniacal somnambulism, a sign of repressed filicidal tendencies her mother will reenact from beyond the grave.

The mechanics of the story are advanced through a shocking peripeteia: in a freak accident, Charlie is decapitated while Peter drives her to the hospital as she suffers an allergy attack. The family's half-hearted attempts to grieve an unloved grandmother are now compounded by the unimaginable grief prompted by the death of an innocent. Meaningful communication within the family unit comes to halt, save for blaming and recrimination, and Peter withdraws further. Annie returns to therapy, where she meets Joan (Ann Dowd), a sympathetic grandmother who recently lost her son and grandson. At the film's approximate midpoint—62 minutes into a 124 minutes-plus-credits running time—the plot undergoes a second peripeteia, in which Joan invites a skeptical Annie to a séance. After witnessing Joan's deceased grandson miraculously, invisibly respond to her commands, Annie rushes home, hoping to conjure Charlie in her own séance. Peter and Steve are nonplussed, fearing Annie has been overtaken by manic, delusional grief. As always, Steve remains passive and seems incapable of derailing the horrors to come.

At this point, the "therapeutic" first half of the film gives way to a supernatural second. Annie becomes further drawn into Joan's mysticism, but the demonic forces revealed by Joan begin to overtake Annie. What viewers have long suspected is revealed as fact: Annie's mother, not merely schizophrenic but demonic, has orchestrated, from beyond the grave, the film's horrors, including her own granddaughter's beheading. (Joan, it turns out, likewise arranged the deaths of her son and grandson.) In the film's final half hour, the horror escalates inexorably: Steve is burned alive (a realization of Annie's pyromania), Annie is transformed into a raving demon, and Peter jumps to his death, only to be resurrected and led to the backyard treehouse, where the coven over which Annie's mother had presided congregates. In the treehouse, a mock-pagan space in suburban America, the resurrected Peter becomes the new bodily host of bi-gendered King Paimon, God of Mischief, who has long awaited the male host Annie's mother had promised.

HEREDITARY AND GRIEF

In assessing *Hereditary*'s deployment of grief, the present analysis advances, including Elisabeth Kübler-Ross's five stages of grief, the failed therapeutic and supernatural suturing in the film, narcissistic chosenness, the religious denial of death, and maternalism. Despite the film's presumed elevation of grief, however, *Hereditary* fails to "elevate" its themes beyond the trappings of standard horror paradigms. Put another way, Aster's mannered style does not entirely camouflage his old-fashioned, decidedly pedestrian subject matter.

ELISABETH KÜBLER-ROSS AND THE FIVE STAGES OF GRIEF?

A convenient means to rationalize inexorable loss, Elisabeth Kübler-Ross's familiar five stages of grieving have become ubiquitous in popular culture, referenced in everything from stand-up comedy routines to new-age psychobabble to the film appraised in this chapter (McCallum 2019). The contrived linearity with which Kübler-Ross presented her model has condemned it to parody and caricature. Obviously, grieving follows no finite or definite sequence; it often follows no sequence at all. At best, Kübler-Ross offered a descriptive rather than prescriptive account of grief, based mainly on her anecdotal observations of hospice patients. A coping strategy rather than a philosophical inquiry, Kübler-Ross's description does nothing to redress the existentialistic claims of Kierkegaard, Schopenhauer, Otto Rank, and other theorists who posit grieving not as a temporally bounded experience prone to resolution but as something immanent in human consciousness. For the existentialist, all humans are embroiled in a perpetual process of grieving for themselves, for humanity, unlike the lower mammals, is cursed with the foreknowledge of its own mortality. People might parcel out stretches of grief for departed loved ones, but they always carry within themselves a cosmic grief that no five-step process can mitigate. As Ernest Becker suggests in *The Denial of Death*, repression becomes a necessary tool to overcome ever-present fears of decay and annihilation (1997). Only when people repress their narcissistic desires for immortality can they accede to the busy-work of postindustrial lifestyles.

Those who conceive of grief as a circumscribed, medicalized process imply that people must *consciously* incorporate loss into themselves, attempting to undo the subconscious mechanisms of repression that psychoanalysis claims are inevitable. Posited as a conscious process, both introspective and extrospective, grieving becomes effortful and laborious. People often say that they are "working" through pain and grief. But why should grief be tethered to notions of work while other types of suffering are not? Perhaps it is because contemporary society, influenced by the Kübler-Ross model, believes that the achievement of linear goals results only from work, and the final stage of "acceptance" can only be a "work product." By framing grief as labor, people convince themselves of its finitude. But even if this were true, one must ask what lies on the far side of grief. Do people labor through grief merely to return to the normal state of repressed living, a state in which they are overwhelmed with *unworkable*, Schopenhauerian laments for their cosmic mortality? Furthermore, how many people truly "accept" their own mortality? To acknowledge something is not necessarily to accept it; one may recognize the annihilatory facts of material reality and curse them all the same.

With some effort and labor, it is (probably) possible to wedge *Hereditary*'s storyline into the Kübler-Ross model, as some critics have attempted.[6] However, there is little reason to do so, for the film's conclusion hardly suggests fatalistic "acceptance." Peter is coerced into a cruel fate he neither labors toward nor consciously accepts. If anything, *Hereditary* inverts viewers' assumptions of "working through." The family has little opportunity to grieve the anticipated loss of the ailing family matriarch or the more shocking loss of their young daughter. As the deceased mother's being becomes not a figment of Annie's grieving imagination but an exteriorized, demonic force, "loss" becomes a presence that devours those who attempt the harrowing trials of grief. The "loss" thus incorporates the grievers, not vice versa.

For all its rampant grief-strickenness, *Hereditary* makes no clear statement about the meaning of grief. By no means does the film's elevated style automatically produce elevated thematic meanings. It might be that *Hereditary* is closest in spirit to Kubrick's *The Shining*, another self-referential exercise in technique, lacking in moral resonance or intellectual depth. Like many supernatural horror films, *Hereditary* concerns itself with an initial ontological crisis (i.e., the existence of a metaphysical world) but neglects to explore the actual ramifications of that crisis. Horror centered around ghosts, hauntings, possessions, and so forth too often pivots to organized religion and hoary Christian tropes—priests, lapsed faith, exorcisms, covens, Satan—to avoid ontological complexities beyond the grasp or interest of most screenwriters. Sophisticated audiences assume that liberal Hollywood filmmakers do not believe in hell or Christian demons: these are merely culturally received tropes, easily exploited to elicit predictable audience responses (perhaps true believers respond more intensely). Borrowing such tropes, however, threatens to de-elevate the film's "elevated" horror, as director Aster tethers his themes not to generally irrational fears but to easily dismissed faith systems per se.

THE TWO HALVES OF GRIEVING IN *HEREDITARY*

The psychological-therapeutic approach to grieving that marks the first half of *Hereditary* turns out to be useless, a red herring. Once Joan is introduced, demonism and supernaturalism overtake the "realistic" psychology of Annie's group therapy sessions. While Aster asserts that the two halves are organically integral, one feels a certain disappointment (not horror) that the first half's multilayered attempts at psychologizing are (re)solved (or undermined) by the second half's doctrinaire supernaturalism, derived from medievalist nonsense. The profoundly mysterious process of grieving suggested in the first half becomes short-circuited and co-opted by a fairytale ending that, for all its devilishness, is far less mysterious. Much as Paimon colonizes Peter, so does the film's tidily satanic resolution forestall a deeper investigation of grief. This forestalling, of course, is the lynchpin of the film's horror: the therapeutic narrative of the first half must be derailed. Without the supernatural peripeteia, Annie could (through her therapy sessions) theoretically incorporate grief into her being. The film's horror necessitates that grief become exteriorized as an incorporeal and non-incorporable presence. It is common enough for children to guiltily, subconsciously wish for their parents' deaths. *Hereditary* offers a diametrically opposed narrative: the family matriarch *consciously* and guiltlessly plans her children's deaths.

If the process of grieving calls for introspection, little lurks within these characters, who become swallowed up in the film's overweening, objectivizing style. They are reactive and situational creatures, careening from one impossible incident to the next with barely a reflective pause. In place of a dynamic inner psychology, Annie arrives pre-equipped with a litany of psychological disturbances, including somnambulism, pyromania, and a repressed desire to murder her children (the unconscious legacy of her own filicidal mother). Annie's sleepwalking attempts to immolate her own children signify the submergence of her mother's evil within her own unconscious. Ultimately, her will proves no match for her mother's demonic legacy. Yet grieving in itself has little to do with this sequence of events. Even if Annie did *not* grieve her mother's death, the film's satanic conclusions would still come to pass. There does not seem to be a *causal* relationship between grief, which theoretically provides a path to control and normalcy, and the chaotic monstrosity associated with horror.

The weakness of Annie's will is reflected through her dollhouse, a macabre microcosm of her shattered familial environment. This aesthetic reconstruction of the family space and its dilemmas at first seems to offer her both respite and control. The dolls populating the house have a fetishistic, totemic quality, as if she were practicing a kind of crude sympathetic magic of her own. However, her mother's lurking demonism renders her attempts at control impotent; mothering lifeless dolls cannot substitute for her failure to mother a family at death's door. In her final, possessed state, Annie becomes herself puppet-like, controlled by her own, transubstantial mother. The dollhouse's conceit of art-as-therapy is insufficient: the dollhouse is too perverse and sterile a means of recreating a broken world and broken family. Annie's aestheticized manner of grieving turns out to be merely an illusion, while her own mother's satanic "fantasy" turns out to be real. More generally, if grieving becomes an emotional vehicle through which exterior forces—coded as "the devil"—exploit weakness, it is only because conventional, linearized approaches to grieving are impoverished (or perhaps delusional).

NARCISSISTIC CHOSENNESS IN *HEREDITARY*

In analyzing *Hereditary*, two linked observations can be made. First, Annie's deceased mother turns out to be radically Machiavellian, at least in the caricatured sense of Machiavelli that Christopher Marlowe presented in the prologue to *The Jew of Malta* (Marlowe 2013, 9–10). For reasons left unexplained, her demonisms alienated her from the rest of her family, who assumed she was schizophrenic (an alternate break from material reality). Rather than sharing her power with her family, she sacrifices them to fulfill prophecies—presumably, familial sacrifice is part and parcel of the devil's bargain. Obviously, the film identifies the family unit as a site of horror, not a refuge. But is it the goal of "evil" to destroy the family, or does "evil" merely reveal the destructive tendencies that already underlie nuclear family structures? Second, the film's horror is rooted in the narcissistic desire to be "chosen" for an extraordinary life: Annie's mother is (somehow) able to access demonic powers forbidden to others, while Peter, in a tragic sense, is specially selected to host a fairly prominent figure from Christian demonology. Just as humans cannot stand their own mortality, they must believe they are specially, magically chosen for greatness. This is the motivating force behind Protestantism, for instance, whose adherents claim "personal" relationships with Jesus Christ. Narcissistic chosenness also explains belief in an imminent apocalypse, which must occur within the intimate window of the adherent's fragile lifespan. Supernatural horror reimagines chosenness negatively, yet the sense of cosmic specialness remains. As protagonists are improbably singled out for harassment by a spirit or monster, they acquire a special knowledge of and connection to supernaturalism denied to the average citizen. In *Hereditary*, Peter is specially chosen only to be negated. His "pagan" treehouse rebirth, a parody of Christ's resurrection, mocks organized religion's wish-fulfillment fantasy of life after death. Ascending into the treehouse, Peter will have an afterlife, but only as not-Peter, as an empty shell housing an alien force. Reborn thus, Peter becomes a *literal* antihero—not the romantic antihero of an action film, who bitterly or begrudgingly serves humanity, but a horrific antigod who serves only himself.

In the film's climax, Peter is surrounded by members of the coven before jumping from a window to his death. Shown only in brief flashes, the coven members, like Annie in her possessed stage, are animalistic, growling, filthy creatures. Not merely opposing Christian divinity, their profanity embraces and embodies humanity's animalistic nature, which the civilizing process has striven to deny and camouflage. Ernest Becker argues that the narcissistic desire for immortality and the revulsion at humanity's mammalian origins animate a primal fear of death, a fear that mediates all of life's meanings (Becker 1997, 2–3). A post-Freudian, Becker suggests that much of what Freud claimed were basal problems—the Oedipal complex, castration anxiety, and so on—were symptomatic of a deeper, stultifying fear of one's own mortality. To repress a mortal fear and trembling that otherwise would paralyze them, people develop personalities armored with "character," an idea Becker adopts from Wilhelm Reich's *Character Analysis*. This character armor, fashioned "for the precise purpose of putting it between [ourselves] and the facts of life," is a "special tour-de-force that allows" people to ignore the incongruity between egos they wish were timeless and bodies they know are decadent (Becker 1997, 59). Neurotically armored with numerous repressions, people "thrive on blindness" and accomplish "a peculiarly human victory: the ability to be smug about terror" (Becker 1997, 59).

This defensive ego function—smugness in the face of terror—reverberates throughout the horror genre. In the most general sense, horror films repeat the comforting religious illusions of the afterlife: audiences look into the face of terror—as terrific as filmmakers can manage—only to congratulate themselves on the stoicism and impassivity with which they experience a given film. Audiences emerge from the horrific experience unmoved and unscathed. Conflating the horrors they have witnessed with the very real terrors that human mortality incites, audiences are heroically reborn as the theater's houselights come on. Through its grimacing, animalistic images of the coven in its climax, *Hereditary* more specifically parodies Reich and Becker's notion of egoistic armor. In conquering mortality, the monstrously transformed coven has returned to a drooling, primeval state, not an angelic one. The coven's members have blasphemously broached two irreconcilable realms, combining eternal life with the filth associated with human decay. The coven has "smugly" defeated death, yet only by sacrificing its character armor—everything that makes humans "civilized"—and succumbing to a premodern belief system in which people become indentured servants to a negative religion.

The smugness that people conflate with heroism in the face of death relates, too, to the present discussion's original theme of "elevated horror"—that is, horror that *asks to be taken seriously*. Even a child can act smugly in the face of badly acted slasher movies and phony gore. But can audiences be equally smug in the face of an artist's apparently sincere—if thematically underdeveloped—attempt to grapple with mortal grief? If so, then human smugness is indeed an effective means of denying death, as people "frighten away reality" as if banishing a vampire with a crudely symbolic cross (Becker 1997, 59).

In the foreword to Ernest Becker's *The Denial of Death*, Sam Keen states, "the main task of human life is to become heroic and transcend death," a futile ambition reflected in horror films that cultivate in their audiences a "smugness" toward images of death and, in the case of *Hereditary*, grief and grieving (1997, xiii). This smugness is not merely a futile personal exercise; as a public sign of hubris and arrogance, it can be exploited, organized, and politicized. Keen suggests that "ideological conflicts between cultures . . . become battles between immortality projects" and "holy wars" that aim to determine whose image of immortality will emerge triumphant (1997, xiii). In the far more trivial realm of horror cinema, another (though equally egoistic) immortality project brews: a contest between horror filmmakers, who specifically trade in images of violent death, and spectators, who heroically armor themselves and emerge unmoved by filmmakers' best, most sadistic efforts. Willfully enduring mythic horror—and smugly refusing to grieve in the face of that horror—becomes a culturally acceptable means for adolescents and adults to test their character armor. Before adolescence, the average person's egoistic character is still developing; thus, horror is deemed inappropriate for insufficiently armored children, for whom everything is play and who still confuse reality and fantasy, the body and the imagination. At the same time, the child before the age of socialization does not recoil at filth as adults do. Horror is only a suitably smug test for the socialized, civilized human, whose desire for immortality cannot be reconciled with a body spoiled by Freudian anality and steeped in what Becker calls "creatureliness"—everything that reminds people of their fetid, organic animal nature (Becker 1997, 87). Though *Hereditary* refuses gratuitous gore, its occasional shocks are steeped in images of creaturely decay. Without warning, the film suddenly cuts to Charlie's severed head, covered with swarming, devouring insects. In a scene in which Annie hallucinatorily sleepwalks, viewers see insects pour from Peter's mouth while he sleeps, a reminder of the insectoid earth to which all return. For Becker, mystical and religious systems forestall mortality and provide a "manic defense and denial" of human fragility (Becker 1997, 41).

One might say that *Hereditary* ups the stakes, daring its audience to smugly deny not only death but the possibility of grieving, a facet of one's character armor that the film presents as a human frailty to be exploited by uncontrollable forces. The film, intentionally or not, reveals the pitfalls of armoring oneself too thickly with acculturated structures (the nuclear family) and rituals (funerals, group therapy) that turn out to be destructive, deceptive, or useless. People are so heavily and neurotically armored, in fact, that in denying death they also deny life: "We repress our bodies to purchase a soul that time cannot destroy; we sacrifice pleasure to buy immortality; we encapsulate ourselves to avoid death. And life escapes us while we huddle within the defended fortress of character" (Becker 1997, XIII). Yet an important question remains: is Peter, who exists only to die and be emptily reborn, tragically blinded by his armor, or did he never have sufficient armoring to begin with?

RELIGION, DEATH, AND *HEREDITARY*

The pivot from a therapeutic denial of death (the testing of character armor) to an expressly religious denial of death (the desire for bodily transcendence) is mirrored in *Hereditary*'s pivot from a psychologizing first half to a horrifically supernatural second half. The film's first half centers around Annie's trips to group therapy, where she theorizes about the ways in which her mother's schizophrenia had ruptured three generations of her family. As soon as Joan is introduced, the film drops all psychotherapeutic pretenses in favor of spiraling, creaturely horror. Though director Aster has claimed that the film's two parts are inextricable, one strains to reconcile, thematically, the first half's individualistic psychologizing and the second's objectivizing supernaturalism. On the surface, the film posits something ludicrous: that Adlerian esteem-building, Maslovian self-actualization, and other possible outcomes of humanistic group therapy are no match for the devil's minions. Recall, however, the mutually allegorizing relationship between religion and the family structure that Freud established in *The Future of an Illusion* and *Civilization and Its Discontents*. Upon coming of age, children recognize their life-giving parents are no longer godlike. Realizing their own creaturely mortality and unable to undo their existence (i.e., return to the womb), the parentally disenchanted create social structures—organized religions—that offer a comforting afterlife granted by a quasi-parental deity. Christianity perfects the illusion by making God the Father indivisible from a son, Christ, who embraces his mortality but unwittingly possesses an immanent transcendence. In the figure of Christ, one finds the same denial of death proposed by eternal demons and monsters; the crucial difference is that Christ was a cosmic masochist, absorbing the sufferings of all rather than inflicting pain on a specially chosen few, as do cinema's inordinately sadistic monsters.

Through its supernatural reality, *Hereditary* inverts the conventional allegories that thread psychology together with religion. The demonism of Annie's mother adapts the schizophrenic split between the delusional mind and the reality-bound body to the structure of Christian religiosity, which seeks to transcend death through piety, devotion, and sacrifice. This "adaptation" obviously becomes travestied by the form of the coven's demon worship. Piety and devotion are expressed toward a god of destruction, not redemption. Sacrifice becomes the particular Machiavellian sacrifice of one's own children, an inversion of Christ's unparticularized, undifferentiated sacrifice for humankind. Notably, unlike many films about demonic possession, such as William Friedkin's *The Exorcist* (1973) or Damiano Damiani's *Amityville 2: The Possession* (1982), there is no crisis-stricken priest character through which audiences can negotiate contrary elements of faith and reason. The clergy are entirely absent, in fact. Unlike most possession narratives, *Hereditary* does not employ hand-wringing priests to confirm and legitimate the organized religion from which demons spring.

MATERNAL GRIEF

So far, the present discussion has analyzed the ways in which *Hereditary* incorporates and reflects the denial of death in general terms. For Becker, this denial is at the heart of self-conscious human experience. People must attempt to repress their fear of death, whether through religion, art, or other sublimated means, in order to participate in the business of everyday life. Without these systems of repression and sublimation, they would drown in their own cosmic grief, unable to function. People's repressions, Becker says, are part of their character armor, the heroic personality system they construct for themselves and through which they adopt a stoic or "smug" attitude toward their own mortality (Becker 1997, 57). Conspicuous in *Hereditary*, however, is the thinness and inadequacy of Peter's character armor. A typical high school upperclassman, he is precisely at the age when his Reichian armor, though not completely wrought, should have produced an ego independent of his mother. After the film's first peripeteia, Charlie's horrific accident, the film focuses more intently on Peter's relationship with Annie, now in a state of ceaseless hysterics. The crux of the film, arguably, is not the accident itself but Peter's reaction in the aftermath. After a fatal accident, a normally developed teenager would call 911 and, in a state of panic, wait for police and an ambulance to arrive. Bizarrely, Peter does nothing of the sort. Leaving Charlie's severed head on the road, he drives away with the remainder of her body wedged in the backseat. Returning home, he makes sure his parents are asleep and then climbs silently into bed, tucking himself into a nearly fetal position. Peter's response to death is not so much traumatic as it is infantile. A normally armored adolescent would take responsibility for the accident, not sneak back home and curl into a ball. Peter's response evinces not a neurosis of character—that is, what one accepts as normally rationalized behavior—but the sort of willful ignorance found in traumatized but *pre-neurotic, unarmored* children. Rather than relying on *unconscious* mechanisms to deny the reality of death, as an adult would, Peter *consciously* retreats into infantile blindness. Only the following morning do Annie and Steve learn of Charlie's death, as they find her decapitated torso in the car (the moment of discovery occurs offscreen). Shortly thereafter, a pent-up Annie releases her fury at the dinner table, where she (sensibly) accuses Peter of refusing to take (adult) responsibility for his actions. Peter's infantilism is reinforced in the climax. As Peter hides in the attic while a demonized Annie pounds on the attic's trapdoor, he helplessly cries, "Mommy!" as saliva dribbles from his mouth.

One need not be a strict Freudian to see in Peter's infantilism a failure to break from his mother, just as Annie cannot free herself from her own mother. Freud traced the male child's failure to become independent to castration anxiety, but Peter's powerlessness extends far beyond routine Oedipal struggles. In the larger scheme Freud sketches in *Civilization and Its Discontents*, the child's powerlessness in the face of life and death dovetails with religious mechanisms. The young male child sees his mother as godlike, the provider of milk, comfort, love, and life itself (Freud 2010, 33–45). This unwitting deification entails a dual problem. "On the one hand," Becker says, "the mother is a pure source of pleasure and satisfaction," a "goddess of beauty and goodness, victory and power" (Becker 1997, 38). But the boy must also try to break free from his mother's dazzling omnipotence, lest he lose "the feeling that he has aegis over his own powers" (Becker 1997, 38). The life-giving mother thus threatens to erase the boy's autonomy, his life, and, by extension, his life-giving capacity to deny death. The domineering mother in *Hereditary* is made literally rather than figuratively monstrous, embodying the animal nature from which the child must flee. At the same time, the boy's horror is "a tissue of fantasy inseparable from his own fantastic project of becoming father of himself," an outcome ironically realized when not-Peter finally ascends the pagan treehouse and becomes reborn as Paimon, a patriarch who "re-fathers" him into an afterlife (Becker 1997, 39). As a horror film, *Hereditary* obviously subverts the fantasy: the afterlife becomes not a chance at parentless independence but a total loss of self, a final descent into filial servitude.

CONCLUSION

This analysis began by sketching the contours of contemporary horror film production, noting how A24 has positioned itself as a brand in the genre that foregrounds human dread and grief in both the marketing and narrative of a film—a strategy this essay termed as "elevating grief." Yet *Hereditary* deploys the theme of grief only as a smokescreen; rather than truly examine how these characters might grieve impossible, incomprehensible losses in the long term, the film pivots to more familiar horror territory, albeit presented with a degree of style and artistic commitment seldom found in the genre. By picturing the denial of death as the gateway to a host of immortal or immaterial monsters, the filmmakers make audiences think twice about their neurotic denials and begin to conceive of life (and death) differently. If immortality opens the door for immortal monsters, perhaps mortality has gotten a bad rap. *Hereditary* complicates this formulation by locating horror within the factory of mortality, the family, and by suggesting that humans cannot break free from their ghostly pasts.

While familial disorder and perversion often haunt the narratives of horror films, many "faithful" specimens of the genre find conservative ways to reinstate normalcy and enforce closure. Such closure usually entails the recuperation of patriarchal order in the film's dénouement. Because tales of possession most often derive from Catholic belief systems, this patriarchy is typically represented by the character of a troubled priest who reclaims orthodox faith in an apparently godless, post-Enlightenment world. The clichéd priest character always has a dual function: he offers an identifiable character through which audiences can negotiate faith and reason (as suggested above), and, as a man, he reinstates conservative, patriarchal control after ninety or so minutes of pleasant carnage and blasphemy. *Hereditary* notably denies this trope, instead completely subsuming its family within a matriarchal occultism. Not only does the story deliberately exclude the usual savior-priest, but the family, saddled with a weak, ineffectual father, cannot muster enough patriarchal force to counter the film's two devilish matriarchs. Clearly, the film's vision of maternal horror might posit its own conservative platitudes. The resulting storyline casts maternalism (rather than femininity in general) in a monstrous light, reiterating the psychoanalytic cliché of the castrating, suffocating mother whom weak men fail to cast off. By locating the character of adulthood in the traumas of childhood, psychoanalysis claims that humans cannot free themselves from the ghosts of the past. For all of its "elevated" style, *Hereditary* literalizes this basal metaphor, plumbing the depths of the grief-stricken psyche only to excavate the smothering spirits that other, indeed lesser films have envisioned again and again.

BIBLIOGRAPHY

A24. 2018. "Hereditary | Frighteningly Good | Official Promo HD | A24." *YouTube*. June 13, 2018. www.youtube.com/watch?v=megmpfx1fzc/.

Barber, Nicholas. 2018. "Is Horror the Most Disrespected Genre?" *BBC*. June 14, 2018. www.bbc.com/culture/article/20180614-is-horror-the-most-disrespected-genre/.

Barnes, Brooks. 2018. "The Little Movie Studio That Could." *The New York Times*. March 3, 2018. www.nytimes.com/2018/03/03/business/media/a24-studio.html.

Baron, Zach. 2017. "How A24 is Disrupting Hollywood." *GQ*. May 9, 2017. www.gq.com/story/a24-studio-oral-history.

Becker, Ernest. 1997. *The Denial of Death*. New York: Free Press.

Bradley, Laura. 2019. "This Was the Decade Horror Got 'Elevated.'" *Vanity Fair*. December 17, 2019. www.vanityfair.com/hollywood/2019/12/rise-of-elevated-horror-decade-2010s/.

Chen, Nick. 2018. "How Ari Aster Made the Best Horror Movie of 2018." *Dazed*. June 12, 2018. www.dazeddigital.com/film-tv/article/40328/1/hereditary-horror-film-ari-aster-interview/.

Church, David. 2021. "Apprehension Engines: The New Independent 'Prestige Horror.'" In *New Blood: Critical Approaches to Contemporary Horror*, edited by Eddie Falvey, Joe Hickinbottom, and Jonathan Wroot, 15–33. Cardiff: University of Wales Press.

———. 2021. *Post-Horror: Art, Genre, and Cultural Elevation*. Edinburgh: Edinburgh University Press.

Ehrlich, David. 2015. "The Distributor as Auteur." *Slate*. September 30, 2015. slate.com/culture/2015/09/profile-of-the-independent-film-distributor-a24-the-company-behind-spring-breakers-and-room.html.

Falvey, Eddie. 2021. "'Art Horror' and 'Hardcore Art-Horror' at the Margins: Experimentation and Extremity in Contemporary Independent Horror." *Horror Studies* 12 (1): 63–81.

Freud, Sigmund. 2010. *Civilization and Its Discontents*. New York: W.W. Norton.

Gardner, Kate. 2019. "Please, Stop Calling Your Scary Movies 'Elevated Horror.'" *The Mary Sue*. March 18, 2019. www.themarysue.com/stop-calling-scary-movies-elevated-horror/.

Gleiberman, Owen. 2018. "How Did *Hereditary* Get a D+ From CinemaScore? For the Crime of Being More Artful Than Sensational." *Variety*. June 10, 2018. variety.com/2018/film/columns/how-did-hereditary-get-a-d-plus-from-cinemascore-1202839120/.

Gottlieb, Akiva. 2018. "Indies Fight to Survive as Marketplace Undergoes Radical Changes." *Variety*. April 23, 2018. variety.com/2018/film/features/indies-fight-to-survive-world-of-blockbusters-1202754499/.

"*Hereditary* (2018)." n.d. *The Numbers*. Accessed June 22. 2022. www.the-numbers.com/movie/Hereditary-(2018).

"*Hereditary*." n.d. *Script Slug*. Accessed July 22, 2022, www.scriptslug.com/script/hereditary–2018/.

Keen, Sam. 1997. Foreword to *Denial of Death*, by Ernest Becker, xi–xvi. New York: Free Press.

Knight, Jacob. 2018. "There's No Such Thing as an 'Elevated Horror Movie' (and Yes, *Hereditary* Is a Horror Movie)." *Slash Film*. June 8, 2018. www.slashfilm.com/558818/elevated-horror/.

Kohn, Eric. 2018. "'Hereditary': The Year's Scariest Movie Required Years to Make and Painful Experiences No One Will Discuss." *IndieWire*. June 8, 2018. www.indiewire.com/2018/06/hereditary-ari-aster-interview-inspiration-history-1201972348/.

Lieberman, David. 2016. "A24 Says It Will Boost Film and TV Operations with Raise in Bank Credit Line." *Deadline*. February 23, 2016. deadline.com/2016/02/a24-boost-film-tv-operations-increase-bank-credit-line-1201707778/.

Marlowe, Christopher. 2013. *The Jew of Malta*. Edited by James R. Siemon. New York: Bloomsbury.

McCallum, Rebecca. 2019. "*Hereditary* and the Five Stages of Grief." *The Evolution of Horror*. April 16, 2019. www.evolutionofhorror.com/blog/hereditary-and-the-five-stages-of-grief/.

McNary, Dave. "Katz, Fenkel, Hodges Launch A24." *Variety*. August 20, 2012. variety.com/2012/film/news/katz-fenkel-hodges-launch-a24-1118058061/.

Nordine, Michael. 2022. "A24 Films Ranked from Worst to Best." *Variety*. March 17, 2022. variety.com/lists/a24-horror-films-ranked-worst-to-best/.

Platts, Todd K. 2021. "Cut-Price Creeps: The Blumhouse Model of Horror Franchise Management." In *Horror Franchise Cinema*, edited by Mark McKenna and William Proctor, 111–27. New York: Routledge.

Platts, Todd K., and Mathias Clasen. 2017. "Scary Business: Horror at the North American Box Office, 2006–2016." *Frames Cinema Journal* 11. framescinemajournal.com/article/scary-business-horror-at-the-north-american-box-office-2006–2016/.

Rao, Sonia. 2019. "How the Indie Studio behind 'Moonlight,' 'Lady Bird' and 'Hereditary' Flourished while Breaking Hollywood Rules." *The Washington Post*. August 5, 2019. www.washingtonpost.com/lifestyle/style/how-the-indie-studio-behind-moonlight-lady-bird-and-hereditary-flourished-while-breaking-hollywood-rules/2019/08/01/47094878-a4dc-11e9-bd56-eac6bb02d01d_story.html/.

Rose, Steve. 2017. "How Post-Horror Movies are Taking Over Cinema." *The Guardian*. July 6, 2017. www.theguardian.com/film/2017/jul/06/post-horror-films-scary-movies-ghost-story-it-comes-at-night/.

Sharrett, Christopher. 2021. "New Horror Cinema and the Return of Politics." *Cineaste* 46 (2): 27–31.

NOTES

1. On the complexity and debate of these labels see: Church, David. 2021. *Post-Horror: Art, Genre, and Cultural Elevation*. Edinburgh: Edinburgh University Press.

2. See, e.g., Ehrlich, David. 2019. "The Evils of 'Elevated Horror'—IndieWire Critics Survey." *IndieWire*. March 25, 2019. www.indiewire.com/2019/03/elevated-horror-movies-us-1202053471/.

3. See especially, Church, David. 2021. "Apprehension Engines: The New Independent 'Prestige Horror.'" In *New Blood: Critical Approaches to Contemporary Horror*, edited by Eddie Falvey, Joe Hickinbottom, and Jonathan Wroot, 15–33. Cardiff: University of Wales Press. As well as Falvey, Eddie. 2021. "'Art Horror' and 'Hardcore Art-Horror' at the Margins: Experimentation and Extremity in Contemporary Independent Horror." *Horror Studies* 12 (1): 63–81.

4. We stress "Western" because the Japanese ghost story—consider Kenji Mizoguchi's *Ugetsu* (1953) or Kaneto Shindo's *Onibaba* (1964)—offers an alternate model of "slow-moving" horror, emphasizing repressed tension rather than overt sensation.

5. See, for example, Falvey, Eddie. 2021. "'Art Horror' and 'Hardcore Art-Horror' at the Margins: Experimentation and Extremity in Contemporary Independent Horror." *Horror Studies* 12 (1): 63–81.

6. See, for example, McCallum, Rebecca. 2019. "*Hereditary* and the Five Stages of Grief." *The Evolution of Horror*. April 16, 2019. www.evolutionofhorror.com/blog/hereditary-and-the-five-stages-of-grief/.

PART II

Loss and Gender

Grief and Motherhood/Womanhood

Chapter 4

To Make You Feel My Love
Jennifer Kent's The Babadook (2014), *Motherhood, and Loss*

Rebecca L. Willoughby

Jennifer Kent's debut film, *The Babadook* (2014), *is* a horror film, but one that defies easy classification. In it, an exhausted widow and her young son are set upon by a supernatural wraith called "Mister Babadook," who springs from the pages of a mysterious children's book. Is this a possession film, drawing scares from a long tradition that includes such canonical entries as William Friedkin's *The Exorcist* (1973)? Is it a "relentless psychological thriller" comparable to Stanley Kubrick's *The Shining* (1980) (Kenny 2014)? Is it, as some of the film's marketing might suggest, a monster movie, wherein the titular Babadook terrorizes a hapless family until they find within themselves the resources to combat it? Just where, exactly, does the central horror of this film come from?

The Babadook's treatment of grief and loss contributes to this murkiness, the widow's "widowhood" at the center of what drives the darkness. In the end, the film locates the excesses of the horror genre in Western culture's expectations of parenting (particularly motherhood, particularly of the single variety), and in how those expectations, in this specific case, compound the psychological demands of self-care in connection with grieving. How is a woman beset by both intended to cope?

The narrative of self-sacrifice when it comes to love is a familiar one, one certainly not exclusive to the horror film. The trope of one individual willingly coming to harm, or even death, in order to save or spare the cherished other can be found in stories across literature and film. Though often love is the privileged emotion in these narratives, the concept of love and loss is intertwined. Manifestation of personal traumas is a particularly common subject of horror films, specifically supernatural horror. Narratives of ghosts frequently contend that those haunting the living are doing so because of "unfinished business" in the real world, as in M. Night Shyamalan's *The Sixth Sense* (1999). Demons are frequently metaphorical as well as literal.

Possession films, in particular, explore personal trauma in a unique way. The possessed person is vulnerable due to age, circumstances, or even loss. One of the most well-known possession films of the horror canon, *The Exorcist,* conforms to this basic tenet. The child of a single mother, Regan MacNeil feels her father's absence, which creates a gap in her life.[1] Father Damien Karras, who is later taken over by the demon, is struggling with his faith, the lapse of which is another form of uncertainty or loss.

While (most typically) demons take advantage of vulnerability, inserting themselves into the gaps created by absences in the lives of the possessed, the ways in which these entities are defeated are also of interest to this examination. It is in the restoration of some aspect of the possessed—an acknowledgment of the missing piece, a willing emotional (or sometimes literal) sacrifice—that the negative energy is driven out, in other words, the healing of whatever fissure created the space in which nefarious forces work.

The Babadook builds on this framework and creates significant shifts in how the spaces caused by loss, the grieving process, and emotional healing are presented. While not a demon, the Babadook embodies a host of negative and depressive thoughts and feelings experienced by Amelia (Essie Davis) and her son Samuel (Noah Wiseman), feelings created by the loss of Samuel's father, Oskar (Ben Winspear) on the night of Samuel's birth. The trauma experienced by these two characters and Amelia's inability to heal create the space into which the Babadook inserts itself.

Many critics have described this scenario as a classic representation of Sigmund Freud's "return of the repressed."[2] According to Freud, repressed emotions may return in more extreme forms, thereby providing the basis for monstrous resurgences at the center of many horror films (2003). Adolfo Aranjuez supports this notion in "Monstrous Motherhood: Summoning the Abject in *The Babadook*." Here, Aranjuez observes that both the presence of the Babadook figure as an embodiment of loss, as well as the appearance (and re-appearance) of the children's book from which he springs "powerfully evokes . . . the 'return of the repressed'" (2018, 123). As a personification of Amelia's grief, the Babadook is "a product of tragedy, a manifestation of grief that was born, as was Samuel, on the night Amelia's husband was killed" (Kidd 2014).

Yet for all the critical acknowledgment of Amelia's repression, few have examined the reasons Amelia represses her grief. Closest to this exploration is Amanda Konkle's "Mothering by the Book: Horror and Maternal

Ambivalence in *The Babadook*" which asserts that "the real monster in the film is the pressure to be the perfect mom that comes from the ideologies of intensive mothering" (2019, 1). This viewpoint suggests that Amelia must repress her grief in order to appear to be a good mother, that she has simultaneously lost her individuality as well as her husband and must subsume her selfhood for the purpose of mothering Samuel. The pressure of this assumption is certainly a significant aspect of the narrative and contributes to Amelia's mental dissolution. As Konkle writes, "the horror of being judged by the same standards as other, wealthier mothers" seems, on the surface, to be the primary stressor in Amelia's daily life (2019, 4). But this assertion does not adequately address the trauma and loss that are at the core of Amelia's breakdown, though Konkle does acknowledge that "the traumatic loss of her husband corresponds to the traumatic loss of her selfhood when she became a mother" (2019, 4).

While Konkle and others have addressed multiple facets of Amelia's role as a mother and that role's associated social expectations, still other scholars and critics have examined the ways in which loss and grief can be seen to be the primary drivers of Amelia's descent into madness. Most significantly, Paul Mitchell's "The Horror of Loss: Reading Jennifer Kent's *The Babadook* as Trauma Narrative" outlines the stages of grief and the processing of traumatic events that fuel the manifestation of the Babadook and feed Amelia's destructive behavior, particularly toward Samuel. Mitchell proposes that the narrative of the film illustrates Amelia's "process of recuperation" from post-traumatic stress disorder caused by Oskar's death, and that journey toward healing is figured particularly in her ability to "express her trauma" (2019, 191). This expression is a form of grieving and healing in itself, and therefore an expression of self-care.

Significantly, most of the current scholarship examining *The Babadook* does read the appearance of the Babadook creature as a manifestation of Amelia's repressed grief and anger, a part of the grieving process that, although harrowing for both Amelia and Samuel, effectively allows her to confront her toxic feelings and move beyond them. This examination, then, builds on those acknowledgments and recognizes Amelia's terrifying ordeal as an extreme representation of the process of fostering self-care—a manifesto expressing the importance of consistent and supported self-care in mental health.

THE MOTHER-SON DYAD

Amelia Vanek is frequently judged by others to be a bad mother due to her son Samuel's behavior at school, with other children, and in public spaces. At best, onlookers sympathize with her challenging situation, yet she is also made to feel uncomfortable by Samuel's bald references to the underlying reasons for it [00:07:43–00:08:04]. At worst, she is rejected because of her dedication to her seemingly disturbed child. Amelia does not seem to fall neatly into either category of horror-film mothers as articulated by Barbara Creed: the de-sexualized, benevolent caregiver or the domineering roommate, the former characterized by Chris, Regan McNeil's mother in *The Exorcist*; the latter most famously illustrated by Norman Bates's mother in Alfred Hitchcock's *Psycho* (1960) (1993).

To be fair, in the first half of the film, Samuel's behavior does little to endear him to those around him or to viewers. As Glenn Kenny notes in his review for *RogerEbert.com*, Samuel is "a needy clinger who won't let his mom sleep," and he terrorizes his classmates and other children, at one point shoving his cousin out of a treehouse, breaking her nose (2014). In these ways, his characterization, both in act and in appearance (his school uniform alluding to the buttoned-up jacket and shorts of Damien Thorn in Richard Donner's *The Omen* [1976]) recalls many previous possession films wherein the Terrible Child trope finds its most solid traction (Wells 2000). Yet, as Konkle notes, *The Babadook* is not a film about the "endangered child, but the terrors that plague the mother" (2019, 2). Through the film's progression, viewers come to understand that it is, in fact, Amelia who is "possessed."

The reason for this possession is a deep trauma—the loss of Amelia's husband, Oskar, on the night of Samuel's birth. This trauma's inter-connectedness with Samuel's birth creates an environment where trauma is subsumed in Amelia's obedience to the social expectations of motherhood that surround her.[3] From that comes what Amanda Konkle has called "maternal ambivalence," a state which influences Amelia's every waking moment, and which psychotherapist Rozsika Parker defines as "loving and hating feelings for [. . .] children exist[ing] side by side" (2019; 2005, 1). If it is implied that good mothers make sacrifices for their children, then Amelia certainly has, to the point where her own identity has eroded. Her devotion to Samuel in the intervening years since Oskar's death is clear. Kent provides numerous examples of Amelia caring for Samuel, even when it is difficult. Yet, at this point in her small family's life, Amelia is finally sent spiraling into madness, triggered by the confluence of two circumstances—her neglect of herself in this tragic scenario and the mounting societal expectations that she continue this devotion.

Figure 4.1 Amelia shows Samuel a monster-free closet. Kent's framing illustrates Amelia's feelings of entrapment in the mother-son dyad as she appears hemmed in by blackness on either side, Samuel clutching her waist. Left: Noah Wiseman (as Samuel Vanek). Right: Essie Davis (as Amelia Vanek).
Source: The Babadook (2014)

Kent's skillful direction and thoughtful *mise-en-scene* leads viewers to empathize with Amelia's perspective in spite of a superficial "bad mother" label, deftly using the present moment (the days surrounding Samuel's seventh birthday) as an indicator of years of neglected self-care. Viewers come to understand the mental anguish and loss that Amelia has endured through Essie Davis's masterful performance as well as in the oppressive and shadowy set design of the monochromatic Vanek residence. Kent uses the visual and auditory techniques of the horror film to illustrate Amelia's unravelling yet contextualizes that breakdown in terms of loss and grief in the narrative and in symbolic content. Representatives of the social norms of motherhood are also on display, shown to strongly contribute to Amelia's feelings of entrapment in parenthood, compounding her depression and inability to process her bereavement.

As a horror film, *The Babadook* takes an audacious stance on the intersection of grief and motherhood, highlighting the competing demands of parenting and motherhood and the fact that self-care is an integral part of dealing with loss. Further, Kent's treatment of Samuel and of the society surrounding Amelia suggests that the pressures of motherhood may, in fact, compound and complicate the interior life of women, bringing those negotiating complex emotional states to moments of crisis. In drawing its horror from both the return of the repressed and the competing demands of parenting amid working through grief, *The Babadook* rewrites the narrative of the possession film, throwing into dramatic relief how social pressures and expectations of motherhood intensify grief and loss, and stressing the importance of self-care in dealing with mental illness in addition to physical maladies.

THE MOMENT OF TRAUMA

The opening of the film revisits the moment of trauma that has shaped Amelia's life in the seven years since its occurrence. In a disorienting sequence, Amelia floats through the muffled sounds of screeching and crashing, bits of shattered glass dancing in the air around her swirling hair. High contrast lighting focuses on Amelia's bright face whirling in the darkness.[4]

Paula Quigley has noted that the close-up framing of this opening scene is continued throughout the film (2016, 61, 66–67). This technique, appearing so early in the narrative, serves to encourage the audience to identify with Amelia through the details of her facial expression over anything else. Further, using frequent close-ups eliminates many opportunities to discover context. In essence, Kent puts viewers in Amelia's subject position. In particular, the director often employs a full-front, one-point perspective in these close-ups, confronting the audience directly with the visage of the traumatized character.[5] This technique is important in this initial sequence as the audience's experience mimics Amelia's own, and the continuation of Amelia's central framing encourages empathy with her perceptions as she navigates an increasingly illusory and hostile environment. Here, in the initial moments of the film, viewers experience the repetition of Amelia's trauma in a dream, learning of the symbolic and surreal interior state.

This repetition of the moment of trauma ends with Samuel's voice waking his mother. The conclusion of the original moment of trauma is also connected to Samuel's birth.

SCENES OF RELUCTANT MOTHERING

The exposition of the film, following Amelia's traumatic and repetitive dream sequence, involves a series of scenes illustrating Amelia's daily lived experience with Samuel. The child also has bad dreams, though viewers assume they are of a more typical, monsters-under-the-bed variety. Samuel leads Amelia through a routine of checking common monster hiding places. In these moments, Amelia's demeanor appears worn and resigned, and the composition of images tightly frame Amelia and Samuel together, depicting their isolation and closeness, as well as visually gesturing toward Amelia's unspoken feelings of entrapment. Once she has calmed Samuel, he sleeps in her bed, and a series of shots show his kneading fingers and gnashing teeth disturbing Amelia and keeping her awake. A final overhead shot shows the mother and child, Amelia's back turned to her son. Clearly, this is an indication of her illicit desire to escape him, yet the bed itself serves as a visual box, holding the two inside. As Shelley Buerger notes in "The Beak That Grips: Maternal Indifference, Ambivalence, and the Abject in *The Babadook*":

> Much of the discomfort inspired by the first two acts of the film results from the viewer's awareness of Amelia's frustrated desires to break free of her maternity coupled with what seems to be a lack of proper feeling for her son. The tension is further heightened by the way in which Amelia's physical being is almost entirely, if reluctantly, subsumed by her responsibilities of motherhood. Her personal space, her body and her sexuality, have all been co-opted against her will by her son, Samuel's demands. (2017, 37)

As the film progresses, evidence of Amelia's feelings of entrapment mounts. She frequently rebuffs Samuel's physical affection, only addressing his constant pleas for attention when he acts out, breaking windows and threatening other children at school with his homemade monster-defense weapons. In one instance early in the film, she recoils from a particularly ferocious hug from Samuel, whereas moments before she seemed to soften and relax as he stroked her cheek.[6]

Through all of this, it is clear that Amelia understands the expectations of the society around her—she offers her sister Claire (Hayley McElhinney) and her neighbor Mrs. Roach (Barbara West) generic reassurances about their well-being, makes simple jokes with co-workers, apologizes to a stranger for an awkward moment in a supermarket, and defends Samuel when school officials propose separating him from his classmates due to "significant behavioral problems" [00:06:28–00:06:34]. To the few people who may glimpse a small part of Amelia's struggles, she says nothing, continuing to repress her innermost feelings by seeming to assume they are inappropriate to share or that it would be embarrassing to ask for help. This is the behavior of the "good mother," who unfailingly supports and defends her child, giving selflessly of her own stores of energy and offering heavy emotional labor without complaint. For Amelia, this work is undergirded by the loss that she has experienced, and she buries those feelings to focus entirely on her son. While these moments of reluctant parenting are discomfiting enough, the additional layers of Kent's film will show that the repressed is complicated and exacerbated by these external forces of society.

Parenting and Grieving Vs. Self-Care

In *The Babadook*, Amelia's refusal to engage in the grieving process and release toxic emotions amounts to an extreme neglect of her own self-care. Further, Kent's film illustrates the failures of various facets of society to support healthy practices in managing mental health as part of overall health.

Self-care as an idea has come to some prominence in the last twenty years, supported by the World Health Organization and the United Nations as a means for reducing worldwide health-care costs. The practice has also enjoyed popular recognition as an important part of overall personal health. However, most common definitions of self-care refer most specifically to physical health, and the WHO has defined the idea as:

> What people do for themselves to establish and maintain health, and to prevent and deal with illness. It is a broad concept encompassing hygiene (general and personal), nutrition (type and quality of food eaten), lifestyle (sporting activities, leisure, etc.), environmental factors (living conditions, social habits, etc.), socio-economic factors (income levels, cultural beliefs, etc.), and self-medication. ("What Is Self-Care?" n.d.)

Recent societal emphasis on mental health concerns, particularly anxiety and depression, necessitate expanding this view of self-care to include mental health in the definition of "health" more broadly, especially because of the acknowledged connections between mental health and physical manifestations of mental health issues. For instance, throughout a film like *The Babadook*, viewers *see* the physical ramifications of diminishing mental health.[7] Amelia's lack of sleep, her social conflicts, and her complex relationship with her son all contribute to her haggard appearance and daily dysfunction in the world she and Sam inhabit.

The International Self-Care Foundation recognizes that "self-care can only be undertaken by individuals themselves, although the broader environment can provide vital assistance or present significant barriers" ("What Is Self-Care?" n.d.). The organization emphasizes that "community-level action to support people in self-care" is a necessary component of making self-care possible ("What Is Self-Care?" n.d.). In other words, societal pressures that are contradictory to self-care are counterproductive not only to the individual, but to the health of society in general. Amelia and Sam's interactions with the police, doctors, and social workers illustrate the ways in which those outside their insular day-to-day life fail to support Amelia, and in fact actively work to judge and threaten her even as she struggles.

Modern society creates additional obstacles to practicing self-care. A wide array of factors common to daily life in the Western world demand time, attention, and energy; likewise, they can include expectations for contributions to the workplace, home, family, and to communities. These demands frequently privilege others over the individual, requiring that the individual put the interests of others ahead of her/his own to conform to what it means to be successful in all areas of life. Those external entities frequently assume the stability and health of the individual, failing to account for internal tribulations that individuals may be navigating at any given time. A common sentiment that encourages refraining from judgement of others addresses this assumption, asking that before demands are made of others—either societal or personal—that one pause to consider the possible internal battles they may be experiencing. This social paradigm shift is grounded in the increasing cultural understanding of self-care.

Self-care, as a concept, prioritizes the individual before others, with the understanding that an unwell individual will contribute less successfully to society. Therefore, the idea is contextualized as caring for our one's ability to most productively participate in relationships as well as society at large. Physically and mentally healthy individuals can also more successfully deal with obstacles that may arise in life. According to the International Self-Care Foundation, practicing self-care is a process, a cyclical one that asks the practitioner for consistent self-reflection—act, monitor, recognize, evaluate, act ("What Is Self-Care?" n.d.). More specific theories about the processes of self-care come from the medical field, where practitioners, again, most commonly refer to physical health in terms of the maintenance of disease, yet this characterization could apply to mental health as well. Theories of self-care for chronic illness often discuss three dimensions of self-care, which include self-maintenance, self-care monitoring, and self-care management (Riegel et al. 2012). Self-care maintenance refers to illness prevention, which Amelia is beyond when the narrative begins. Self-care monitoring, though most often referring to testing and recognition of symptoms of illness, would seemingly also be beyond Amelia's grasp in the film, as she appears to ignore many of the warning signs of her imminent psychotic break. Yet the concept of self-management is one to which this examination will return in order to consider the resolution of the film.

Amelia's everyday life (and her own refusal to process Oskar's death and its impacts on her) contains none of the self-reflection upon which self-care monitoring would seem to insist, nor does her environment facilitate these considerations. In fact, Kent's representation of Amelia's life indicates that her environment "presents significant barriers" to her self-care, best illustrated in the isolation she and Samuel experience, as well as Samuel's demanding nature—his own processing of his mother's trauma and trauma response (Riegel et al. 2012, 202).

In the few moments in the film where viewers might observe Amelia participating in self-care, her efforts are either thwarted or disingenuous.

The first of these moments comes as Amelia has seemingly lulled Samuel to sleep after the initial discovery of the sinister Mister Babadook bedtime story. Clearly, she is disturbed by the contents of the book. A few subsequent shots depict her reluctant parenting as she doggedly reads a different book to Samuel while he writhes and cries in her lap, then tweaks and kneads her groggily after he falls into an uneasy sleep. After some late-night television that suggests romance and even eroticism, Amelia retreats to her bedroom, takes a vibrator from her sewing basket, and gets into bed. This is the first time in the film where Amelia is shown tending to her own needs, and she has done so only after her obligations to Samuel have been met. As Amelia comes closer to climax, the creepy theme associated with the appearance of the book recurs, and from an angle above her head, viewers see her bedroom door swing open. Her climax is then interrupted by Samuel frantically jumping onto her bed, claiming the Babadook is in his room.

Significantly, sexual needs are another area not directly addressed by the definition of self-care, an oversight made even more problematic because of the vital role sexual and emotional health plays in overall personal health (Daugherty 2016). With this scene, Kent's film importantly brings a discussion of these aspects of Amelia's well-being to the forefront and connects the sexual and emotional dimensions of life with her trauma and loss.

Another important moment occurs the day after when Amelia claims Samuel is ill because she oversleeps and is late for work. When her co-worker, Robbie (Daniel Henshaw) learns how stressed Amelia is, he offers to cover her shift so that she can return home to care for her son. It is significant that in this moment Robbie also articulates, "You don't have to be fine, you know" [00:19:13–00:19:16]. He appears to normalize addressing external and internal forces leading to stress, but Amelia ignores his encouragement of this healthy practice even while she takes him up on his offer.

Rather than go home, Amelia wanders through a shopping mall, the photography now diffuse, light, and ethereal. The camera lingers on her reflection in shop windows, and watches as she eats an ice cream cone on a plush, solitary bench. Though she has not taken Robbie's suggestion that she mine her psyche for the reasons why she might feel overwhelmed and desperate, she does take time for herself in this scene, choosing time away from her son as a possible way to heal, at least momentarily. As she leaves through the parking garage, viewers see her watch a young couple kiss passionately in an adjacent car, a scene which links two moments of indulgence and suggests the underlying reason for her depression: the loss of her husband. This brief interlude in Amelia's day ends when she discovers a series of missed calls from her sister, Claire, claiming that Samuel has been terrorizing his cousin with tales of the Babadook.

It is important to note that these moments of self-care do not serve to ease the burden of loss or the effects of repression that Amelia is suffering, though both instances are linked to elements of her struggle as a single parent. Additionally, each of these instances ends with Samuel's needs—his fears, his monster obsession. He characterizes his focus on these creatures as preparation for an upcoming battle with unseen adversaries, a way of protecting his mother. However, at this point in the film, Kent's direction privileges Amelia's perceptions. By depicting both Amelia's strained relationship with her son (stemming from the connection he shares with the loss that haunts her) and her inability to find some small solace in self-care to allow herself room to grieve, Kent's film illustrates the pressures Amelia faces in dealing with loss.

As Amelia is unable to find personal space throughout her struggle to fulfill her motherly role, several moments in the film serve to illustrate the negative ways in which society views her and Samuel in spite of her efforts. The most prominent one occurs at Claire's daughter's birthday party. Amelia sits at a table surrounded by other women—friends of her sister—as Samuel clings to her, whining when Amelia tries to separate from him. Once she finally convinces him to leave the room, the conversation turns to Amelia's previous work as a writer and the circumstances of the other women at the party. One woman obliquely refers to Amelia as "disadvantaged" because she has lost her husband then complains about her own situation of "having the kids 24/7" as a result of her husband's increased workload and not being able to find time for the gym [00:29:35–00:29:56]. It is obvious that the circumstances Claire's friend is articulating is a mere inconvenience compared to Amelia's day-to-day situation. She icily rebukes the complaint, forcing the woman to recognize her own privilege and highlighting the continued strain Amelia is experiencing. The composition of camera shots in this scene emphasizes Amelia's oppression. The women are standing around the table, facing Amelia, who is seated; their height and dark clothing appear imposing, a metaphorical wall of assumptions. Their judgement is a notable external factor inhibiting Amelia's ability to perform self-care, as they add to her anxiety and feelings of isolation. Significantly, Amelia's outburst at the party is an example of the thinning of the veneer of Amelia's seeming ability to cope that begins when the Babadook is introduced into the narrative. The release that Amelia may feel in lashing out at Claire's friend allows her some truth, a trend that will continue in the extreme as Amelia's mental state deteriorates and she begins to exhibit signs of possession.

That possession can be equated with Amelia's ability to give voice to the feelings that she has suppressed and that are forbidden by the society that surrounds her is a symptom of the social disease that *The Babadook* examines, one that forces women to bury any negative feelings toward motherhood and one that puts limitations on the acceptable strategies employed in grieving a loss.

THERAPEUTIC POSSESSION

Possession gives Amelia the ability to face the reality of her loss, to begin to heal. Societal expectations of motherhood and social pressures related to the appropriateness of grieving are no match for the Babadook, a physical manifestation of Amelia's repressed feelings of mourning for her husband and sublimated ambivalent feelings towards Samuel. While in the throes of the Babadook's influence, Amelia, like Samuel and Oskar themselves, according to Mrs. Roach, is finally able to give voice to the anguish she has felt over the past seven years, albeit in a violent and dangerous way.

In this forbidden expression and its connection to possession is the intersection of the treatment of loss and the connection that expression has to the horror genre. Several moments in this section of the film visibly recall *The Exorcist*—the shaking bed, the cracking walls, the vomiting. These are only the most direct homages to a specific possession film; the whole of Kent's production design (courtesy of Alex Holmes) evokes the darkness and oppressive atmosphere that characterizes Amelia's state of mind, as well as recalls iconic horror film tropes. In this extremity, such horror tropes allow Amelia to begin to realize the extent of the effects of her repression. The scenes of possession in the film also include several moments of the same high-contrast lighting seen in the film's initial traumatic moment and suggests the trauma's return.

Though Amelia has been slowly spiraling toward a full-on wrestling match with her pent-up feelings, the depiction of her possession provides the

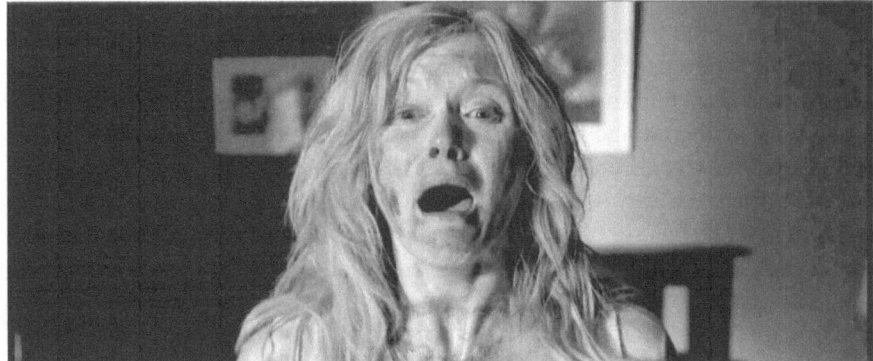

Figure 4.2 Amelia experiences the loss of her husband once more in an expressive close-up, revealing the depth of her grief. The full-front angle of the shot gives additional emphasis to the intensity of these repressed feelings now coming to the surface. Essie Davis (as Amelia Vanek).
Source: The Babadook (2014)

clearest expression of her internal battle, as well as includes the most direct pieces of dialogue addressing loss, depression, and anger.

Amelia's possession reflects horror genre expectations and shows the extreme nature of Amelia's emotions. In an interview with *The Dissolve*, Kent identified this film as one in which she intended to illustrate loss, saying, "I've lost people, I've lost my dad, I know what that feels like, and it feels like it's never going to end. So I think it's important to have stories that can help you through" (Ehrlich 2014). In *The Babadook*, Amelia's behavior during her possession by the monster is violent—both in word and deed—but ultimately truthful. She says hurtful things to Samuel (who by this point knows that the woman he sees is not his mom), but they are things that are understandable given the circumstances of her trauma. She is also able to state in one sentence what underpins the entire film: "I haven't been good since your dad died. Not good at all. I'm sick. I need help" [01:14:19–01:14:35].

Eventually, Amelia is able to rid herself of the Babadook by experiencing love for Sam. The film draws on early scenes of Sam's weapon and trap-making to prepare viewers for his trapping Amelia in the basement—the site of repression—where she confronts her grief. He ties her up, and admits that he knows she does not love him, as he says, "The Babadook won't let you" [01:16:47–01:16:49]. A close-up of Amelia's face shows the internal struggle she experiences, the rage and despair of the Babadook on the one hand and her own maternal impulses on the other. When she frees her hands and attempts to strangle her son, he reaches out to repeat the same stroking of her cheek from the start of the film, the one gesture that reaches her. This gesture triggers her ability to "get it out." She vomits a stream of Babadook-black bile onto the basement floor before collapsing. This scene, like many in this section of the film, is lit using a bright white light, a single bulb hanging from the ceiling, which mimics the headlights present in Amelia's dream in the opening of the film.

As part of the film's finale, Amelia is forced to relive the circumstances of Oskar's death one last time in order to overcome it. Near the end of the film, viewers may believe that Amelia has expelled (literally, in that stream of black bile) her demons and that the dénouement is imminent. But Samuel remembers: "You can't get rid of the Babadook" [01:19:03–01:19:05]. Amelia's healing process is not as simple as expelling her anger and hurtful wishes toward her son.

Once more, from the darkness, emerges a likeness of Oskar. Unlike an earlier moment wherein Amelia was confronted with and then embraced Oskar's image in the basement, she realizes immediately that her trauma is about to be replayed. Her realization is significant—she has begun the process of self-care monitoring. She can prepare. The other difference in this scene is that Oskar's mirage speaks the same words to her as he had originally, not the manipulative words of the Babadook who urged Amelia to kill her son. The dialogue, in which Oskar encourages her to "keep breathing" during labor and observes that he thinks it will rain, is a real expression of her past exposed [01:20:28–01:20:44]. Viewers hear and see the moment of the accident, complete with the bright white light. Over the next few minutes, Amelia is plunged once more into the depths of mourning. When she is again threatened by the Babadook, she understands that that experience—the loss, grief, rage, and anguish she has repressed for so long—means that she has endured much more, overcome so much, and she no longer cowers. She releases a horrific primal scream, forcing the Babadook to back down. It retaliates once more with a shriek of its own, coupled with the bright white light, before retreating to the basement, where it will now be trapped—but only to a certain extent.

FINAL AMBIVALENCE

The ending of the film is a complicated and nuanced statement regarding repression and acknowledgment of emotional pain, providing much fodder for consideration of how both the internal challenges and external pressures of *The Babadook* have played out. On the day Samuel and Amelia are celebrating his birthday, Amelia is able to plainly tell the social workers checking up on Samuel that her husband was killed the day her son was born (just as Samuel is happy to tell them why his cousin is not coming—because he "broke her nose in two places") [01:26:00–01:26:20]. It is even suggested that Mrs. Roach knows about the supernatural and violent events in the Vanek household when Amelia alludes to the stitches she received when Samuel stabbed her in the leg with a kitchen knife while she was possessed. Flowers bloom on the trees and in Amelia's garden. The Babadook has been relegated to Amelia and Samuel's basement, where Amelia returns periodically to feed it worms, telling Samuel that he can see it "when you're bigger" [1:27:01–1:27:03]. Amelia's response to the Babadook here is an example of self-care management or a response to signs and symptoms of illness (Ziguras 2013). She is able to manage the shrieking creature, calm it, and feed it the worms she and Samuel have gathered from the garden.

Though the Babadook is inhabiting the original, horror-film site of repression, the Babadook is no longer being repressed; in contrast, the end of the film clearly illustrates that Amelia is tending to the creature, this embodiment of a pain that will never leave her. Her healing has come in the form of acknowledgment, making peace with the scars—both physical and emotional—that have led her to this point. Her willingness to discuss that pain with Sam in terms that are appropriate for him is even more evidence that she has turned a corner in her dealing with grief and loss and come to an understanding and practice of self-care.

BIBLIOGRAPHY

Aranjuez, Adolfo. 2018. "Monstrous Motherhood: Summoning the Abject in *The Babadook*." *Screen Education* 92: 122–128.
Bradshaw, Peter. 2014. "The Babadook review—a superbly acted, chilling Freudian thriller." *The Guardian*. October 23, 2014. https://www.theguardian.com/film/2014/oct/23/the-babadook-review-chilling-freudian-thriller.
Buerger, Shelley. 2017. "The Beak That Grips: Maternal Indifference, Ambivalence, and the Abject in *The Babadook*." *Studies in Australasian Cinema* 11 (1): 33–44.
Clover, Carol. 1993. *Men, Women and Chainsaws: Gender in the Modern Horror Film*. Princeton, NJ: Princeton University Press.
Creed, Barbara. 1993. *The Monstrous Feminine: Film, Feminism, Psychoanalysis*. Oxon: Routledge.
Daugherty, Timothy K., Hannah M. Julian, Nicole M. Lynch, Stephanie J. Chen, Tanya L. Whipple, and Austin F. Ginsburg. 2016. "Beyond the Absence of Disease or Infirmity: The Case for Sexual Wellness." *College Student Journal* 50 (3): 404–8.
Ehrlich, David. 2014. "The Babadook director Jennifer Kent talks about drawing horror from life." *The Dissolve*. December 1, 2014. http://thedissolve.com/features/emerging/834-the-babadook-director-jennifer-kent-talks-about-dr/.
Freud, Sigmund. 2003. *The Uncanny* (Trans. David McLintock). London: Penguin.
Kenny, Glenn. 2014. "*The Babadook*." *RogerEbert.com*. November 28. 2014. https://www.rogerebert.com/reviews/the-babadook-2014.
Kidd, Briony. 2014. "Umbilical Fears: Jennifer Kent's 'The Babadook.'" *Metro* 180: https://metromagazine.com.au/umbilical-fears/.
Konkle, Amanda. 2019. "Mothering by the Book: Horror and Maternal Ambivalence in *The Babadook*." *Feminist Encounters: A Journal of Critical Studies in Cultural and Politics* 3: 1–12.
Mitchell, Paul. 2019. "The Horror of Loss: Reading Jennifer Kent's *The Babadook* as a Trauma Narrative." *Atlantis: Journal of the Spanish Association of Anglo-American Studies* 41 (2): 179–96.
Parker, Rozsika. 2005. *Torn in Two: The Experience of Maternal Ambivalence* (New and revised edition). London: Virago.
Quigley, Paula. 2016. "When Good Mothers Go Bad: Genre and Gender in *The Babadook*." *Irish Journal of Gothic and Horror Studies* 15: 57–75.
Riegel, Barbara, Tiny Jaarsma, and Anna Strömberg. 2012. "A Middle-Range Theory of Self-Care of Chronic Illness." *ANS: Advances in Nursing Science* 35 (3): 194–204.
Wells, Paul. 2000. *The Horror Genre: From Beelzebub to Blair Witch*. New York: Wallflower Press.

"What Is Self-Care?" *International Self-Care Foundation.* https://isfglobal.org/what-is-self-care/.

Ziguras, Christopher. 2013. *Self-care: Embodiment, Personal Autonomy, and the Shaping of Health Consciousness.* London: Routledge.

NOTES

1. Other examinations of this film suggest that Regan's positioning on the cusp of adolescence is a tenuous life stage (see Carol Clover, *Men, Women, and Chainsaws: Gender in the Modern Horror Film*, 1993), an idea which also lends itself to creating vulnerability.

2. Peter Bradshaw, writing for *The Guardian*, brings it right out in his review title, and Adolfo Aranjuez, Paula Quigley, and Amanda Konkle, among others, have noted this connection to Freud's concept, so often invoked in horror as the psychological origin of a monster or monstrous behavior.

3. It's significant, though, that two other characters who are seemingly closest to Amelia—her next-door neighbor, Mrs. Roach, and her coworker, Robbie—at several points provide opportunities to express her hidden feelings in a safe way. That Amelia does not take advantage of these opportunities speaks to the depth of her entrenchment in these social mores surrounding motherhood and grieving.

4. This lighting cue is one that will be repeated throughout the film in moments where Amelia is working through her grief, suggesting she is shining a light on her trauma in order to make it visible and initiate the healing process. That this lighting is so directly connected to the moment of Oskar's death and re-appears at various moments of crisis is significant—in many ways, she must repeatedly revisit and even re-experience this trauma in order to lessen its impact on her mind and heart.

5. Kent continued this technique in her 2018 film, *The Nightingale*, particularly early in the film where she isolates her protagonist's face during a brutal rape scene, a trauma for that character that drives her actions for the entire remainder of the film.

6. Importantly, this gesture and the response it elicits will also be repeated later in a moment of crisis with the Babadook.

7. Possession films are prime examples of depicting this kind of physical deterioration, and the technique of matching the exterior of the victim of possession to their interior, beleaguered state can be seen in films as wide-ranging as *The Exorcist* (Friedkin, 1973), *Amityville II: The Possession* (Damiani, 1982), and more recent films such as *The Exorcism of Emily Rose* (Derrickson, 2005), *The Conjuring* (Wan, 2013), *The Rite* (Hafstrom, 2011), and *The Devil Inside* (Bell, 2012), to name a few.

Chapter 5

The Myth of the Natural Woman
Horror and Grief in Ari Aster's Midsommar (2019)

Aspen Taylor Ballas

Grief is not the typical affect we link to the horror genre. Whereas grief is normally associated with the loss of a person or thing for whom one has deep love and affection, the horror genre is dominated by visual gore, monsters, and grotesque anomalies that viewers are invited to loathe. Apart from these differences, grief and horror strike similar visceral chords. Together, grief and horror capture fear and curiosity of death and the unknown. They are reminders of our mortality and the fragility of our corporeality, prompting us to explore our existential condition and the uncertainties guiding our lived realities.

According to Darryl Jones, "Horror as a cultural form maintains a dialogic relationship between radicalism (the urge to confront) and conservatism (the desire to control)" (2018, 15). This dialectic is active in Ari Aster's 2019 horror film *Midsommar*, as the central character, Dani (Florence Pugh), is forced to suppress her melancholy and grief within the social context of her American college experience. In *Midsommar*, grief is employed thematically as a horrific excess that must be subjectively controlled in the feminine body to prevent it from manifesting in the social world. Dani's grief threatens to disrupt the lives of the young and carefree men in her social circle. The film's Americanized treatment of grief stands in stark contrast to the radical, collective embrace and performativity of grief in the small Hälsingland village of Hårga that the group of college students will later travel to. In both cases, grief is an obstacle that can either be approached through acts of suppression

(American setting) or sublimation (Scandinavian setting), neither of which are devoid of consequences.

Midsommar's commentary on grief is further complicated by its symbolic use of nature and womanhood, being two ideological categories historically used as scapegoats for establishing tangible meaning around death and correlative states of uncertainty. The foundation of Simone de Beauvoir's well known *The Second Sex* (1949) consists of the archetypal roles of women used to aid in the construction of social hierarchies, which continue to hold a strong grip over the ideological, social, cultural, and emotional orders, among others, that influence the lives, autonomy, and well-being of women through history and around the world. Aster's *Midsommar* makes use of formal cinematic elements to represent a carnivalesque shift of power, reversing these social and political hierarchies outlined by Beauvoir. Furthermore, the myth of woman and nature helps form an allegorical perspective of grief. Like women and nature, grief is treated as a category of chaos that must be subdued.

Midsommar's symbolic triad of nature, womanhood, and grief are delivered as a lattice, of sorts, on which spectators can rely for conceptualizing the aesthetic beauty and uncanny horror of grief. On a larger scale, this lattice allows spectators to consider social perceptions of grief, the meaning behind the joint suppression of these categories, and therefore, possibly gain a more holistic understanding of the political valences of grief. All in all, *Midsommar* presents an *ecology of grief*, not only made up of the inner thoughts and emotions of grieving individuals but the environmental, social, and ideological elements of the world, through which grief is processed and felt.

The central character, Dani, is a young college student. Predisposed to panic attacks and loneliness, Dani's mental and emotional conditions are worsened by the unstable relationships in her life. The film introduces Dani in her small, dark apartment, scarcely lit by a desk lamp and the glows emitted from the screens of her laptop and cellphone. A low-angle shot reveals her sitting in a chair. This angle is often used to make characters look powerful and commanding, however, in this case, the power is not reserved for the hesitant and fearful Dani but rather the overwhelming grief that seems to engulf her. Dani's physicality exposes her inner turmoil, as her oversized sweater falls below her fingertips, which she uses to wipe the tears from her eyes. Despite being inundated with technological interfaces, it is clear that Dani is alienated and alone. Worried about the well-being of her family following an ominous message received from her sister, Terri (Klaudia Csànyi), Dani's screens represent empty voids as she fails to contact her mother (Gabi Fon) and father (Zsolt Bojàri) over the phone. "I can't anymore—everything is black—mom and dad are coming with me—goodbye," the message cryptically reads in an open email thread on Dani's screen, to which Dani replies with frenzied questions that go unanswered [00:03:04]. Finally able to reach her boyfriend, Christian (Jack Reynor), over the phone, long awkward breaks in their conversation prove that despite making contact, Christian is notably distant and unavailable.

"How's the sister situation?" Christian asks reluctantly before dismissively asserting that everything is probably fine. The sighs and pauses that spill from Christian cause his sympathy for Dani to register as synthetic—as a mere shortcut for expediting their uncomfortable conversation. Not only does Christian fail to support Dani during this exchange but he aggressively blames and denigrates her, as he reminds her, rather dismissively, that Terri shows this behavior "every other day" before unfairly suggesting that Terri's bi-polar disorder persists because Dani lets it [00:04:41–00:05:07]. Through this conversation, it becomes clear that the couple's relationship is already strained, and Dani's feigned composure is performed out of the fear that not doing so will push Christian further away. These fears become palpable in the scene that follows of Dani nervously pacing around her apartment while speaking to a girlfriend. These anxious movements are captured through an indirect shot of a body-length mirror, which warps Dani's face and figure—a visual representation of emotions plaguing Dani from the inside out.[1]

The couple's instability is reconfirmed when Christian and his friends—Mark (Will Poulter), Josh (William Jackson Harper), and Pelle (Vilhelm Blomgren)—sit around a booth in a local pizzeria. Here, Mark stridently expresses his disapproval of Dani and her emotional dependence on Christian. In the midst of urging Christian to end things with Dani, she calls again. Upon answering, Christian is met with an inconsolable Dani, whose cries and screams are so heavy and near surreal that the only way to properly represent them cinematically is to accompany them with the unsettling, dissonant sounds of violins. These non-diegetic sounds play after the scene transitions to the crime scene, wherein it is revealed that Terri has carried out a horrendous murder-suicide in a fit of mental illness, taking the lives of Dani's parents as well as her own. As a slow tracking shot moves through Dani's family home—where Terri has strategically siphoned car exhaust into their parents' bedroom and through a gas mask donned by Terri—a duet of string instruments plays a dissonant harmony, one instrument sustaining a droning bass note while the other swells at a higher pitch, oscillating as though it is incapable of resolving. As the lurid details of the crime scene compound, so too the cacophonous sounds crescendo. Dani's cries rejoin the audible friction at the same time that the camera cuts from the crime scene to Christian approaching Dani's apartment from a dark and snowy street, onto which Dani's cries spill out in a hauntingly impossible reverberation. A wide-angle shot shows Christian attempting to comfort Dani on her small loveseat, which appears cramped and incapable of accommodating the two, again, managing to visually inscribe the surplus of Dani's grief into the scene. Dani, who lies in a fetal position across the chair, is cradled, rocked, and shushed by Christian, framing her grief as an infantilized, deeply susceptible form—a combination that gains significance as the film progresses.

Despite Christian's literal presence, he nonetheless fails to mitigate Dani's grief, which is augmented by the somber, eerie, and dissonant harmonies of cries and string instruments. As the camera zooms in on the couple, it does not stall on a two shot but supersedes them, ultimately focusing on a full frame of the blizzard raging outside of the window behind them. In this moment, Dani's grief is echoed in the chaotic and relentless force of nature, transforming her emotional state into a visual allegory.

After crying herself to sleep, Dani awakens to Christian trying to leave undetected, tiptoeing away in a manner similar to the cliché of a man secretly departing in the aftermath of a one-night stand. Similar to the previous scene, where Dani's grief finds symbolic representation in the snow, here her grief is also represented as feminine; as an emotionally demanding and burdensome affect no different from the way femininity is oftentimes portrayed in heteronormative sexual relationships. Following the theme of emotional dependency in the opening scene and the visual infantilization in the scene prior, Dani is quickly depicted as "needy," which is only amplified in comparison to Christian, whose affection seems labored, otherwise appearing detached and disingenuous. Dani's familial circumstances have produced an inopportune time for Christian to end their relationship, complicating the web in which the two are entangled. To make matters worse, unbeknownst to Dani, Christian is planning to take a trip to Scandinavia with Mark, Josh, and Pelle.

Christian's fraudulent performance that he genuinely cares about Dani's grief is shared by Mark and Josh. As a group of graduate anthropology students, the male characters lean into the notoriety historically attached to the discipline. Traditionally, the voyeuristic, Eurocentric, male anthropologist, is deemed a pragmatic, central bearer of truth, using their perspective to interpret and record cultures and traditions geographically and ethnically distinct from their own. The anthropological task of archiving these—arguably biased and self-serving—interpretations of distant cultural practices according to Eurocentric truths has given shape and meaning to the present realities and the ongoing hierarchical orders that structure social relationships in the world today. This includes the Enlightenment-era shift away from nature towards technology; tradition towards science; emotion towards rationalism. Framing these early anthropological archetypes in the context of *Midsommar* is useful, insofar as it paints a clearer picture of the pragmatic, individualistic, and emotionally detached group of male characters, the social environment they control, and therefore, the inability for Dani's grief and anxieties to be addressed, explored, or reconciled within this social context.

This is evidenced when Dani, after catching Christian, offers to accompany him to the party he was heading to in his clumsy departure. Supervising sound editor of *Midsommar*, Gene Park, discusses the important role of sound in an interview with Jennifer Walden. Park's description of "a really quiet underlying room tone that is more felt than heard" captures this particular scene of the couple at the party (Walden 2019). Although sound is being drowned out, a bridge between Dani and viewers forms an allegiance of emotional numbness. A close-up of her face causes Dani to appear as though she is in a daze, briefly bending her mouth into a smile or looking at others in her circle to show that she is listening; however, the muffled sound of the loud music and the dialog exchanged suggests that Dani is occupying another realm. Already ostracized from the group, Dani's grief produces an additional layer of alterity. However, Dani is quickly pulled back into reality when Josh shares the details of their trip. As their long list of plans compound, the camera methodically gains distance from the group—initially capturing each character in close-ups and medium shots, the camera then cuts to two shots, before ending in long and wide shots of everyone standing in awkward and estranged silence. After leaving the party, Dani and Christian begin arguing over her unawareness of the trip. Once they enter Dani's apartment, the mirror is used again to suggest Dani's grief and alienation. On the right side of the frame, Dani is shown standing against a wall; to her left is a mirror that frames Christian sitting on the other side of the room. This use of the mirror is disorienting as it causes both characters to visibly face in the direction of the viewer as opposed to one another. In one sense, this reinforces the distance between the couple despite their spatial intimacy on-screen, but in an arguably more powerful sense, this effectively sutures the viewer into the emotional whirlwind of the characters, mediating the emotional disconnection between the two. This mirror effect is again reinforced in the following scene, when Josh, Mark, and Pelle sit in an apartment living room. As the group plans their itinerary, Christian alerts the rest of the men that Dani is on her way up. A loose frame remains on the group of men as Christian walks towards and past the camera where the entryway is positioned. While waiting at the door, Christian is only made visible through a large mirror that fills the wall above the heads of Pelle and Mark. It is through this poorly lit reflection of Christian's that he delivers the unwanted news that Dani has been invited on the trip to Europe. Christian is now marked by this estrangement that was previously reserved for Dani, who eventually enters the apartment and shares the dark, distorted mirror-space with him. This mirror *mise-en-scène* is apt for summarizing the social disconnection as well as the group's scrutiny that both Dani and Christian face.

Against the wishes of Mark and Josh, Dani accepts the invitation, launching the group of five on their travels to Scandinavia. Pelle, the only group member warm and welcoming towards Dani, is from the Swedish village where the group is headed to experience and study the midsommar tradition. Dani's presence proves to drastically alter the group's dynamics during their time in the Swedish village; not only does the hierarchy of the group change, but the behaviors and emotions that are deemed socially acceptable do as well. Dani, initially an unwanted excess, transforms into the most crucial figure of the group, as she is the one who will eventually be crowned May Queen, thereby becoming a pivotal figure in the completion of the village's midsommar ritual. By contrast, the once powerful and domineering men individually succumb to sacrificial roles, falling victim to intense, ritualistic violence for each day of the midsommar festival. Based on Dani's ascending social position and the violent decline of her companions, the final two-thirds of *Midsommar* turns deeply carnivalesque. Alongside the shifting social positions, the treatment of dark, secretive affects, such as melancholy and grief, are able to transcend beyond Dani's subjective position, making heavy imprints on the objective world.

In this new setting, dominated by nature and archaic pagan-like rituals, Dani's grief assumes a new appearance as it is no longer suppressed in the old environment but sublimated into the social practices of the Swedish villagers. In fact, the spatial transition from America to Sweden is cinematically unique. It begins with Dani in the same apartment of the previous scene, where Pelle admits that he is happy and excited that Dani is joining them. Pelle then shares his own experience of losing his parents at a young age and finding community in the Swedish village to which they are bound. However, Pelle's recognition and kind regards has an adverse effect on Dani, whose smile slowly morphs into a frown. Seeing her grief reflected beyond herself proves to be overwhelming. In the act of escaping to the bathroom of the apartment to regain composure, Dani is followed by a bird's eye view through the hall and into the bathroom, when suddenly, upon crossing the threshold, Dani is shown to be inside of an airplane bathroom. Again, Dani's grief is portrayed as an excess that cannot be resolved within the confines of the scene, forcing it to transitionally spill over into another location and another time. Dani's grieving appears to transform alongside her social and spatial circumstances, made all the more apparent in the scenes that follow.

In the Swedish setting nature, womanhood, and grief begin to meld into a larger statement worth reflection. Some of the major examples that fuse the trio include sex, conception, and labored breathing, the fertilization of land, the cycle of life and death alongside the changing seasons, and the personification of nature. Clearer descriptions of these examples will follow with the intention of showing how Dani's sublimation of grief is cathartic and recognized within the new Scandinavian setting but also a horrifying display of the social and existential burden that the woman's condition historically carries in tow. In the chapter titled "Biological Data," Simone de Beauvoir begins her studies of the woman and female organisms at the biological level. From insects and fungi to vegetables and mollusks, Beauvoir seeks to understand reproductive functions and how they have evolved into the contemporary (ideological) conception of women. While Beauvoir acknowledges the difficulty of reducing female humans to gametes, she uses this science as a foundation for explaining the complexities that arise when the basic necessities of reproduction are transformed into myths that concretely shape and structure human life (Beauvoir 2011, 52, 26).

Mythologies of nature have shaped women through time and in the context of *Midsommar,* the wanton horrors of womanhood, nature, and grief come to the fore. Women are the producers of life, but life is a struggle that ultimately leads to death. As a result, the tumultuous cycle of life and death is symbolically assigned to women. These pressures become further amplified in lieu of the dialectical relationship of the sexes (active male/passive female). Beauvoir arrives at the woman, whose child-bearing role in nature has led to the relinquishing of her individuality, reducing her to nature itself. Meanwhile, man "considers himself a fallen god," cursed in his descent "from a luminous and orderly heaven into the chaotic obscurity of the mother's womb . . . He would like himself to be as necessary as pure Idea, as One, All, absolute Spirit" (Beauvoir 2011, 199). Unfortunately, for man, he is mortal, corporeal, and limited in his body, where he must exist "in a place and time he did not choose" (Beauvoir 2011, 199). Consider the masculine/feminine dichotomy in *Midsommar,* which overshadows the relationship between Dani, Christian, and his friends. The latter are composed, decisive, and controlling as they freely and emotionlessly plan, survey, and document their surroundings while Dani is timid, emotional, and compliant with the plans in which the men include her, more or less out of pity. However, upon the group's arrival in the Scandinavian village, this unforgiving sexual divide assumes new meanings of horror and new sacrificial roles. As the group speeds towards their destination, an aerial shot moves in the opposite direction of their approaching car before quickly flipping directly overhead, then upside down in one continuous take. The lingering upside down shot of their voyage is symbolically apt in foreshadowing their upcoming experience: disorienting and founded on the complete reversal of power.

The Scandinavian setting of *Midsommar* is historically important, marked with some of the earliest evidence of pagan religious practices. In reference to ancient pagan societies (like the Sami people of the same region) dualism was a strongly held belief. For example, life was a balance of oppositional forces, composed of, but not limited to body-spirit, life-death, light-dark, and masculine-feminine elements. The pagan roots with which *Midsommar* is identifying is crucial for understanding the horror that these characters are set to face: a relentless balancing act or violently forced equilibrium that is embedded in their new environment. To clarify this point, consider the following scene of the group's arrival to the Swedish village.

After being greeted with psilocybin mushrooms in a picturesque field of green grass and wildflowers, Mark insists that all group members ingest their mushrooms at the same time because not doing so will result in "totally separate trips" [00:27:50]. By peer-pressuring Dani and Christian into taking the mushrooms with everyone else, Mark further exposes his neurotic need to have control over situations. Furthermore, being the character who fawns over the mere idea of Swedish women and excludes Dani for being more emotional than she is sexual, Mark reinforces his self-assigned role as the all-powerful patriarch of the group. However, Mark's authoritative control quickly dwindles when the group is shown sitting in the field well into their psychotropic "trip." Curious of the time, Mark asks Christian who then informs him that it is late into the evening, to which Mark protests, "What do you mean? That can't be right. The sky is blue. That feels wrong, I don't like that" [00:29:00]. The bathos injected into this scene, while comedic, also exposes the shifting scales of their environment; no longer is Mark's forceful and pragmatic perspective being catered to. Mark becomes paranoid and uncomfortable, trying to cope by demanding that everyone lie down with him to synchronize their hallucinations, growing increasingly frantic when no one abides.

During this same scene, Pelle asks the others, "Can you feel that? The energy coming up from the Earth?" [00:29:54]. At that moment, Dani looks down at her hand to find blades of grass growing through her flesh and bones. Pelle claims that the trees are breathing; that nature knows how to instinctively stay in harmony; that nature is capable of mechanically doing its part. Here, Aster switches to a low angle, subjective shot. The tree the group sits beneath appears to "swell and deflate with psychedelic life" (Razowski 2020, 25). This effect is then carried over to the background of grass in a medium shot of Dani.

Not unrelated, this scene can serve as a commentary on the white, western, and wealthy search for neo-pagan spirituality and roots by "returning to nature" or living off-the-grid, popular in the so-called "back to lander" movement among others. While Dani and Pelle prove to have a deeper connection to nature during their "trip," the involvement of the others appears detached, hasty and superficial. These sugarcoated revisions of modern mushroom "trips" and consumeristic "festival culture" clash with the more ancient and earnest pagan relationships to nature and ritual wherein human sacrifices worked to appease the gods and goddesses who were believed to regulate and supply natural elements for human well-being and survival. Ultimately, the fantasy of "returning to nature" precludes, but is nonetheless rooted in, the sobering and practical rituals of sacrifice for survival against the chaotic phenomena of nature and death to which humans have forever been susceptible. Dani and Pelle's traumatic relationships with death suggest that they have the potential to cross this more daunting threshold.

Human sacrifice may not be a staple of modern humanity; however, death remains a natural phenomenon that humans cannot escape. With Dani's grief at the forefront, the group's adventure into the spiritual realm is pre-conditioned by these primal, terrifying aspects. Their American worldviews are upended as daylight stays well into the evening and trees begin breathing. As Mark's futile protests make clear, all attempts of certainty and individual agencies are quickly overturned. However, this initial "trip" is only the first of many misadventures awaiting the group. As the film progresses, each character proves to be at the whims of nature, or, at the very least, its sanctification through the midsommar rituals that ensure its order.

Despite this important ideological and environmental shift, Dani's anxiety does not subside, but her grief and anxieties do begin to manifest in different ways. In "Contesting Tears: The Hollywood Melodrama of the Unknown Woman," Stanley Cavell explains the importance of the melodrama, as an outlet that enables women to tell their story or begin their search for one (2019, 259). Cavell describes a "chief negation" of traditional narratives, like the institution of marriage, for example, and the ways in which the most familiar and well-known concepts can lead to originality and creativity (2019, 261). The ability to reimagine the world requires a loosening of the rigid systems, behaviors, and beliefs that preexist. The brilliance of Aster's *Midsommar* appears to have a similar effect outlined by Cavell, insofar as the film allows spectators to plunge into Dani's inner turmoil in a new way, not by necessarily straying from the symbolic representations normally attached to grief (i.e., the woman and nature) but animating them in a way that begins the critique of common and readily accepted social narratives. No longer suppressed, Dani's grief does not dissolve but begins to take on new concrete forms. This shifting aesthetic display of Dani's pain invites viewers to contemplate grief as it affects humans subjectively while also contemplating the material expressions of grief.

One of the first instances that Dani's grief becomes imprinted on the world is after an anxiety attack arises during their drug induced "trip." Dani runs into an outhouse which is completely dark inside. While lighting a match, Dani's reflection not only becomes visible but the haunting face of her sister wearing a gas mask appears in the mirror to Dani's right. As the match loses spark, Terri's presence dissipates along with the energy of light, resulting in Dani's lone reflection, her face now distorted in the mirror despite the mimetic reflection shown initially. Dani's reflection becomes misshapen at the same time that Terri disappears, a transformation that can be interpreted as a transference of affective energy. Dani's grief is momentarily given a shape in matter, but, without this externalization, Dani's grief inflates within, misshaping her reflection once again. Dani's reflection appears to frighten her more than Terri's ghost, causing Dani to run out of the outhouse and into the woods, where she falls asleep and dreams of her mother, father, and Terri sitting together on a couch, engulfed by darkness apart from a flickering, low blue lighting and paired with amorphous, static-like sounds. In the dream, Dani's mother and father appear dead or sleeping while Terri, who sits on the far end of the couch, is awake. Her head slowly turns toward the camera, proving that she maintains a level of awareness in whatever supernatural realm she is operating from within. While somewhat eerie, this dream seems to have a healing, rejuvenating effect; the shot that follows the dream sequence is a close-up of Dani's face, dewy and glowing, slowly rising out of a deep sleep as opposed to an abrupt and panic-stricken jolt that is oftentimes displayed in characters awaking from nightmares.

In a sense, Dani's dream suggests that she is approaching a modicum of peace, despite the fear and discomfort that led up to her dream and catharsis. This can be found in the immediate scenes that follow. After backpacking through the woods, the group arrives at Pelle's village. Three villagers play whimsical flutes as the camera pans over a beautiful Swedish landscape, sprinkled with yellow wildflowers, and a background of blue skies and hills of various shades of green. For the first time in the film, Dani appears to smile, not in a matter that is forced to alleviate awkwardness, but as a genuine

Figure 5.1 Amidst a panic attack, Dani seeks refuge in an outhouse. Devoid of light and electricity, Dani strikes a match, revealing her own reflection in the mirror alongside a haunting apparition of her deceased sister over her right shoulder. Left front: Florence Pugh (as Dani). Right back: Klaudia Csányi (as Terri).

Source: *Midsommar* (2019)

display of happiness. Another side of Dani begins to show as she makes warm conversation with Father Odd (Mats Blomgren). Odd welcomes the group individually, shaking the men's hands one by one with a "Hello" before giving Dani a hug and welcoming her "home," a gesture that implies both a preconditioned and permanent presence attached to Dani alone. Specifically directing his remarks towards Dani, he states, "We are so very happy to have you" [00:37:13]. Not only does this foreshadow Dani's arrival as being supernaturally manifested on behalf of the Hårga cult but it initiates the development and rounding of Dani's character, as the compassion and thoughtfulness that fills her is finally being nurtured and reciprocated. "I love what you're wearing," Dani tells Odd, gesturing towards his floor-length white vestment. "It's kind of girly, no?" [00:37:24]. Odd jokes, pulling the skirt outwards and dancing on his tiptoes, before speaking sincerely of the cultural meaning attached to the vestment, as a midsommar tribute to nature's intersexed qualities. Readily, the conflation of nature and gender is established within this new environment, again, gesturing towards masculine and feminine principles in pagan belief systems. This initial blurring of sexual distinctions may possibly serve two purposes: first, to balance the power dynamics and inequalities embedded in the group of college students. Suddenly, Dani appears happy and relaxed while the men exchange subtle looks of uncertainty and confusion. This second purpose of the blurred distinctions is related to the first: to introduce viewers to the ideology that governs the new setting—one able to produce different outlooks and responses to Dani's grief, which has proven difficult to reconcile and resolve.

The theme of sex, conception, birth, and death continue to play a role in the midsommar traditions, all of which coalesce to produce a larger commentary on grief and anxiety. The act of breathing, for example, begins as a way for Dani to cope during her anxiety attacks. However, cleansing breaths are also practiced in the midsommar traditions, like the women taking sharp breaths in tandem with one another, releasing a forced exhalation before the May Queen competition. The rhythmic control of breath is taught to Dani by Karin (Anna Åström) after they imbibe a drug-infused tea; however, Dani performs a similar breathing pattern when she blows out her birthday candle days before. In a two shot, Dani waits for Christian to finish singing "Happy Birthday" on the right side of the screen. On the left side of the screen, Christian holds up a small loaf of cake in which a single candle burns between them. In the background, directly above the cake, a deep-focus shot reveals a small circle of villagers, who sway back and forth in unison while singing over a newborn baby. In this single shot, the treatment of life and birth between the two cultures is placed in juxtaposition, managing to exaggerate the collective (Hårga) and individualist (American) distinctions between the two. The narrative symbolically links the principles of life with breath and energy. Alongside

Dani blowing out her birthday candle, breathing is ceremoniously incorporated into the May Queen competition which is used to celebrate and bless the fertility in both women and crops. After Dani wins May Queen, Christian is also pulled into a cabin, where he is required to inhale (i.e., breathe in) an analeptic steam for his vitality and stamina as he has been chosen to impregnate Maja (Isabelle Grill). Essentially, the restorative breaths are symbolic of life, energy, and fertility but also tied to grief, as the patterns were initially presented to viewers in the midst of Dani attempting to subdue her anxiety.

Following her win of the May Queen and blessing the crops for the community, Dani sets out to find Christian. After Dani approaches a cabin, she glimpses Christian and Maja together through the peephole. Abrupt sadness and pain leaves Dani sobbing on the floor of the sleeping lodge, where she is quickly surrounded by the congregation of women. Each of the women wears an embroidered white dress and flower crown, providing a visual uniformity to the shared affect that ensues. Huddled around Dani on the ground, the women mirror her by resting on their hands and knees. Inga (Julia Ragnarsson) kneels opposite Dani. Looking her in the eyes, Inga and the surrounding women replicate Dani's facial expressions and audible cries. This display of collective grief contrasts the impersonal treatment and isolation that the grieving Dani previously faced in America.

However, there remains something deeply disturbing in this more communal embrace of her grief. Like the child's game of mimicry, the women's mirroring of Dani's trauma adds elements of surreal insincerity. Registering more as a mocking performance than a genuine cathartic release, these displays of collective grief noticeably arise in two other scenes surrounding death and loss: the first being the Attestupa ceremony, in which two elders jump off a cliff to their gruesome death. In this first instance, the villagers observe the sacrifices made before them. An extreme long shot of the community shows each member in mourning, however, it looks less like a natural response and more like a staged interpretive dance, as the sounds and movements translate as choreographed and overstated. Much like the violins that are paired with Dani's cries early in the film, the collective mourning carries a similarly dissonant and supplementary tone.

The other scene in which this collective grief is presented is in the concluding scene, in which the closing ceremony of the midsommar festival is carried out. In this ceremony, nine human lives are sacrificed; among them are Josh, Mark, and Christian. Initially, Dani was predisposed to loneliness because her anxiety and grief were diminished and suppressed; now, Dani and her emotions are the focal point of an entire village. Dani sits in the center of a circular platform, in the middle of the field and before the rest of the community. Almost lost beneath a large pile of fresh and brightly colored flowers, which cover the chair on which she sits and give shape to her oversized dress and crown, Dani's face continues to exude sadness. Just below this platform is Christian, who sits in a wooden wheelchair; however, the white cloth of his frock, which hangs down and conceals his legs and feet, dwarfs him within the contraption, almost like an infant in a baby carriage—this is fitting, as those sacrificed are said to be reborn. "Wherever life is in the process of being made—germination and fermentation—it provokes disgust because it is being made only when it is being unmade; the viscous glandular embryo opens the cycle that ends in the rotting of death," Beauvoir writes (2011, 199). Now that Dani is Queen, the verdict of the chosen members for sacrifice resides with her. Without revealing her decision, the scene unfurls with Christian and the rest of the sacrifices being loaded into the barn, grotesquely staged, and set aflame. As the barn is swallowed by fire, Dani cries hysterically and attempts to run but the weight of the flowers composing her dress and crown make it nearly impossible for her to make ground. Once the fire has consumed nearly all of the barn, leaving the skeletal frame and scabs of yellow paint, a cross dissolve slowly brings Dani's face into the center of the frame at the same time that remaining bits of the edifice fall to the ground. A chaotic combination of imagery—including the garish blanket of flowers, Dani's disturbed expression, the cult dancing in the background, and the towering flame that lingers in the cross-dissolve—is sustained until Dani's frown slowly makes its way into a contented yet maniacal smile. The film presents Dani's catharsis as a consolation for her long-repressed anxiety and grief.

The flowers that swallow Dani by the end of the film are significant in their own right, as they prohibit her movement as though she is wearing a straitjacket and chains. The lightweight and delicate objects produce an unbearable weight; an allegory for the larger ideological themes of grief, nature, and the cycle of life and death which have symbolically and parasitically attached themselves to the narratives of womanhood throughout history. As the queen and female ruler of the congregation, Dani has begun hardening into the myth, the nature, the folklore, the fairy tale, all of which are common forms of social sublimation. This somewhat horrific and demented imagery prompts viewers to gauge which is more horrific: the tortured and repressive treatment of grief either reserved for the individual or its reproduction through an arcane form of sublimation. The real horror of *Midsommar* is marked by these two extremes of failure: the failure to express grief in the overly synthetic and civilized American setting *and* the failure to contain grief as a natural excess, difficult to rationalize and, therefore, reserved for mythos. For this reason, the stale and confined treatment of grief in the film's opening is not the only horror in *Midsommar* but the existential threat that women and nature symbolize—mythological reservoirs of chaos, affect, and emotion that cannot be overcome but rather can only be unleashed. Again, Beauvoir writes:

Being conceived and born is the curse weighing on his destiny, the blemish on his being. And it is the warning of his death. The cult of germination has always been associated with the cult of the dead. Mother Earth engulfs the bones of its children within it . . . In most folk representations, Death is woman, and women mourn the dead because death is their work. Thus, Mother Earth has a face of darkness; she is chaos, where everything comes from and must return to one day; she is Nothingness. (2011, 200)

The horror lies in the symbols that have become the pillars supporting our conceptual understandings of death, grief, and womanhood, regardless of the moral structure that these pillars work to reinforce.

In Claude Monet's *Poplars on the Epte* (1891), rows of poplar trees are shown winding into the distance, decreasing in size to capture layers of depth between foreground and background. In the foreground is the Epte River, reflecting leaves and branches in an impressionistic but recognizable fashion. Broken up by white clouds is a bright indigo sky. The poplars resemble shadows, composed of dark blues and burgundies. Just above the center of the painting, there appears to be a face loosely formed by collections of poplar leaves. Looking at this painting for an extended period may begin to expose other faces to the observer but the one in the center is the most noticeable and pronounced. Given their similar discourse of nature, *Midsommar* can be put in conversation with Monet, particularly after Dani has won the title of May Queen. Dani is encouraged to step on a platform that is then lifted above the heads of the villagers while she remains standing. An extremely loose frame shows the profiles of the villagers walking, Dani overhead. While it is easy to focus on Dani's precarious position as she labors to keep her balance in this scene, the face of her deceased sister, Terri in the gas mask, is superimposed into the trees that form the forest in the background. Like this shot in *Midsommar,* Monet and other early symbolists relied on nature as a vehicle for the expression of emotion. The face in the trees heightens the sensibilities of viewers, rendering Dani's repressed, interiorized emotions as something worldly. In psychology, the phenomenon of spotting faces in everyday things is called "face pareidolia." Producing a cinematic motif out of this natural human faculty becomes increasingly meaningful on the topic of horror and grief, as it plays into the mind's power to create faulty *and* convincing illusions, while furthermore revealing the tendency to imbue such illusions with personal meaning and heightened emotions.[2] Strange feelings are invoked when spotting these faces, because as viewers, these images simultaneously validate yet deceive our senses, alienate and yet connect us to the unknown. Like Monet, Ari Aster uses these faces to present both the impasse and the interface between the external world and the subject's innermost emotional states, between an outpour of grief and an influx of horror.

Figure 5.2 A procession unfolds to celebrate Dani (Florence Pugh), who has just been crowned the May Queen. In the background, a superimposed face of Dani's deceased sister (left, top corner), Terri is faintly visible in the trees and bushes. Extending from the Terri's mouth area and to the right are brown and light green leaves that are distinguishable from the rest of the forest, creating detail and depth that resembles the long tube that Terri used to siphon gas into her mask while carrying out her suicide.
Source: Midsommar (2019)

While offering complicated and thought-provoking commentary on grief, *Midsommar* arguably succumbs to essentializing the triad of woman, nature, and emotion. Although the film presents these categories in the context of a cultish veneration of an archaic and primitive past, it can be argued that the narrative and imagery reproduce the same myths that are at the core of its critique. For the same reason, *Midsommar* opens a debate regarding the carnivalesque and whether the parading of these socially and politically suppressed categories are effectively radical or simply a temporary subversion of oppressive and/or repressive norms. Regardless, horror, like grief, is effectively used as mythology or lore to give definition to the social phenomenon that humans struggle, and more so fail, to understand. In the case of most horror films, the monster, the murderer, the contagion must be destroyed, but this destruction is successful only momentarily. Together, protagonists and viewers are typically granted a minute or two for rejoicing in the overcoming of their existential threat. However, the last few seconds of these films manage to subvert expectations with cliff-hangers, such as the well-known sequence from John Carpenter's *Halloween* (1978), in which Laurie Strode (Jamie Lee Curtis) pushes Michael Myers (Tony Moran) out of the second-story window. An initial glimpse of the serial murderer laying stiff on the ground assures viewers that he is dead; however, a subsequent shot out of the window reveals no trace of Myers, leaving no one safe. Similarly, in Tobe Hooper's *The*

Texas Chain Saw Massacre (1974), Sally (Marilyn Burns) manages to escape from the cannibalistic family of murderers, narrowly outrunning Leatherface (Gunnar Hansen) and jumping into the back of a stranger's pickup truck. From Sally's point of view, the distance between her and Leatherface grows, leaving him standing, with chainsaw raised, defeated in the middle of the road. Although Sally managed to survive, Leatherface continues to stalk travelers in the crook of some Texas woods.

A less literal translation can be made regarding the opening scene of *Midsommar*. A sequence of shots reveals dark and capacious woodlands, blanketed with snow. The cold and empty landscape produces a mood of solitude and stillness. These images paired with a Swedish song[3] performed a cappella by a feminine voice creates a complex blend of the whimsical and the melancholic. Just as the film lulls spectators into this new and unusual state of darkness and contentment, the obtrusive sound of a telephone jars viewers, abruptly undoing the trance that briefly moves those who relinquish themselves to the aesthetics. While there is something dark and unfamiliar about these establishing shots, the true horror registers when a familiar, modern device intervenes. Almost inversely, the film encourages the audience to confront, embrace, and gain familiarity with the visceral content toward which they have been primed not to pay much attention. Dani's introduction in the film asks viewers to home in on her grief and anxiety: she is set in a small, dark apartment amid the glowing screens of her electronics, the *mise-en-scène* suggesting her overwhelming loneliness and alienation. This insular environment proves incapable of accommodating Dani's grief. By the end of the film, Dani's personal struggle with pain and grief becomes enmeshed in the pagan midsommar festival, representative of love and life, but also a prolongation of death and despair. Only through a climactic scene of death rituals and human sacrifice does something come to life in Dani as she is no longer required to deaden herself and blunt her emotions to appease others in her environment. In the end, nature becomes the medium through which grief is expressed and accommodated.

Perhaps, *Midsommar* prompts viewers to conceive of an *ecology of grief*, which is at once deeply subjective, as well as intersubjective; at once influencing while being vulnerable to one's social, political, and environmental surroundings in the wake of loss. Grief and the elaborate human response to it, stands as one of the most defining human qualities, and, therefore, contending with grief means a deep, thoughtful, and even horrifying look into humanity's core.

BIBLIOGRAPHY

Aster, Ari. 2019. *Midsommar.* DVD. A24.

Beauvoir, Simone de. 2011. *The Second Sex.* (Trans. Constance Borde and Sheila Malovany-Chevallier). New York: Vintage Books.

Cavell, Stanley. 2019. "Contesting Tears: The Hollywood Melodrama of the Unknown Woman." In *Philosophers on Film from Bergson to Badious: A Critical Reader*, edited by Christopher Kul-Want, 255–70. New York: Columbia University Press.

Jones, Darryl. 2018. *Sleeping with the Lights On: The Unsettling Story of Horror.* United Kingdom: Oxford University Press.

Krlic, Bobby. *Midsommar (Original Motion Picture Score).* Milan Records, July 2019. *Spotify,* open.spotify.com/track/6JAFr2i1lWnkLHPCAMFx1C?si=601a29f f8c6942c1.

Monet, Claude. 1891. *Poplars on the Epte.* Tate Gallery, United Kingdom.

Razowski, Joanna. 2020. *Midsommar: Screenplay.* Independently published.

Trier, Lars von. 2009. *Antichrist.* DVD. Pyrmont, NSW: Paramount Home Entertainment.

Walden, Jennifer. 2019. "Designing the Deeply Disturbing Sound in 'Midsommar.'" *A Sound Effect.* July 17, 2019. www.asoundeffect.com/midsommarsound/.

NOTES

1. Mirrors play an important symbolic role throughout *Midsommar,* as pending analyses will show, generally reflecting Dani in dark and distorted ways that confirm the haunting measures of her grief.

2. It appears as though Ari Aster was inspired by Lars von Trier's film, *Antichrist* (2009), which similarly tackles the intersection of womanhood, grief, and nature; the two also share visual motifs. After the loss of their child, a husband (Willem Dafoe) and his wife (Charlotte Gainsbourg) travel to their remote cottage in the woods to help the wife in her mourning process. As the couple travels by train to their woodsy destination, the speed of the train blurs the dense greenery outside of the window. Sudden flashes of light break through the heavy foliage at times, and superimposed in the light are a variety of screaming, grief-stricken faces. See: Trier, Lars von. 2009. *Antichrist.* DVD. Pyrmont, NSW: Paramount Home Entertainment.

3. Interestingly, this song is not listed on *Midsommar*'s official soundtrack, despite the fact that the opening song, "Prophecy," dissolves into the acapella voice. In a way, this adds to the mystery of the distant and ethereal voice that entrances viewers. See: Bobby Krlic, "Prophecy," track 1 on *Midsommar* (Original Motion Picture Score), Milan Records, 2019, *Spotify.*

PART III
Loss and National Identity
Grief and History

Chapter 6

O Father, Where Art Thou?

Grief and Cannibal Culture in Jorge Michel Grau's **Somos lo que hay** *(We Are What We Are) (2010)*

Megan DeVirgilis

During a pivotal scene in Jorge Michel Grau's Mexican cannibal film, *Somos lo que hay* (2010), Patricia (Carmen Beato) and her youngest son, Julián (Alan Chávez), are driving with a dead prostitute in the trunk of their car. Julián and his brother had brought her home earlier in the evening for their cannibal ritual, but in a fit of rage, and behind the pretext that the prostitute was unfit to consume, Patricia bludgeoned her to death. They drop her off at the corner where they found her, and Patricia warns the other prostitutes to stay away from her family or they would meet a similar fate. At this point in the film, the family has just found out that their patriarch and the leader of their cannibal rituals has died, and they are struggling with how to move forward without him. Patricia is feeling sidelined, so she accuses Julián of always defending his older brother, Alfredo (Francisco Barreiro). She recounts how, as children, the boys were inseparable. She recollects how they would wrap themselves as a taco, excluding their sister Sabina (Paulina Gaitán), whose only option was to be the salsa. She lets the memory sit for a moment and then utters, "We are monsters, Julián," as if realizing it for the first time [00:50:14].[1] This scene is crucial to the greater message of the film in that the outer persona of this anything-but-maternal character—angry, controlling, violent—peels back for a brief moment, letting both viewers and her son see that she is a complex character whose grief spurs self-reflection, regret, and nostalgia. In a departure from the trend in familial horror of depicting middle- and upper-class families in a way that supports the self/other and victim/monster dichotomies, this is an economically impoverished family where the distinction between good and evil is blurred, suggesting that they can co-exist within us, especially within a corrupt and exploitative society. They are monsters who suffer a significant loss and seemingly insurmountable challenges. Some members of the family are forced down a path of self-discovery that exposes the vulnerabilities and cruelties of the nuclear family within patriarchal society, leading to the family's eventual dissolution and the emergence of a new order. This chapter will take character-centric and historical approaches to *Somos lo que hay*, exposing how its treatment of grief and horror tropes challenge historical processes and outmoded social structures.

Somos lo que hay is set in modern-day Mexico City and takes place over the two-day period that follows the sudden death of the family patriarch. The family dynamic itself—its internal power struggles, the relationships between its members, and the degree to which they each grieve and cope with their loss—is what drives the film. Once five, the family becomes four: Patricia (the oppressive and distraught mother), Sabina (the cunning and beautiful teenage daughter), Alfredo (the eldest son and a closeted gay man), and Julián (the slightly younger, self-assured, more violent son). The family struggles to find cohesion after the father's death. Sabina thinks Alfredo should be the family leader, which entails his stalking victims and bringing them home for the ritual. However, he is hesitant to take on that role. Julián thinks he is more adept than Alfredo to be the leader, although a series of mishaps prove him to be clumsy and a liability to the family's survival. Patricia mostly keeps herself locked in her room, awaiting what she is certain is the family's demise. Eventually, she concedes that the ritual must continue, but on her terms. After threatening the group of prostitutes, she has sex with a taxi driver (Noé Hernández), then brings him home to be the next victim. Unbeknownst to the rest of the family, however, Alfredo is also on the hunt, but when Patricia sees his victim, Gustavo (Miguel Ángel Hoppe), is a young gay man—confirmation of Alfredo's sexual identity—she refuses to eat him, and a fight erupts in the film's climax. Gustavo manages to escape, while the taxi driver is brutally killed and subsequently prepared for the ritual. The young man alerts the police, which integrates the main plot with the sub-plot of two corrupt detectives who are pursuing the family, attempting to solve a case and earn their fifteen minutes of fame. One of the detectives, Octavio (Esteban Soberanes), is mistakenly killed by police officers right as he is closing in on Alfredo and Julián. The other detective, Owen (Jorge Zárate), manages to locate and enter the family's home, but is soon killed by Sabina and Patricia as they prepare the taxi driver's body. More police arrive on the scene, leading to a shoot-out where both sons die, Sabina is mistaken for a victim, and Patricia escapes from the rooftop, only to be hunted down and killed by the prostitutes she threatened earlier in the film. As a result, neither the origins nor the details of the ritual itself are revealed to the audience. The final scene shows Sabina escaping from a hospital, walking unnoticed into an outdoor market, and spying a young man who is presumably her next victim, evidently continuing the ritual on her own.

Somos lo que hay engages with a long tradition of familial horror that both supports and subverts conservative family values concerning sex and gender. According to Barry Keith Grant, issues of gender are integral to horror, but its treatment is heterogeneous (2015, 7–8). Films that support conservative sex and gender norms can do so in a variety of ways. Promiscuous women tend to be peripheral characters who are tortured and/or killed off, while men or women with same-sex tendencies or atypical gender behavior can be associated with monstrosity, if not embodied by the monster figure itself. As Harry Benshoff observes, "the words 'monster' and 'homosexual' are seen to overlap to varying but often high degrees" (2015, 117). Alternatively, horror films can subvert these norms by challenging ideas of monstrosity, deviating from simplistic portrayals of female characters, exploring various gender and sexual identities in a positive light, and so forth. This subversion can also come in the form of parody. The *Scream* franchise is an obvious example. In the first installment, Sydney (Neve Campbell), the film's female protagonist, consents to sex with her boyfriend, oblivious to his warped ulterior motives. A psychopath who kills by the tenets proposed by Carol Clover's "Her Body, Himself" (1987), Billy (Skeet Ulrich) can only murder Sydney if she is no longer a virgin. However, even after losing her virginity, Sydney prevails against Billy's attempts to murder her. This is a watershed moment in horror history because a female character's survival is no longer determined by her sexual history. Sydney, therefore, breaks from the prescribed confines of the "Final Girl" role (Clover 1987). The subversion and confirmation of conservative family values can also coexist in the same film, and tends to be the norm, even in contemporary horror cinema. This is arguably because even if a film implicitly or explicitly subverts traditional sex and gender norms, films are still cultural products of a tenuous ideological framework that reveals the constant conflict between conservative and progressive ideals.

Horror films treat patriarchal norms in a similar way. Patriarchy within the framework of bourgeois capitalism is based on problematic sex and gender ideals that oppress women and non-conforming gender and sexual identities in order to maintain its hierarchy and "moral order." Horror films that align with bourgeois ideology tend to depict strong male leads who destroy "evil" forces represented by the likes of effeminate male villains, gender-ambiguous monsters, promiscuous *femme fatales*, and supernatural forces. These figures and forces threaten the hearth/home, heteronormative sexual practices, and procreation within the confines of marriage. Films that explore patriarchal crisis and other vulnerabilities of the nuclear family subvert these norms by encouraging viewers to question their validity. According to Kimberley Jackson, "patriarchal crisis has been a hallmark of family horror since the 1960's" (2016, 2). This crisis can be directly observed in *Rosemary's Baby*, Roman Polanski's 1968 classic psychological horror film: "We can see in *Rosemary's Baby* the radical beginning of patriarchal failure: of paternity refused, denied, abandoned, hated; of patriarchy simultaneously terrified and terrorizing in the face of its increasing impotence; of patriarchy maddened by paradoxical desire for its own annihilation" (Sobchack 2015, 181).

Other horror films explore patriarchy's failings by relegating the father figure to the sidelines or eliminating him completely. The first *Scream* (1996) film represents the former, and *The Sixth Sense* (1999) the latter. But in *The Sixth Sense*, would exhausted mother Lynn (Toni Collette) have been able to help her son without child psychologist Malcolm Crowe (Bruce Willis) stepping in? In her introduction to *Gender and the Nuclear Family in Twenty-First Century Horror*, Jackson examines the feminocentric horror films *Carrie* (1976) and *Aliens* (1979), noting that "despite the absence of strong patriarchal figures in these films, the females [sic] still cannot fully free themselves from the fetters of patriarchal oppression" (2016, 10). The dominant ideology is not completely destroyed. Arguably, most horror films tend to operate within and inevitably support patriarchy. However, as the following analysis will suggest, *Somos lo que hay* offers the possibility of an alternative order where loss and grief allow for the blurring of the binary distinction between masculinity and femininity and the eventual toppling of the gender hierarchy. Ultimately, the film challenges conservative family values by suggesting that the traditional family structure is inherently defective and therefore an impossible ideology.

Regarding Alfredo's character in particular, it is important to draw attention to a significant cultural factor when discussing familial horror in Latin America in relation to familial horror in the United States: *machismo*. According to Gustavo Subero:

> Historically, *machismo* was introduced and instituted by the conquistadors as a reaction to the indigenous people's interpretations of sexuality and gender. Some male-to-male sexual practices, as well as some transvestitic practices, were found amongst the indigenous people of America but were deemed as sinful and amoral in the eyes of the European invaders. (2014, 7–8)

This same author goes on to define *machismo* as "the configuration of generic practices that adhere to the ideas of patriarchy that guarantee the power of men and the subordination of women" (2014, 9). There are parallels between *machismo* and American ideas of masculinity, but they are not one in the same because they are born of distinct historical and ideological realities, which extend to family structure and religious attitudes. Andrés Lema-Hincapié and Debra A. Castillo note that the *macho* is not uniform in representation, especially with respect to the degree to which they display traditionally feminine qualities, such as weeping (2015, 2). Vek Lewis echoes this idea, attributing heterogenous forms of representation in film to the effective changing of the times:

> If *cinemachismo*, to reiterate the use of [de la Mora's] phrase, is first born out of the revolutionary programme of modern patriarchal nation-state formation and collective identity, films made in more recent times should, and will, with all the attendant socio-cultural changes, map male bodies and masculinities in perhaps different ways, even as traditional gender discourses continue to circulate alongside emergent ones. (2009, 185)

American horror films also map male bodies in inconsistent ways, across the genre and at times within the same film, but while American horror films tend to support conservative family values, Latin American horror challenges dominant ideological norms at the intersection of gender, marriage, and nation. It is within this particular tradition of familial horror that *Somos lo que hay* belongs.

While this chapter will primarily explore grief within the parameters of horror's familial subgenre, it is important to note that *Somos lo que hay* borrows from and contributes to several subgenres, specifically, zombie films, body horror, queer horror, character-driven horror, and of course, cannibal films. According to Carlos Gerardo Zermeño Vargas, "Grau seems to be looking for a bridge between his cannibals and the zombie figure: living beings that appear dead, monsters that eat monsters" (my translation) (2014, 82). This is most evident in the opening scene, where a man, who is later revealed to be the father, stumbles through an outdoor mall while clutching his stomach. He soon begins to throw up a tar-like substance and falls to the ground. Within seconds, a cleaning crew drags away his corpse, wiping away his bile just before a pair of unwitting shoppers walk by the very spot, a clear homage to George A. Romero's *Dawn of the Dead* (1978).

The film also engages in varying degrees with body horror and queer horror, both of which suggest patriarchal crisis. Tony Williams links body horror to patriarchal hysteria, and this is most evident in *Somos lo que hay* in the scene where Sabina and Patricia begin to prepare the taxi driver's body (2014, 18). Patricia has slept with both the film's adult male figures—her husband, and a stand-in meant to fill the vacancy her husband left. And while her husband provided a degree of economic stability through his watch repairs, and symbolic economic stability through the "capital" he brought home in the form of bodies, the taxi driver stand-in *becomes* the capital, suggesting patriarchy has effectively been consumed. Another way the film suggests the fall of patriarchy is through its association with queer horror. Viewers, like Alfredo himself, are unaware that a large part of the motivation behind Alfredo's insecurities, grief, and overall distress stems from his sexual repression. Once he decides to return to the night club to meet Gustavo, both he and the audience realize that he will not only embrace his same-sex desires but use them to lure in potential victims for the ritual.

Because of such developments, the film can easily be read as a character study, placing it within a burgeoning trend in global horror cinema. However monstrous this family may be, its members fight their own monsters, both internal and external. In his *New York Times* piece on the recent upswing of character-driven horror, Jason Zinoman writes:

> These movies have confronted liberal racism, economic worries and family dysfunction; and while horror has always reflected the social and political concerns of its day, if you had to pinpoint a unifying theme that distinguishes this renaissance, it's the ominous danger of overwhelming grief. A character coping with the death of a loved one is the new car of teenagers heading to a cabin in the woods. (2018)

Films such as *The Others* (2001), *El orfanato* (*The Orphanage*) (2007), *Orphan* (2009), and *Hereditary* (2018) are prime examples. In these films, mothers have lost children, and their grief acts as a catalyst for behaviors and events that motivate suspense and horror, revealing, in most cases, unimaginable cruelty and despair within the parent/child relationship and within the human mind itself. What is interesting about *The Others* and *Hereditary* is that the families are also coping with the loss of the father and the mother/grandmother, respectively, further aligning them with the specific themes and concerns of *Somos lo que hay*. Religion and ritualism also play an important role, as they tap into fears of what we can and cannot control, what we can and cannot escape, what we can and cannot be ultimately consumed by.

Somos lo que hay most explicitly engages with the cannibal film tradition, a vastly heterogenous subgenre that has marked histories in American and Italian cinema. Cannibal films experienced what can be considered a boom in the 1970's and '80's with American films such as *The Texas Chainsaw Massacre* (1974), *The Hills Have Eyes* (1977), *Eating Raoul* (1982), *C.H.U.D.* (1984), *The Hills Have Eyes Part II* (1985), and *The Texas Chainsaw Massacre 2* (1986). These films included a wide range of concerns, campiness, and horror tropes, and saw a range of critical reception. *The Hills Have Eyes* is one of the most recognized from this time period, and it lays the groundwork for the majority of the problematic elements in *Somos lo que hay*. In "Ideological Formations of Nuclear Family in *The Hills Have Eyes*,"

Lorena Russell argues, "As is often the case in films centered on family ideology, gender identity and expression function as markers of individual growth" (2010, 111). She later adds, "The audience is invited to consider the horror that lies within the human capacity for violence, and to recognize that none of us are so different from the Others that haunt us" (2010, 112). In *Somos lo que hay*, Sabina and Alfredo experience powerful epiphanies that allow them to shatter ideological barriers, and, as a result, invite viewers to challenge traditional ideas on Otherness and monstrosity. From the Italian cannibal boom of the same time period, *Cannibal Holocaust* (1980) and *Cannibal Ferox* (1981) are among the most recognized. Both engage the myth of ritual cannibalism. The films were banned in several countries for their obscenity and violence, including rape and gruesome body horror, and years later served as the inspiration for Eli Roth's *The Green Inferno* (2015), which was also met with negative criticism for its portrayal of indigenous savagery. *Somos lo que hay* clearly engages with this particular tradition in cannibal films, although it turns it on its head by placing the ritual cannibals in a megalopolis that, ironically, occupies what used to be the Aztec capital, Tenochtitlan.

It is important to acknowledge that reading this film exclusively within the parameters of horror traditions limits its possibilities. It is also a family melodrama, a bumbling-cop/detective thriller, and a coming-of-age story. The relationship between horror and family melodrama, according to Vivian Sobchack, dates back to *Rosemary's Baby*, the horror/science-fiction mashup that relocates the locus of horror to the nuclear family. While horror deals with familial chaos and science-fiction with social chaos, from the 1960's onwards, "the events of family life and social life have been commonly and increasingly experienced as convergent" resulting in a conflation of horror, science fiction, and family melodrama (2015, 174).[2] Although Sobchack's position relates to American cinema, *Somos lo que hay* can certainly be analyzed within this pattern. Some of its classic horror tropes include a monstrous Other, suspense, torture, cannibalism, death and corpses, blood and gore. Its science-fiction elements, though not as prominent or shocking to viewers, are also clearly established: occult spirituality, ritualism, and a "doomsday" ideology portrayed through the excessive ticking clocks. The characteristics of family melodrama, however, are its most interesting, revealing, and thoughtful: loss of the patriarch, coping with grief, collapse of hierarchy, and internal struggles such as those for validation and acceptance. As Sobchack suggests, the overlap between these seemingly different genres expresses the convergent shortcomings of bourgeois ideology at the familial and greater social levels (2015). This is extremely evident in *Somos lo que hay*, but the family also provides the necessary context for a coming-of-age story. The adolescent children are forced to face who they really are while they are grieving. They are mourning the loss of their father and of their childhood, however strange and violent that may have been. Slavoj Žižek suggests that every horror narrative can be accurately understood by eliminating the horror/monstrous element (2006). In this case, such an approach magnifies the fact that the film is truly a family melodrama and coming-of-age story. Cannibalism and its accompanying horror tropes merely represent the familial and societal horrors that cannot otherwise be translated into images.

The film is also a product of a long Gothic tradition, and within that, a specific Mexican filmic tradition that adapts European Gothic conventions to express contemporary national horrors.[3] This is most acutely evidenced in the dark and lugubrious *mise en scène* meant to elicit a strong response from the viewer. While the film is set in modern-day Mexico City, and not an isolated rural area, its depiction of a depraved, ravenous cityscape recalls the streets of Bram Stoker's *Dracula*, Oscar Wilde's *The Picture of Dorian Gray*, and other turn-of-the-century Victorian-Gothic novels. The consistent gray-green palette conveys the moral bleakness of society as depicted in *Somos lo que hay*, while temporal and spatial ambiguity create an overwhelming sense of perilousness and confusion. There is a strong focus on time in the hundreds of clocks on the walls—part of the dead husband's trade, but also a staunch reminder that time is running out—while the layout of the home is ambiguous and unnerving. The home itself is organized, though dirty and sparse, with numerous clocks, candles, and mirrors being the only décor. According to Paul Julian Smith: "Late in the film, mirrors and knives glow ominously in the candlelight. It's a handsome *mise-en-scène* that owes something to that cosmopolitan reinventor of horror—who also eludes the established tradition of Mexican auteurship—Guillermo del Toro" (2014, 154). As handsome a scene as it is, it presents the family home as a place of horrors, reflecting anxieties and fears surrounding the nuclear family—from gender and patriarchy to marriage and the parent/child relationship.

In true Gothic form, the house and characters of *Somos lo que hay* harbor damning secrets that oppose societal norms. The first is the universal cultural taboo of desecrating a human body through murder and consumption. Jennifer Brown suggests: "Traditionally the idea of the human body is that it is sacred and, therefore, above and beyond the category of edible or inedible. This notion is overturned through cannibalism; the consumption of human flesh by human flesh upsets the most fundamental boundary between the 'self and else'" (2013, 7).

The second secret is that Alfredo is gay, something that he appeared to hide from himself with relative success, but that he could not hide from the rest of his family. At one point, Julián calls him a "maricón" (faggot) and Sabina quickly tells him to be quiet, as if the secret were known to all, yet also unspeakable.[4] The third secret/taboo is the possibility of incest between Sabina and Julián. He is clearly in love with his sister, and even though she can be authoritarian with him, she also responds to his advances. In an incredibly revealing scene, Julián and Sabina are standing behind a curtain, gazing out the window with their fingers resting on the windowpanes. In a close-up, viewers see Julián's hand inching towards Sabina's, a moment of affection cut short when Patricia pulls the curtain down to expose their illicit behavior. She does not say a word but glares at Julián while Sabina looks down at the floor, ashamed. Their embrace during Sabina's bath is another scene that suggests there is an incestual relationship between the two. The last two secrets are especially important within the context of their grief because the father's death provides the characters with the opportunity for sexual freedom. The secrets also reveal the breakdown of strict moral codes within the nuclear family structure.

According to Gabriel Eljaiek-Rodríguez, "Grau's commentary is directed not only toward this family in particular, but toward the Mexican family as an institution" (2018, 84). The film conveys this idea in various ways. First, frame-within-frame shots reveal that the characters are trapped within their grief and monstrosity and that their home is hindering their growth. Additionally, Grau uses tracking shots. After Sabina informs the family of their father's death, the camera cuts to an empty chair at the head of the dining room table, a symbol for the loss they have just experienced. The camera then tracks from Patricia to Alfredo, finally landing on Sabina and Julián sitting on the staircase, thereby establishing the supposed hierarchy after the death of the father. In another crucial scene, the camera cuts to Sabina treating Alfredo's wounds in the bathroom. She comforts him, albeit sternly, letting him know that there is no other way forward than through him. Still, she can help him accomplish what needs to be done. She talks with her back to him, looking at their mirrored reflections. According to Stacy Rusnak:

> The camera tilts up, and Sabina is brought into focus while Alfredo becomes a blur. This movement of the camera and the rack focus foreshadow the ending of the film, when Sabina will emerge as the head of the family. In the intimate space of the bathroom, patriarchal conservatism is literally "flushed away" as the cinematography underscores Sabina's emerging status as the leader of the family. (2017, 317)

It appears that Sabina, if only symbolically, will occupy the seat at the head of the table, but by the end of the film it becomes clear that not only the father must be replaced, but the entire hierarchy/order to which he belonged and which he supported. The film confronts the vulnerabilities and contradictions inherent to patriarchy and the Mexican family, and therefore makes possible a new order where traditional sex and gender norms are abolished.

Each family member processes her/his grief in different ways, but the film suggests that, collectively, their outmoded beliefs and practices must inevitably come to an end. Patricia experiences the typical stages of grief: anger, disbelief, bargaining, depression, and finally, acceptance. The problem is that Patricia's acceptance entails allowing Alfredo to step into the traditional role her husband held, thus ignoring the failings of the patriarchal structure. When Sabina first announces that their father is dead and Alfredo drops the basket of watches he was holding, Patricia grabs some of the items and smashes them on the ground. Afterwards, she displays mood swings, fits of violence, and more crying. She also locks herself in her room for long stretches of time, leaving the children to figure out how to survive on their own. When Alfredo and Julián return from their botched first attempt at securing a victim for the ritual, she admonishes them: "Your father dies and you two go out to hunt?" [00:22:28]. She appears to want to mourn his loss, discontinue their ritual, and await whatever tragic fate this would entail. Once she realizes that her children are continuing the ritual without her, she becomes angrier, bludgeoning to death the prostitute her sons drive home for the ritual. She is by no means going to relinquish any power to Alfredo, but at the same time, she is a woman who is lost and uncertain of how to proceed. She contemplates her character and the family's morality, but by the time they approach the prostitutes, her anger and sense of moral superiority have again emerged, revealing her most monstrous qualities are borne in part of her social and familial environment, and her own innate propensity towards evil. Her presence and behavior throughout the film echo deep-rooted systemic and cultural biases and their resulting oppression throughout Latin America, and this oppressive environment ultimately causes her particular demise. (It is incredibly telling, and satisfying, that she dies at the hands of the prostitutes she judged and despised.) In a sense, her death represents the death of outdated ideological practices and structures such as corporal punishment, authoritarianism, homophobia, sexual repression, *machismo*, gender hierarchy, and even the traditional nuclear family.

Like his mother, Julián cannot envision a familial structure outside the confines of a violent and predatory man. His first reaction upon hearing the news of his father's death is not to cry, but to go to his sister, a sign that he does not experience his father's death in the same way as the other members of the family. He profits from his father's death. Julián is the sibling most like his father—he engages in extreme violence and taboo sexual behaviors—and he is also the male figure in the household who most adheres to *machismo*, expressing disdain towards Alfredo's timidness and his sexual identity. Julián is the one who best fits the societal "mold" to oversee and make decisions for the family. He sees his father's death as an opportunity to garner more responsibility and power, and also to explore his erotic feelings for his sister.

But in doing so, he ignores limits and engages in risky behavior that leads his sister to support Alfredo as the new head of the household.

In stark contrast to Julián, Alfredo's world appears to close in on him from the moment he hears of his father's death. As previously mentioned, he is at first in shock, dropping all his father's watches to the floor. Next, he experiences disbelief. In one of the film's early scenes, he sits with his sister and brother in a corner of the upstairs hallway. They are trying to make sense of what is happening, and what their next steps should be. Sabina and Julián have accepted the fact that their father is dead and that they need to move on with the ritual, but Alfredo has not. He says his father is just lost, prompting Julián to correct him: "Dead. Dad is dead." After a brief discussion, Alfredo insists, "It can't be. He must be alive, and we need to wait for him" [00:15:11]. He eventually goes through the motions of trying to secure their next meal, but his inability to follow through with the prize or please his mother feeds his insecurities and sense of hopelessness. At one point, through tears, he asks Sabina, "This is what it's like living without Dad?" [00:39:50]. Alfredo's grief and inability to fully accept the present circumstances appear to be fueled by unreasonable expectations from his mother, herself an abject figure who is still beholden to oppressive sexual and familial norms. According to Barbara Creed, "We can see abjection at work in the horror text where the child struggles to break away from the mother, representative of the archaic maternal figure, in a context in which the father is invariably absent (*Psycho, Carrie, The Birds*)" (2015, 44). Conversely, it is possible that Alfredo was trying to break away in a literal sense. Earlier in the film, he sits alone on his bed and pulls a small object out from under the mattress. A reverse shot reveals that he has been hiding the gold watch the client from the market scene accused their father of taking too long to repair. Another shot shows Alfredo looking away from the watch and towards the empty, blurred hallway, his guilt and grief evident. The film quietly suggests that Alfredo was hiding the gold watch to finance something of his own (possibly an escape?), but his father's death thwarted his plans, and he is left torn between his own needs and those of his family.

At first, grief holds Alfredo back, but it also acts as a catalyst for exploration and acceptance of his contra-normative sexuality, his "monstrosity." His loss grants him the freedom to pursue what he wants, but only outside the literal and symbolic confines of his home. After the fiasco with the prostitute and his emotional scene with Sabina, the film cuts to Alfredo on a bus, his eyes focused on fragmented parts of other bus riders' bodies. There are cutaways to a hand and elbows before his gaze shifts to Gustavo walking down the street with his friends. Their eyes meet, setting in motion a cat-and-mouse chase that ends with Gustavo kissing Alfredo outside the bathroom of a club. While the bus ride is symbolic of awakening to the idea that people are just flesh, eventually eaten in a dog-eat-dog society, the kiss causes Alfredo to reconsider *his* body, and what he can do. According to Subero: "Although his transformation is not immediate, the kiss is the facilitator that begins the process of transformation through which he realises that his queer masculinity can be accepted and assumed as a valid form of male sexuality, and that it should not handicap his role as the new patriarch in the household" (2016, 87).

At first shocked and horrified, Alfredo breaks away from Gustavo and runs back to the train, crying and defeated. On the train, however, a guardian-angel figure gives him a note that reads, "You are alive," prompting him to finally embrace who he is and run back to Gustavo [00:56:04].

The kiss and Alfredo's subsequent realization are crucial in terms of his grieving process. He has now accepted his father's absence and his place as head of household. Moreover, he can now vocalize his grievances towards his mother. Patricia is not happy to see Gustavo in her home, but Alfredo stands his ground, telling her, "From this point on, I decide what the family does." She replies, "Say that again," thinking he will back down. He repeats himself, and she slaps him. This sequence recurs a few more times until he finally screams what he dared not say before: "Why do you hate me so much? Why have you always hated me? I didn't ask to be born this way" [00:58:40–00:59:27]. Here, Alfredo could be referring to his cannibalism or to his own sexual identity, or both. As Subero observes, "Cannibalism becomes a metaphor of a crisis of sexual categories in which women and gay men are no longer at the mercy of machismo and rebel against patriarchal normativity" (2016, 83). Cannibalism provides a horrific yet appropriate image for what his mother, in essence a microcosm of society, perceives as sacrilege.

What is most interesting about Alfredo's grief as a path towards realizing his potential and worth is the fact that once he embraces his inner sexuality/killer/cannibal, he becomes more human. As Subero accurately points out:

> Although assuming his homosexuality helps him to become a monster—like the rest of his family—the film constructs him in ways that call for the audience to identify and relate to his dilemma as a closeted gay man. Alfredo's apparent self-loathing and his depiction as a social outcast throughout the story seem to operate at the level of the diegesis as a tool to elicit spectators' sympathy by means of humanising the monster figure. (2016, 94)

The film evokes this sympathy through specific scenes, such as Alfredo curling into a ball when his mother smashes the watches on the ground and, later, his contemplation of the gold watch. However, when Alfredo realizes that his needs and those of his family do not have to be mutually exclusive, he successfully overcomes his guilt and grief, therefore securing the audience's sympathy. This is further cemented in his self-sacrifice. Once the shoot-out moves to the second floor, Julián and Sabina find themselves trapped in a bedroom across from Alfredo and Patricia, who urges Alfredo to break out through the fire escape with her. Alfredo senses they are doomed, so he runs across the hallway to his siblings, suffering a shot to the shoulder. He manages to move over to Sabina, bite her in the face and on her arm, and then place something in her hand before Julián shoots him with the detective's gun. Julián is then shot by the police, and Sabina is mistaken for a victim.[5] A shot of her being lifted into the ambulance shows her opening her hand to expose the same note given to Alfredo the previous evening: "You are alive." She nods, finally understanding that his plan ensured her survival and the continuation of the ritual. Alfredo's death is therefore sacrificial and cathartic: he needed to die in order for the nuclear family to be dissolved, making way for a new order outside the confines of patriarchy and *machismo*.

From the beginning, Sabina was clearly the member of the household most suited for leading the family. Although her initial reaction was to cry at the news of her father's death, she skips anger and disbelief and moves right into acceptance. She is the voice of reason within the family, and the one who expresses the need to move on with the ritual. She is also manipulative, telling Alfredo what he needs to hear, distracting their mother, and leaning into Julián's advances to keep him steady and compliant. The brothers have no idea where to begin with the ritual, so she suggests first finding a young victim under the bridge and later bringing home a prostitute. It is clear that she understands the practice of cannibalization, and the parallel between the family's and the homeless children's and sex workers' invisibility and exploitation. She is also the one who appears to have paid the most attention to their father's ritual teachings, proving herself an expert when it comes time to prepare Owen's body. Sabina is a combination of the stereotypes and excesses of masculinity and femininity: a born leader and a *femme fatale* with an inclination towards violence and manipulation. Although the horror genre narrative tends to support the status quo, it is also: "An excellent vehicle to provide a language for the reimagination of a self in constant transformation: a self that is regendered, ungendered and regenerated through the multiple possibilities of the monstrous body as a space that both disrupts and challenges social assumptions of the gendered body" (Subero 2016, xxi). Sabina seems to understand that by moving seamlessly between attitudes and behaviors associated with both masculinity and femininity, she can help ensure the completion of the ritual, which arguably speaks to the fluidity of gender roles.

Sabina not only disrupts notions of the gendered body but also of the family. Without her family's insecurities, rivalries, injustices, and missteps weighing her down—characteristics of an outmoded sex and gender hierarchy—she is free to carry out the ritual on her own terms. She represents both the mother and father figures, a new brand of leader altogether, and it is not happenstance that when she hunts for her next victim in a market, she ultimately conflates men and capital. In a strong departure from Clover's "Final Girl" theory, Sabina proves she is anything but catatonic. She was the one in power behind the scenes, but in entering the market (public sphere), she understands that she can use her strengths to lure in victims, just as she had suggested Alfredo do earlier in the film. Her desexualized white hospital gown can, in this context, be understood as a sign of rebirth. She has overcome her grief and is now standing in the ashes of patriarchal conservatism, most acutely represented by the behavior of her unhinged mother, her brother's sexual advances, and a ritual she was deemed unfit to lead. The bourgeois traditional model has become obsolete, and viewers cannot help but cheer her on. This nudge toward sympathy is enhanced by a change in the film's score from somber chamber music to a plucky and hopeful crescendo, and the look of triumph in her eyes.

The perseverance of the cannibal ritual can be further understood within the context of colonialism. As Jennifer Brown observes:

> Fear of the Other is often expressed through images of being literally and metaphorically consumed by that Other. Cannibalism has a long history of being used to "other" particular groups. The configuration of colonial subjects, working classes, women, homosexuals, Christians and non-Christians, as cannibalistic is suggestive of the fear and repulsion these groups evoked at various times. (2013, 4)

In the case of Latin America and the Caribbean, the representation of Indigenous Peoples as cannibals can be seen in maps and chronicles drawn and written by Spanish and European explorers, fomenting the idea of a landscape and demographic that *needed* to be conquered. According to Carlos Jáuregui: "Since the first encounters, Europeans reported cannibals all over the place, creating a sort of semantic affinity between cannibalism and America. In the sixteenth and seventeenth century the New World was culturally, religiously, and geographically constructed as some sort of Canibalia" (Eljaiek-Rodríguez 2018, 3).

The first documented account of cannibals in the "New World" is in Christopher Columbus's diaries. In the account of his third voyage, he claims that natives warned him against going near specific areas where people engaged in man-eating practices, and in the account of his fourth voyage, he claims to have seen these men for himself; or at least, he found men whose "gestures" were an indication of their cannibalistic behavior (de las Casas n.d.). Although Columbus never actually found proper evidence of anthropophagi, his familiarity with writings on the East (where he mistakenly thought he had found an alternate route to in his voyages) led him to believe he would. As Persephone Braham notes:

> Columbus's readings of the apocryphal fourteenth-century text *The Travels of Sir John Mandeville* and Marco Polo's accounts of his travels to the East had acquainted him with the varieties of monstrous beings he could expect to encounter in the Indies, which included anthropophagi as well as dog-headed and otherwise fantastic figures within a generally anthropomorphic classificatory system. He therefore expected to meet anthropophagi in his travels and he did, notoriously, coin the word *cannibal*. (2008, 50)

Most likely, upon hearing the word "Carib," the name of a Caribbean indigenous tribe, he mistook it for "ca*n*ib," and thought he had reached the empire of Genghis Khan (*Gran Can*), where, according to chronicles, natives engaged in anthropophagi. Thus, the Latin American cannibal was born.

Amerigo Vespucci went on to corroborate Columbus's false accounts, citing that an anthropophagus had confessed to having eaten parts of over two hundred men, but all of these early accounts of ritual cannibalism were challenged when William Arens published *The Man-Eating Myth* (1979) (Sartori 2009, 269). According to Brown, the text "argues that cannibalism, as a widely practised cultural phenomenon in the non-Western communities of the world, probably never existed and is, in fact, a racist myth" (2013, 4). Even today the myth persists because it has become embedded in the fabric of colonial discourse, Latin Americans' view of themselves and their origins. From Sor Juana's mystic poems to Borges' minotaur and beyond, Latin American authors have established their connection to monstrosity, taking ownership of various images imposed upon them. But the idea that a pre-Columbian monstrous Other lurks just beneath the surface of Latin Americans, although borne of racist myth, is also a source of anxiety and fear. As Enrique Ajuria Ibarra suggests: "European colonisers brought forth a mythical vision of the conquered lands that haunts the region under the guise of a colonial past and of more ancient systems of belief that are always in the process of being unearthed, recognised and remembered with detachment, fear and awe" (2019, 268). Without a doubt, horror provides an appropriate context to explore the unearthing of these fears.

It can be suggested that *Somos lo que hay* both conforms to and dismantles the image of the indigenous cannibal created as a justification of Spanish conquest and colonial rule. Clearly, Grau links cannibalism with monstrosity through his implementation of horror tropes and enactments of a disturbing ritual, but while the family is at times cruel and violent, they are also struggling with their own inner demons and external obstacles: grief, non-normative sexual desires, an oppressive hierarchy, and poverty.

Therefore, the film challenges the traditional us/them and victim/monster dichotomies. It also challenges the civilization/barbarity dialectic that has fueled horrific practices throughout Latin America with the end goal of repressing the barbarous Other. Family horror is often understood in terms of "the return of the repressed" (Williams 2014, 13) and according to Robin Wood, "One might say that the true subject of the horror genre is the struggle for recognition of all that our civilization represses and oppresses [. . .]" (2018, 79). In many cannibal films, the "repressed" can be understood as an autochthonous past or present. In *Somos lo que hay*, the repressed is the "savage Other" that returns in the context of contemporary Mexico City, reclaiming its mythical and actual history atop the ruins of the Aztec capital. The repressed always finds its way out, and the film ultimately embraces this. Moreover, the film explicitly connects grief and the cannibal myth, a myth that undoubtedly helped justify the genocide of millions of indigenous people, resulting in a collective grief over unimaginable suffering and marginalization. Through Sabina's survival and the continuation of the cannibal ritual, it can be suggested that the film imagines a future where this collective grief can be overcome, however destructive that process may be.

While the film represents ritual cannibalism as a product of colonialism, several critics have suggested that these cannibals are products of failed capitalist and neoliberal policies. According to Eljaiek-Rodríguez, "in *Somos lo que hay*, cannibalism is a perverse product of capitalism" (2018, 86). Similarly, Subero suggests, "Grau seems keen to show how the social dynamic of late capitalism means that at some point everybody becomes a cannibal in their desire to consume (or be consumed by) others" (2016, 85–86). The family's poverty and social invisibility speak to this, as does the fact that they prey on other vulnerable populations. As previously mentioned, the film departs from traditional familial horror in Grau's focusing on a lower-class family. According to Ignacio M. Sánchez Prado, this departure is a return to the post-revolutionary trend of invoking the urban working-class, and "resumes the use of the genre as a way to stage the limits of neoliberalism in its moment of profound crisis" (my translation) (2012, 55). Within this framework, "the survival of the 'ritual' can be understood as the inescapable continuation of those monsters that operate in the subterranean spaces of capitalist modernity and can never be fully 'eradicated,' a triumph for those considered 'disposable'" (my translation) (Prado 2012, 59). Interestingly, Williams narrows the scope on this idea by equating it specifically with the family: "Contaminated by capitalist structures, the family is a manipulated unit. It produces everyday monsters" (2014, 184). Viewers are left to wonder: Did late-capitalism contaminate and ultimately destroy the family, or are its mythical indigenous roots, always lurking beneath the surface of "civilized" progress, the true catalyst for the family's demise?

For Rusnak, the dialectical relationship between past and present in the film echoes both colonial and neoliberal struggles. This can be observed in the appearance of *tianguis*, outdoor markets that date back to pre-Hispanic times, which "in comparison with the opening images of the shopping mall, functions as a bridge that links the past and present" (Rusnak 2017, 312). The tensions that arise between the two, she suggests, "allow for a critique of Mexico's legacy of classism" (Rusnak 2017, 312). This dialectical relationship is strengthened through the name of the family's apartment complex, the Bicentennial Projects, a reference to a series of projects that, in an effort to highlight the city's progress and global character, were organized across Mexico City two hundred years after Mexico's independence from Spain. These projects, however, are where the family first mentions their food insecurity, and where their botched ritual takes place. According to Rusnak, "this space will witness the slaughter of the family's ritual feast, echoing the Aztec struggle against Spanish colonialism and critiquing the present neoliberal moment" (2017, 314). Cannibalism as portrayed in the film, more so than a horrific representation of mythical Aztec rituals, becomes a site of meaningful struggle against European ideological, political, and economic processes that have exploited vulnerable populations in the Americas for centuries. Alfredo and Sabina challenge and eventually overcome these destructive practices, while Julián and Patricia remain adherent to traditional violent and oppressive structures, and therefore remain outside the parameters of viewer sympathy.

According to Eljaiek-Rodríguez, "Latin American horror films are spaces where elements from diverse cultures come into contact, creating a product that is capable of representing and interpreting the social complexities of the continent" (2018, 22). By engaging with horror and other film traditions inside and outside of Mexico, and by examining historical and current anxieties within the contexts of grief and cannibalism, this chapter has suggested that *Somos lo que hay* relies on traditional horror tropes yet ultimately deviates from supporting the status quo. The film challenges the moral integrity of late capitalist society and confronts a violent colonial history, and, more acutely, the film questions inherent social, gender, and sexual biases ingrained in patriarchal society. And while the characters' individual and collective grief is what compels them to either conform to or challenge these biases within a redefined familial setting, cannibalism serves as a greater signifier for the horror that ensues when families continue to define themselves according to outmoded norms and processes. All of the family members are cannibals, but by the end of the film it becomes clear why Patricia says to Julián, and Julián alone, "We are monsters."[6]

BIBLIOGRAPHY

Benshoff, Harry M. 2015. "The Monster and the Homosexual." In *The Dread of Difference: Gender and the Horror Film* (2nd ed.), edited by Barry Keith Grant, 116–41. Austin, TX: University of Texas Press.

Braham, Persephone. 2008. "Anthropology, Anthropophagy and Amazons." *Letras Hispanas* 5 (2): 49–66.

Brown, Jennifer. 2013. *Cannibalism in Literature and Film*. Hampshire: Palgrave Macmillan.

Clover, Carol. 1987. "Her Body, Himself: Gender in the Slasher Film." *Representations* 20 (1): 187–228.

Creed, Barbara. 2015. "Horror and the Monstrous-Feminine: An Imaginary Abjection." In *The Dread of Difference: Gender and the Horror Film* (2nd ed.), edited by Barry Keith Grant, 37–65. Austin, TX: University of Texas Press.

de las Casas, Fray Bartolomé. n.d. *Cristóbal Colón: Los cuatro viajes del almirante y su testamento. Biblioteca Virtual Universal*. n.p. https://www.biblioteca.org.ar/libros/131757.pdf.

"El actor Alan Chávez murió en enfrentamiento con la policía." 2009. *Publimetro*. September 20, 2009. https://www.publimetro.com.mx/mx/cine/2009/09/20/actor-alan-chavez-murio-enfrentamiento-policia.html.

Eljaiek-Rodríguez, Gabriel. 2018. *The Migration and Politics of Monsters in Latin American Cinema*. Cham: Palgrave Macmillan.

Grant, Barry Keith. 2015. "Introduction." In *The Dread of Difference: Gender and the Horror Film* (2nd ed.), edited by Barry Keith Grant, 1–13. Austin, TX: University of Texas Press.

Grau, Jorge Michel. 2010. *Somos lo que hay*. DVD. Mexico: Centro de Capacitación Cinematográfica.

Ibarra, Enrique Ajuria. 2019. "Latin American Gothic." In *Twenty-First-Century Gothic: An Edinburgh Companion*, edited by Maisha Wester and Xavier Aldana Reyes, 263–75. Edinburgh: Edinburgh University Press.

Jackson, Kimberly. 2016. *Gender and the Nuclear Family in Twenty-First-Century Horror*. New York: Palgrave Macmillan.

Lema-Hincapié, Andrés, and Debra A. Castillo. 2015. "Introduction." In *Despite All Adversities: Spanish-American Queer Cinema*, edited by Andrés Lema-Hincapié and Debra A. Castillo, 1–15. Albany, NY: State University of New York Press.

Lewis, Vek. 2009. "When 'Macho' Bodies Fail: Spectacles of Corporeality and the Limits of the Homosocial/sexual in Mexican Cinema." In *Mysterious Skin: Male Bodies in Contemporary Cinema*, edited by Santiago Fouz-Hernández, 177–92. London: I.B. Tauris.

Prado, Ignacio M. Sánchez. 2012. "Monstruos neoliberales: capitalismo y terror en *Cronos* y *Somos lo que hay*." In *Horrofílmico: aproximaciones al cine de terror en Latinoamérica y el caribe*, edited by Rosana Díaz-Zambrana and Patricia Tomé, 47–64. Puerto Rico: Editorial Isla Negra.

Rusnak, Stacy. 2017. "Consumption, Cannibalism, and Corruption in Jorge Michel Grau's *Somos lo que hay*." In *What's Eating You? Food and Horror on Screen*, edited by Cynthia J. Miller and A. Bowdoin Van Riper, 309–24. New York and London: Bloomsbury.

Russell, Lorena. 2010. "Ideological Formations of the Nuclear Family in *The Hills Have Eyes*." In *The Philosophy of Horror*, edited by Thomas Fahy, 102–20. Lexington, KY: The University Press of Kentucky.

Sartori, Rodrigo Browne. 2009. "Comunicación intercultural, antropofagia y la canibalización de Caliban en América Latina." *Revista Científica de Información y Comunicación.* 6: 265–82.

Smith, Paul Julian. 2014. *Mexican Screen Fiction: Between Cinema and Television.* Cambridge: Polity.

Sobchack, Vivian. 2015. "Bringing It All Back Home: Family Economy and Generic Exchange." In *The Dread of Difference: Gender and the Horror Film* (2nd ed.), edited by Barry Keith Grant, 171–91. Austin, TX: University of Texas Press.

Subero, Gustavo. 2016. *Gender and Sexuality in Latin American Horror Cinema: Embodiments of Evil.* London: Palgrave Macmillan.

———. 2014. *Queer Masculinities in Latin American Cinema: Male Bodies and Narrative Representations*. London: I.B. Tauris.

Vargas, Carlos Gerardo Zermeño. 2014. "Somos lo que hay y la autofagia social." *Ciencia Ergo Sum.* 21 (1): 77–84.

Williams, Tony. 2014. *Hearths of Darkness: The Family in the American Horror Film* (Updated ed.). Jackson, MS: University Press of Mississippi.

Wood, Robin. 2018. "An Introduction to the American Horror Film." In *Robin Wood on the Horror Film: Collected Essays and Reviews*, edited by Barry Keith Grant, 73–110. Detroit: Wayne State University Press.

Zinoman, Jason. 2018. "Home Is Where the Horror Is." *The New York Times*. June 7, 2018. https://www.nytimes.com/2018/06/07/movies/hereditary-horror-movies.html.

Žižek, Slavoj. 2006. *The Pervert's Guide to Cinema*. DVD. United Kingdom/Austria/Netherlands: Microcinema International.

NOTES

1. All quotes from *Somos lo que hay* are my translations, not the English subtitles.

2. Williams also notes the similarity between melodrama and horror: "Melodrama's hysterical nature as a genre of excess parallels horror, especially in depicting victims created by patriarchal family values" (2014, 22).

3. According to Gustavo Subero, "by the mid-1950s the horror genre in Mexico had become more popular than melodramas and the *Cine ranchero*. Several film studios also turned to horror cinema in order to quench the thirst for horror movies that had spread across the country. As previously suggested, many of these films took as their point of departure well-known gothic horror narratives such as Dracula, Frankestein [sic], and Dr. Jekyll and Mr. Hyde, among others, but with a Mexican twist or flavour

incorporated into the story. From the simple translocation of the story to Mexican lands to the incorporation of certain aspects of Mexican folklore and tradition, these films became embedded in the national imaginary as tales of horror and terror that reflected contemporary Mexico" (2016, 5).

4. According to Benshoff, "Most significantly, when 'homosexuality' (which appeared in the scientific lexicon in 1869) reached common English parlance in the 1880s and 1890s, Victorian England was in the middle of a Gothic renaissance whose legacy can still be felt in contemporary horror films" (2015, 130). Even before then, as Eve Kosofsky Sedgwick notes, early Gothic writers such as William Beckford, Matthew Lewis and Horace Walpole displayed what would by today's standards be considered homosexual behavior or at least queer tendencies (Benshoff 2015, 130).

5. Julián's death in the film parallels the actor Alan Chávez's real-life death on September 12, 2009. Chávez had exchanged gunfire with police and was shot in the heart, dying moments later. He was eighteen years old and considered a promising new face in Latin American cinema ("El actor"). Production had finished on *Somos lo que hay*, but the film had yet to be released.

6. I would like to express my profound gratitude to my wonderful husband, J. DeVirgilis, for entertaining our five-year-old daughter for the entirety of the quarantine summer of 2020 so that I could prepare and write this chapter, and for bringing his expertise on film to the table to help me craft certain phrases with more precision. For supporting me in bringing this chapter to life, and a thousand other things, thank you.

Chapter 7

Sadness Is Rebellion

The Ontopolitics of Queer Loss in The Life and Death of a Porno Gang *(2009)*

Andrija Filipović

Mladen Đorđević's award-winning *The Life and Death of a Porno Gang* (*Život i smrt porno bande*) follows a diverse group of people traveling through Serbia.[1] There, they perform pornographic vaudeville shows (for their own pleasure) and make snuff films (for a foreign businessman). On their journey, the group members die either by their own or the locals' hands until no one remains. It is an ostensibly simple story; nonetheless, the complexities of the film reside in its broader social and historical context. Here, a short history of Serbia's social, political, and economical affairs may help illuminate Đorđević's work.

The Life and Death of a Porno Gang was released in 2009. At the beginning of the twenty-first century, and especially in the years preceding the release of this film, Serbian society was profoundly changing. In October 2000, Slobodan Milošević, dictator for more than a decade during and after the breakdown of the Socialist Federal Republic of Yugoslavia, was removed from office. This followed the NATO military campaign of 1999 and mass protests against election fraud in 2000. Milošević's regime was replaced by an alliance of center and center-right democratic parties which began structural, social, economic, and political reforms with the goal of joining the European Union (EU). Even though there has been a swing back towards political authoritarianism since 2012, the situation remains fluid. This short history is essential for understanding both the changes the LGBTQIA+ community underwent and is still undergoing, and the politics of "queer pessimism" as displayed in *The Life and Death of a Porno Gang*. Within such a deeply cis-hetero-patriarchal environment, queerness is seen as deviant and sick, and queer life is viewed as not worth living. Moreover, this deeply cis-heteronormative society actively tries to erase any possibility of meaningful queer life. In essence, the potential for a rich, full, queer life is virtually nonexistent.

When understood in this context, Đorđević's film can be read as an analysis of the affective structure of queer loss, showing the ways in which the queer community (and difference in general) is treated within contemporary cis-heteronormative, nationalistic, patriarchal, and xenophobic Serbian society. I would argue that Đorđević not only offers a poignant analysis of Serbia's current state of affairs, but that he also underscores particular ontopolitics of queer loss. Instead of taking loss as a structural feature of queer subjects, as is often done in psychoanalytically inspired theories, Đorđević's film calls for an assumption of an ontopolitical position of sadness, even if it might turn deadly (as it does for this film's characters). Queer sadness, in this sense, marks the possibility of rebellion within the devastated social landscape created by cis-hetero-patriarchy which is unable to accept the Other and which is unlivable for those who are not its members. While a grim picture, this is today's cultural climate despite Serbia having an openly lesbian Prime Minister since 2017.[2] Indeed, violence is a fact of everyday life for the queer community in contemporary Serbian society, whether large scale and highly visible such as the anti-gay riots during the 2010 Pride Parade or small scale and insidiously quiet such as the innumerable microaggressions against individuals. Violence is both structural where it is related to cis-hetero-patriarchal societal norms, and systemic where it is related to the state as the source of heteronormative laws and policies.

I will approach this film in a theoretical manner that is inspired by the philosophies of new materialism. In the first part of this chapter, I will explore what I term "geology of loss" in *The Life and Death of a Porno Gang*. Here, "geology" is the exploration of the processes of sedimentation, stratification, and identification of various layers of matter and meaning. In this case, I will unearth all the layers of historical matter sedimented in Đorđević's film, and the ways in which each forms a particular sense of loss, culminating in the loss of the individual lives of the characters. I will also explore the ways in which these processes of sedimentation shape individual bodies and identities, making them susceptible to various experiences of violence and loss. In the second part of this chapter, I will explore the affective ontopolitics of "devastation" as understood through the theoretical framework of new materialism, and show the strata of loss in this film, pointing to particular ontopolitics of devastation as it pertains to queer subjects. The Serbian socio-historical milieu turns out to be a ruined material-semiotic landscape, especially so for the queer community, and so much so that this community needs new ontopolitics based on sadness as rebellion. In this sense, I propose that the Serbian queer community needs queer pessimism that is founded on ontopolitics of devastation and geology of loss.

GEOLOGY OF LOSS

The philosophical concept of geology was first introduced in Gilles Deleuze and Félix Guattari's *A Thousand Plateaus: Capitalism and Schizophrenia* (1980). In this instance, Deleuze and Guattari developed a general theory of stratification, according to which there are various material layers differing in order of magnitude or scale as well as in quality of "becoming." On the plane of immanence, there are the geological, crystalline, physiochemical, organic, and alloplastic strata. These strata are interdependent and mutually causative. In this sense, the concept of geology is tentative to the very materiality of the body, instead of focusing exclusively on a single stratum. Deleuze and Guattari's chapter titled "10,000 BC: The Geology of Morals (Who Does the Earth Think It is?)" gives readers a map of the strata that comprise the Earth and the cosmos. Here, it is revealed that the system of strata that makes up the geology in both the physical and philosophical sense includes three main strata: inorganic, organic, and alloplastic. The inorganic stratum consists of molecular and molar levels: it is made up of formed matter and functional structure. The organic stratum is more complex and cohesive, containing organic compounds and organic systems that make up the organisms: it also possesses the epistratum and parastratum. The epistratum of the organic stratum addresses relations and, as such, it includes at least four types of relations: (1) relations between the outer milieu and inner elements, (2) relations between elements and compounds, (3) relations between compounds and substances, and (4) relations between substances of content and substances of expression. Moving on to the parastratum, it is set up through the capability of the body to act and to be acted upon in three ways: (1) discovery of energy resources, (2) perception, and (3) reaction. The alloplastic stratum includes both the inorganic and organic stratum, but it possesses its own specificities. It is found on the level of society (social machine, *socius*) and, as such, it consists of machinic assemblage of bodies (organic and inorganic), and collective assemblages of enunciation (regime of signs and social institutions).

But that is not all. The inorganic, organic, and alloplastic strata with all their levels and mutual relations are part and parcel of "abstract machines." Deleuze and Guattari define "abstract machines" as a "consolidated aggregate of matter-functions (*phylum* and *diagram*)," and there are three abstract machines that make up the Mechanosphere or Chaosmos (2004, 562). There is the abstract machine of the plane of consistency, which consists of "unformed matters and nonformal functions," and which connects heterogeneous elements (2004, 562). And the other two abstract machines are: (1) the abstract machine of stratification of Earth and cosmos into inorganic, organic, and alloplastic strata, and (2) the abstract machine of overcoding or axiomatic of capitalism, which totalize and homogenize through quantification (compared to the abstract machine of the plane of consistency which mainly functions to deterritorialize). These three and the multiplicity of relations between them make up the Mechanosphere.

What can be concluded with this brief discussion of strata and three kinds of abstract machines is that there is an interdependence of not only abstract machines but of abstract machines and strata as well. In other words, there are the politics of strata, starting from the stratum of unformed matters to the inorganic (as geological, crystalline, and physicochemical), and moving through organic and alloplastic all the way to the cosmos itself, particularly because of the abstract machine of overcoding due to its axiomatic nature. Taking into account the geological aspect means taking into account, at the same time, that the synchronous politicity of space itself, its stratification or sedimentation of strata, and of its diachronic aspect as the processes of sedimentation are durationally long and slow in their creation of strata. Geology shows the politics inherent in the materiality itself in the form of "raw materials" that make the bodies and historical layers, as well as the politics of the energy and sources of energy used to power the movement of the formed bodies within and across milieus. Considering that the concept of geology includes all strata, it also includes the "immaterial," that is the cultural and social aspect of the alloplastic stratum. The cultural or social is not a world unto itself but a heavily striated and coded flux of matter positioned on the plane of consistency just as any other body. Hence, the concept of geology is tentative to both the materiality of infrastructure of the cultural and historical (energy, materials used in creation of cultural artefacts, etc.), as well as the materiality of the cultural itself.

Ultimately, the concept of geology allows for a more careful excavation of the various material-semiotic levels in Đorđević's film. It allows for a more attentive analysis of the loss that is sedimented across all the strata. It also allows the conceptual ground to argue for a particular affective ontopolitics of devastation as presented in the next part of this chapter.

The Life and Death of a Porno Gang opens in late 1998, several months before the NATO campaign against Serbia and more than a year before the fall of Slobodan Milošević. Here, viewers meet Marko (Mihajlo Jovanović), a thirty-year-old fresh graduate of the Faculty of Dramatic Arts in Belgrade who is trying to sell his film treatment. In several shots, Đorđević contextualizes Marko as a rebellious man from a less-than-idyllic middle-class family.

His father is a lecherous businessman, sister is a gold digger, and mother is a housewife. A cut then brings viewers to late 1999 when Marko leaves home to become an arthouse/pornographic film director. Cane (Srđan Miletić), a director/producer of pornographic films, provides funding for one of Marko's films. An insert from Marko's work foreshadows the trajectory of *The Life and Death of a Porno Gang*. Marko's film, *Srem's Herb of Oblivion: A Socio-Political Horror Porno*, is far from the mainstream pornography Cane commissioned. It features a peasant who buys genetically modified soy on credit, but it is substandard quality and does not grow. Desperate and drunk, he penetrates the earth with his penis. From the hole, filled with the peasant's semen and anger (so the narration goes), grows a strange plant. Visually similar to marijuana, this plant becomes a popular drug which delivers erotic hallucinations. However, users also become zombie-like and violent. The film does not meet Cane's satisfaction. And this sets the tone for the rest of the film as Marko tries to evade the infuriated Cane (who wants his funding returned).

Another cut brings viewers to the year 2000. Marko is in-hiding from Cane. He misses the day of Milošević's fall because he is intoxicated. As he says, "I didn't give fuck about it"; and this is true since being indebted to Cane is destroying his life [00:12:41]. This is when the idea of the porno gang is born, and this is the first stratum of historical loss. This part of the film, that covers roughly a year of Marko's life, hints toward the last year of Milošević's rule, but it also shows a particular stance toward political change. The years of Milošević's dictatorship were marked by war, isolation, international sanctions, hyperinflation, but also by oppositional demonstrations and the development of a network of independent cultural institutions funded by the West.[3] These institutions, such as the Open Society Foundation, created an alternative and independent art scene as well as made possible pro-West activism, including gay and lesbian activism. While these years were marked by utter despair because of war and sanctions, they were also marked by hope for effective LGBTQIA+ activism.[4] There was a vision of a future Serbian society built on the ideals of democracy and liberalism (including the liberal market economy). But Marko does not care about that. Instead of being in the streets protesting against Milošević, he spends the day of Milošević's fall in an alcohol-induced stupor. He refuses the optimism that suggests Serbian society will change with the dictator's fall.[5]

In the film, Marko meets Una (Ana Aćimović), a failed theater actress, and devises an idea for a porno theater that incorporates current socio-political issues. He gathers a troupe of performers—an HIV-positive gay couple Džoni (Radivoj Knežević) and Maks (Srđan Jovanović), married heroin addicts Rade (Aleksandar Gligorić) and Darinka (Mariana Aranđelović), two adult-film actors Dragan (Bojan Zogović) and Sofija (Nataša Aksentijević), and a voyeuristic cameraman Vanja (Predrag Damnjanović)—and they set out as a "porno cabaret," creating the first porno theater in the Balkans. With bold taglines like, "Serbs watch out, patriarchy is going out of fashion," the cabaret quickly catches attention. Marko and the cabaret travel through villages all over Serbia while still on the run from Cane and Cane's brother (a member of the police). Considering that it is late 2000/early 2001, the call of ousting patriarchy can only be understood ironically on the part of porno theater troupe as the events that follow will show. This also marks another layer of loss atop the layer of historical loss due to the dissolution of the Socialist Federal Republic of Yugoslavia and Milošević's dictatorship. This layer is made by the sedimentation of cis-hetero-patriarchy and the system of social relations that it entails as well as the economic relations that surround it. This stratum is constituted by the emotional, cognitive, economic, and social loss of all those who do not accept such a system or cannot, for various reasons, participate in it. For the remainder of the film—a series of village cabaret shows interspersed with snuff episodes—Đorđević does not refrain from showing viewers what such a loss means and how exactly it looks for the film's characters (in all its gruesomeness).

The first village porno cabaret show is a resounding success. However, in the middle of the night, a German ex-journalist named Frantz (Srboljub Milin) appears. He offers Marko money to perform snuff plays and shoot snuff films for the black market. The participants are either near death or suicidal; therefore, in Marko's view, the offer is less reprehensible than it may have initially seemed. The next day, members of the village council order the troupe to leave, and later chase them out. At this point, Ceca (Ivan Đorđević), a transgender woman from the village, joins the gang. In a rare move for Serbian film, which often privileges the lives of cisgender women and men, it is her story that viewers hear in greatest detail (besides Marko's). This signals the director's commitment to the most marginalized. While acting in the cabaret, Ceca recounts her life of trauma and isolation. Unsympathetic to her pain, the play's spectators shout, "Slut!" [00:42:25]. She ends her performance with an act of bestiality, shocking the audience into silence. As a result of the provocative show, the gang (women and men alike) are first accosted by the police and then sexually brutalized by the villagers. This is where the interrelation of cis-hetero-patriarchy and socio-economic marginalization becomes the most obvious. As alluded to in her autobiographical performance, Ceca is only able to emotionally relate to animals, and even those relations are predicated on violence. For instance, before Ceca leaves with the porno gang, she kills her favorite goat to protect it from the hands of her father, who physically and sexually abused her. She kills what she loves most to protect it. In other words, the affective bonds that trans people create—and not just between each other or with other human beings but even with animals—are impossible to maintain within the cis-hetero-patriarchal system of rural Serbian communities. Moreover, these scenes that include the villagers show that the villagers themselves are socially and economically marginalized. Their communities are poor and outdated, signaling that young people are leaving the villages to try their luck in the cities. These scenes show the ways in which marginalized classes perpetuate systemic violence, as well as the stratified nature of those who are pushed even further into the social margins, such as Ceca.

Beaten and broke, the group accepts an archetypal pact with the devil, and the porno gang begins to stage snuff plays and record snuff films. The first volunteer is from a nearby village. His scar-covered body suggests pathological masochism. No explanation or context is given for why he is driven to self-harm. Viewers are left to surmise that his suicidal tendencies are the result of his oppressive, rural atmosphere. While being recorded, he cuts himself across the stomach and chest several times, finally slitting his own throat in an abandoned train car. Unfortunately, he does not die quickly, and, in an act of mercy, Dragan kills the villager. Undeterred by the traumatic event, the gang continues performing their porno cabaret plays around the villages. But it is not all work for them. In a particularly phantasmagoric and surprisingly happy scene (given the general tone of the film), they consume some psilocybin mushrooms and orgy away the day in the woods, caressing the trees and having sex with each other. This is where, perhaps, another stratum of loss is hinted at, considering that all bodily pleasures and pains have been instrumentalized for the purpose of either creating the porno vaudeville shows or snuff plays/films. In contrast, this scene shows what happens when bodily pleasure becomes play, uninterested in either representation or any real or symbolic gain. What is lost in these vaudeville shows and snuff plays/films is the bodily capacity for pleasurable play, which then could lead to including what is non-human (such as trees) in the human community. Đorđević, however, does not go further in exploring these potentially utopian perspectives. He allows a glimpse of what a more compassionate world might look like and then returns viewers to a brutal reality. The loss of this bliss is felt acutely throughout the remainder of the film.

The next volunteer for the snuff plays is from a different village, an ex-sniper and veteran of the wars in Bosnia and Croatia. He recounts his horrific combat experiences, and viewers learn that he is dying from liver cancer related to AIDS, which he contracted from a needle exchange during the war. He expresses remorse for killing soldiers, civilians, women, and children alike. The money from the snuff performance will help his family to survive. He is killed by Sofija, who bludgeons him over the head with a large mallet. This snuff play points toward the deep historical trauma that the wars in Bosnia and Croatia created for all ex-Yugoslav nations.[6] The dissolution of the Socialist Federal Republic of Yugoslavia into constitutive republics was enacted through ethno-nationalist projects of these individual states. The wars that led to genocide, mass killings, ethnic cleansing, isolation, and international sanctions resulted in destitution for those who survived, including members of the queer community. Furthermore, the project of the emancipation of the Serbian LGBTQIA+ community that began in 1991 under the influence of Slovenian counterparts was cut short by the beginning of the war, deferring legal and social changes for more than two decades.[7]

The third snuff play is a vigilante justice venture. The gang kidnaps and kills a man from the village who terrorized and sexually assaulted its residents. As a result, the police ambush the troupe and shoot Dragan. From here, the gang continues to disintegrate. Džoni leaves for a monastery they chanced upon in their escape. Maks, Dragan's boyfriend, hangs himself. And the rest succumb to despair—Sofija starts shooting up heroin, Ceca is suffering from the effects of HIV, while others self-medicate with illicit pharmaceuticals.

The last snuff episode is *lapot*—a ritual killing of the oldest family member, based on a legendary ancient custom. An elderly man chooses to die to fund treatment for his granddaughter who was disfigured by enriched uranium left by the NATO bombing campaign to end the Kosovo War and Milošević's dictatorship. This is another stratum of historical loss due to the wars. The 1999 NATO bombing campaign left deep marks in the Serbian national body, especially because it led to the secession of Kosovo and Metohija, the mythic source of nationhood for ethnic Serbs. The aftermath of the bombing campaign also entailed the fall of Milošević in 2000 after mass demonstrations against election fraud, with which the film opens. The *lapot* production is performed in front of clients who specifically paid for this show, including the elderly man's family. However, the event is cut short just before the killing as a result of information that the authorities are nearby. In this sequence, the destruction of the gang continues. Ceca is found dead from an overdose in the barn. The married heroin addicts leave the gang because they "went on this trip to fuck and not to kill" [01:35:10]. Una also leaves. And Marko returns to Belgrade by bus. Months later, in the year 2001, Marko discovers that Sofija and the others, except for Vanja, the cameraman, died in a car crash. However, when Marko attempts to rectify his financial accounts, Vanja is slaughtered by Cane's brother. Marko then meets Una, they make up, and they perform "The Last Snuff Film," as the segment is called. Here, the duo kills Cane. Afterwards, Marko tells Una, "And now I'm going to take you to a romantic place." "A honeymoon?" Una asks. "Something like that," Marko responds [01:45:54–01:46:02]. Marko and Una commit suicide in the ruins of a Roman shrine, cutting open their veins while the camera keeps filming.

The porno gang, with its constitutive multiplicity, works as a "desiring machine" (to use a concept coined by Deleuze and Guattari) connecting all the wretched of the world. But viewers also see, in all its gory glory, the reasons the wretched are made such. As philosopher Steven Shaviro notes, "There is a kind of everydayness to its horror . . . The film's most shocking moments emerge from this background of everydayness, and then quickly recede back into it" (2011). Exploitation by the economic and political elite is largely responsible for the everydayness of the horror that the gang faces. Power clearly resides in the hands of the authorities, from the police to the village councils. The cis-heteronormative patriarchal structure is deadly for everybody, except the white men in power, and socially naturalized as such. The leering, jeering villagers, even though they are impoverished both economically and culturally by being marginalized, act on their cis-hetero-patriarchal impulse in the treatment of the gang's porno cabaret provocations: so much so that they sexually assault the gang collectively in a final act of affirming their patriarchal masculine dominance. The oppression takes its toll, and one by one the gang members are killed off. The honeymoon, it turns out, is possible only in death.

ONTOPOLITICS OF DEVASTATION

The Life and Death of a Porno Gang builds layers upon layers of historical and personal loss, and it grows increasingly grim as the narrative progresses. As it descends into a place beyond hope, viewers glance into the lives of others on the margins of Serbian society: the elderly, the poor, peasants, war survivors (and war criminals), etc. who become the subjects of the gang's snuff plays and films. Ultimately, the film extinguishes itself (rather than spectacularly culminating) in the death of the remaining members of the porno gang. The layers include: (1) the wars in Bosnia and Croatia (as indexed in the second snuff play), (2) the war in Kosovo and the NATO bombing campaign (as indexed at the beginning of the film through the television reports shown in the background and the third snuff play), (3) Milošević's dictatorship, international sanctions and isolation, the dissolution of the Socialist Federal Republic of Yugoslavia, and economic marginalization (as indexed in the destitution of the village inhabitants for whom the porno gang performs), and, finally, (4) cis-hetero-patriarchy (as indexed throughout the film, culminating in the death of all characters). All these strata compose the geology of loss, affecting both queer and cis-heterosexual characters. The landscape made by the movement of these geological strata is a landscape of devastation, where hopelessness remains the only possible outlook. Utter sadness is what viewers are left with at film's conclusion. What is to be made of this? What does it mean for queer politics?

The answers to these questions are inextricably tied to the historical processes homosexuality and queerness were subjected to in Serbia. The first lesbian and gay rights activist group, Arkadija, was not formed until 1991. Likewise, homosexuality was not decriminalized until 1994. In other Yugoslav republics, the situation was different, especially in Slovenia, where the first European gay and lesbian film festival, Magnus, was started in 1984.[8] The Slovenian gay and lesbian scene had a profound, although slow, influence on Serbian gay and lesbian activism, but most activities were curtailed when war broke out in June 1991. Members of Arkadija engaged in anti-war activism, and it was only in 1995, when the war ended, that activities became more focused on improving gay and lesbian rights—and Labris, an organization for lesbian rights, was founded. But again, further action was put on hold due to the worsening political situation during the Kosovo War of 1998–1999. Nonetheless, in the period after the fall of Milošević, during the rise of democratic rule, numerous organizations were started. In Belgrade, Gayten was founded in 2001, Queeria in 2002, Queer Belgrade Collective in 2005, Gay Straight Alliance in 2005, Gay-Lesbian Info Centre in 2009, Centre for Queer Studies in 2010, and Egal in 2015. Organizations were also created outside the capital: Lambda in 2002 in Niš (the second largest city in Serbia), NLO in 2004 in Novi Sad (the third largest city), and Association Rainbow in Šabac in 2004. Some no longer exist (Queer Belgrade Collective, Queeria, Lambda) but others are still active. Some were founded for the express purpose of organizing the Pride Parades (Belgrade Pride as an umbrella organization, for example). These groups and organizations, with the exception of the now defunct Queer Belgrade Collective, are united by an unwavering pro-European attitude, and the single model of a lawfully recognized LGBTQIA+ community as seen through the lens of Western-defined human rights discourse.

The first Pride Parade was organized by Labris and Gayten in 2001, several months after the democratic reforms. It became known as the Massacre Pride because right-wing protestors attacked the participants, leaving dozens injured. The shock of such violence disrupting the optimistic atmosphere, just as Serbian society was becoming more progressive after a decade of being culturally closed, pushed the organization of the next Pride Parade forward to 2004. However, unrest in Kosovo resulted in the parade's cancelation. The next attempt was in 2009, but the government denied permission for fear of further violence. It was not until 2010 that another Pride Parade was finally held, called "State Pride," but, again, groups of right-wing demonstrators, together with some members of the Serbian Orthodox Church, attacked the police and wreaked havoc through Belgrade.[9] Pride Parades have been held annually since 2014, but there are dissenting voices within the LGBTQIA+

community, claiming that the parades are government rainbow-washing to provide an appearance of Serbia's progress on human rights to the EU.

The Life and Death of a Porno Gang shows the ways in the which conditions of possibility for "becoming queer" are produced through the layering of multiplicity of historical strata. The ontology of "becoming queer" is stratified or, rather, it is geological. Such ontological geology is necessarily political ontology: it is geontopolitical. These aspects—ontological, geological, historical, political—intertwine to make conditions of possibility for "becoming queer." Viewers see how the characters are affected by processes of long duration, such as the effects of the dissolution of Yugoslavia or the effects of systemic cis-hetero-patriarchal violence or economic impoverishment. To conceptualize the loss that is specific to "becoming queer" in this film, then, means to include the crushing movement of these layers, to include the devastated landscape this movement creates. The ontopolitics of "becoming queer" is the ontopolitics of devastation, and the sadness is a particular form of relationality between those who identify as queer and the relation of the queer community to the cis-hetero-patriarchy and economic impoverishment under the conditions of devastation.

Fuller and Goriunova define "devastation" as "a kind of becoming in which the virtual is attenuated, depleted in some way, drained of its capacity to be constituent," and it "operates and couples with, protrudes from, and dissolves certain other kinds of becomings that are biochemical, military and economic, sociopolitical, technical and mediatic" (2020, 1). Following Deleuze and Guattari's ontology that includes the concepts of the virtual and actual sides of immanence, Fuller and Goriunova conceptualize devastation as it pertains to the virtual side of reality. They assert that devastations are not "simply a diminution of the stock of entities in the world or the finite number or range of things," nor they are "solely a kind of becoming of nothing in which the nothingness is produced by this or that becoming of some thing" (2020, 1). Devastation does not deal with the actual things, but with the virtuality as such, and hence it actually does deal with the actual but in a roundabout way by the diminishment of the field of potentiality for actualization. More precisely, devastation is "an existing multiplicity, a differential, that fails to actualize, a potentiality that is wounded in a way that makes it implode, that makes it actualize a devastating becoming" (2020, 2). Fuller and Goriunova, then, conceptualize devastation firmly within relational, process-oriented philosophy, which means that this kind of becoming of diminishment must be imagined as anything but lack. Lack, as such, has no place within these relational philosophies such as new materialism. It is reserved for the so-called anti-relational theories inspired by Freudian and Lacanian psychoanalysis. Deleuze and Guattari are critical of the concept of lack, which they tie to a particular construction of subject (made through castration and dependent on signification) that is invalid for the image of reality based on relationality (where subject is imagined as a dynamically changing knot or sedimentation of forces). Within relational philosophies, there is no room for lack, that is, for non-being (or, rather, non-becoming). There is no negation, but only affirmation of differentiation/becoming, and the challenge is to think what is usually taken as negative or pure negation productively, as affirmative of differentiation. Hence Fuller's and Goriunova's attempt to think through devastation is a specific kind of becoming—a becoming of implosion/diminishment of actualization. It is "a kind of becoming in which the virtual is altered, diluted, or maybe enhanced in a sour way," they write (2020, 3). Devastation is not simply destruction, disappearance, or death, but it must be thought as a "form of very active production" in the sense of the "differentiated becoming of the perishing" (2020, 5, 6).

For Fuller and Goriunova, devastation "may sometimes be the only common we are left with," which is an insight that resonates with the characters in *The Life and Death of a Porno Gang* most directly (2020, 10). "Devastation as commons" for those who identify as queer in the film is structural socioeconomic violence. There is no beyond and outside it. It enters the bodies, twists them, pains them, shapes them, and finally kills them. "Devastation as commons" affirms the becoming of perishing of the gang. In other words, it leads to diminishment of virtuality, the potentiality to actualize their affects, and what little is actualized is turned deadly, either in the form of self-destruction (ex. overdose, suicide) or violence toward the gang. This diminishment of bodily relationality is reflected in specific socially recognizable emotional content, that is, this diminishment of affectivity is codified as sadness.

Sadness is an emotion, and an emotion according to philosopher and social theorist Brian Massumi is:

> a subjective content, the sociolinguistic fixing of the quality of an experience which is from that point onward defined as personal. Emotion is qualified intensity, the conventional, consensual point of insertion of intensity into semantically and semiotically formed progressions, into narrativizable action-reaction circuits, into function and meaning. (2002, 28)

An emotion is a socially codified affect. Affect is a relation between the acting and being acted upon, which is how Deleuze and Guattari define the affect following Spinoza (2004, 288). The production of sadness as a socially codified affect is a biopolitical technology which forms individuals and the population through acting on the affective fields of the individual and collective bodies. Sadness colonizes the infraindividual level of individual bodies and the affective atmosphere of the collective body. Massumi defines the infraindividual level as "intensive elements, in intra-action. They are immediately linked variations, held in tension, resonating together in immediate proximity" (2015, 8). Next is the level of the individual's emotions, of social codification of the infraindividually affective intra-acting. The level beyond the individual, the level of the social, picks what has been codified as an emotion and transforms it into a social affective atmosphere through a collective event that is distributed across and within the bodies and "however different their eventual actions, all will have unfolded from the same suspense" (Massuni 2015, 109).

The collective event of suspense, the social affective atmosphere in which the bodies and their actions unfold is, in this case, sadness. Sadness, on the one hand, diminishes the available potentiality for actualization of affects and thus possibility for living otherwise. On the other hand, it naturalizes the affective atmosphere of permanent threat from cis-hetero-patriarchy and socioeconomic marginalization. Sadness as an affective atmosphere is the direct product of the geological movement of devastation. It is the geological movement of all those layers analyzed earlier in the text that produces sadness through the diminishment of possibility for actualization of affects. As Massumi notes, affect produces intensities; intensity is defined as "the strength or duration of the image's effect" (2002, 24). It is directed towards the so-called higher functions, to the depth of the bodies in the form of cognitive processes. In this sense, sadness as diminishment colonizes not only a precognitive level of infraindividual intra-acting, but the cognition as well. It diminishes cognitive capacities. The affective atmosphere of sadness, working on both cognitive and precognitive levels, is instilled as something that defines the whole of existence, which then naturalizes the cis-hetero-patriarchal framework at work within the society, and such framework actively diminishes the potentialities of queer bodies to actualize their affects.

However, given that immanence is the grounding concept in new materialist theoretical framework, it follows that sadness is not only the codified affect that shows diminishment of the possibility of actualization but that it is also, as affect, a possible means of resistance. As Fuller and Goriunova note, "in relation to a commons of devastation . . . new political subjects may arise in contestation of such conditions" (2020, 11). As affect, sadness can also, besides point to the diminishment of virtuality, lead to the increase of one's power to act. In this sense, sadness is rebellion. And it is a rebellion firmly grounded in queer pessimism. Queer pessimism is based on "queerness as negative, the refusal of reified queer identity, insistence against the succession of generations, the critique of the family as the foundational structure of the social order, the critique of politics, conceptions of a destructive *jouissance*," as an anonymous author writes in the online journal *baedan: Journal of Queer Nihilism* (2012). The porno gang's queer pessimism is exemplified in self-destructive practices that are simultaneously a consequence of, retort to, and refusal of heteronormative, patriarchal, and economically exploitative contemporary Serbian society. Instead of representing model citizens, the porno gang's queers are sado-masochistic, bestial, drug users dying of AIDS. Their very process and act of dying precludes the possibility of imagining the succession of generations, that is, the positive LGBTQIA+ politics that can be enacted in the present or projected into the future. In its place, there is the absolute negativity of queer pessimism, which negates both heteronormative and homonormative forms of life. Is there anything beyond? Queer pessimism leads to the erasure of the human by the final act of suicide as well as to the refusal to engage in positive critique with the purpose of bettering of society.

Erasure and refusal are not ahistorical, but firmly located in historical context, and history for Serbia includes a:

> ... sense of exhaustion and depletion ... The feeling of having come too late, of being post-everything (postmodern, posthuman, posthistorical) is probably a worldwide pathology at this point. But it is felt with a particular acuteness in postwar and post-socialist Serbia, torn as it is between a past of vanishing traditions, and a globalized future that somehow never manages to arrive. (Shaviro 2011)

As I have claimed, this historical context is better understood as geology, and a geology of loss more precisely. It is, in this light, even more productive to engage with *The Life and Death of a Porno Gang* as a political text, especially as one imagining what the extinguished future of queer politics may look like in Serbia and elsewhere. Never arriving, or arriving too late, exhaustion, depletion, sadness, and pessimism are the attributes of its overarching affective atmosphere, and there is a strange horror after the implosion of the gang—particularly as the film shuns any representation of what might lie ahead—because there is nothing that can be observed behind it. This void after devastation is more provocative as it questions commonsense approaches to the critique of heteronormativity and mainstream LGBTQIA+ politics. In other words, *The Life and Death of a Porno Gang* asks the fundamental question of whether there is life after social death—that is, how to think beyond representation.

CONCLUSION

I have argued that *The Life and Death of a Porno Gang* depicts a particular geology of loss. This geology of loss is constituted by a multiplicity of layers, including the dissolution of the Socialist Federal Republic of Yugoslavia, wars in Bosnia and Croatia, Milošević's dictatorship, international sanctions and isolation, the Kosovo War and NATO bombing campaign, economic impoverishment and marginalization, and cis-hetero-patriarchy. All these layers bring their own sense of historical loss and affect particular loss in relation to queer bodies. Taken together, these sedimented layers of loss create a landscape of devastation, a specific queer ontopolitics. Devastation is understood as a becoming of diminishment of affectivity, which is socially codified as sadness, among many other emotions. On the one hand, sadness points to the impoverished relationality of queer bodies under the conditions of socioeconomic and historical cis-hetero-patriarchal devastation. On the other hand, sadness is also a means of resistance through queer pessimism. In this sense, sadness is rebellion, marking a non-representational way out of the systemic violence of cis-hetero-patriarchy. Such a way out is figured as death. And indeed, what is pushed beyond this system or leaves it of its own accord might as well be dead for all the system cares since it cannot be represented *within* the system. What is more, the system can only produce sadness and death for it.

Finally, with this film, viewers learn how to think and feel beyond representation. For representation, devastation is only a lack that produces non-being. Queer pessimism leads one out of the representational system, and shows how to think of devastation as becoming, as affirmative differentiation of diminishment of affectivity. For those who identify as queer, that means the possibility of developing ontopolitical frameworks to combat the violent representational system of cis-hetero-patriarchy by other, non-representational means grounded in the new materialist philosophy of relationality.

BIBLIOGRAPHY

Baedan. 2012. "Queers Gone Wild." *Baedan: Journal of Queer Nihilism* 1: (no pages).

Bideleux, Robert, and Ian Jeffries. 2007. *The Balkans: A Post-Communist History.* Oxon: Routledge.

Bilić, Bojan. 2016. "Europe ♥ Gays? Europeanisation and Pride Parades in Serbia." In *LGBT Activism and Europeanisation in the Post-Yugoslav Space: On the Rainbow Way to Europe,* edited by Bojan Bilić, 117–54. London: Palgrave Macmillan.

Deleuze, Gilles, and Félix Guattari. 2004. *A Thousand Plateaus: Capitalism and Schizophrenia* (Trans. Brian Massumi). London: Continuum.

Filipović, Andija. 2019. "We Do Not Know What Queers Can Do: LGBT Community Between (In)visibility and Culture Industry in Serbia at the Beginning of the 21st Century." *Journal of Homosexuality* 66 (2): 1693–714.

Fuller, Matthew, and Olga Goriunova. 2019. *Bleak Joys: Aesthetics of Ecology and Impossibility.* Minneapolis: University of Minnesota Press.

Gočanin, Sonja. 2014. "Počeci LGBT organizovanja u Srbiji–Pismo iz Slovenije koje je pokrenulo istoriju" [The Beginnings of LGBT Organizing in Serbia–A Letter from Slovenia that Launched History]. In *Među nama: Neispričane priče gej i lezbejskih života*, edited by Jelisaveta Blagojević and Olga Dimitrijević, 334–47. Beograd: Hartefakt Fond.

Kajinić, Sonja. 2016. "The First European Festival of Lesbian and Gay Film Was Yugoslav: Dismantling the Geotemporality of Europeanisation in Slovenia." In *LGBT Activism and Europeanisation in the Post-Yugoslav Space: On the Rainbow Way to Europe*, edited by Bojan Bilić, 59–80. London: Palgrave Macmillan.

Massumi, Brian. 2002. *Parables for the Virtual: Movement, Affect, Sensation*. Durham: Duke University Press.

———. 2015. *The Power at the End of the Economy*. Durham: Duke University Press.

Ramet, Sabrina P., and Vjeran Pavlaković. 2005. *Serbia Since 1989: Politics and Society Under Milosevic and After*. Seattle: University of Washington Press.

Shaviro, Steven. 2011. "After Hope: The Life and Death of a Porno Gang." *ACIDEMIC Journal of Film and Media*. http://www.acidemic.com/id137.html.

Spasić, Ivana, and Milan Subotić. *R/evolution and Order: Serbia After October 2000*. Belgrade: Institute for Philosophy and Social Theory, 2001.

Wilmer, Franke. 2005. *The Social Construction of Man, the State, and War: Identity, Conflict, and Violence in Former Yugoslavia*. New York: Routledge.

NOTES

1. Mladen Đorđević's *The Life and Death of a Porno Gang* won twelve awards including the Special Jury Prize at the Boston Underground Film Festival, Best Film at the Buenos Aires Rojo Sangre, and Best Film at the Fantaspoa International Fantastic Film Festival.

2. For more about Prime Minister Ana Brnabić see: Bilić, Bojan. 2016. "Europe ♥ Gays? Europeanisation and Pride Parades in Serbia." In *LGBT Activism and Europeanisation in the Post-Yugoslav Space: On the Rainbow Way to Europe*, edited by Bojan Bilić, 161–89. London: Palgrave Macmillan.

3. For a historical overview see: Bideleux, Robert, and Ian Jeffries. 2007. *The Balkans: A Post-Communist History*. Oxon: Routledge: 233–328. See also: Ramet, Sabrina P., and Vjeran Pavlaković. 2005. *Serbia Since 1989: Politics and Society Under Milošević and After*. Seattle: University of Washington Press.

4. For more about hope in LGBTQIA+ activism in these years see: Filipović, Andija. 2019. "We Do Not Know What Queers Can Do: LGBT Community Between (In)visibility and Culture Industry in Serbia at the Beginning of the 21st Century." *Journal of Homosexuality* 66 (12): 1693–714.

5. For more about how the future was imagined immediately after Milošević's fall, see: Spasić, Ivana, and Milan Subotić. 2001. *Revolution and Order: Serbia after October 2000*. Belgrade: Institute for Philosophy and Social Theory.

6. For more on the wars see: Wilmer, Franke. 2005. *The Social Construction of Man, the State, and War: Identity, Conflict, and Violence in Former Yugoslavia*. New York: Routledge.

7. For more on the project of emancipation of the Serbian LGBTQIA+ community that began in 1991 under the influence of Slovenian counterparts see: Gočanin, Sonja. 2014. "Počeci LGBT organizovanja u Srbiji—Pismo iz Slovenije koje je pokrenulo istoriju" [The Beginnings of LGBT Organizing in Serbia—A Letter from Slovenia that Launched History]. In *Među nama: Neispričane priče gej i lezbejskih života*, edited by Jelisaveta Blagojević and Olga Dimitrijević, 334–47. Beograd: Hartefakt Fond.

8. For more on the Magnus film festival see: Kajinić, Sonja. 2016. "The First European Festival of Lesbian and Gay Film Was Yugoslav: Dismantling the Geotemporality of Europeanisation in Slovenia." In *LGBT Activism and Europeanisation in the Post-Yugoslav Space: On the Rainbow Way to Europe*, edited by Bojan Bilić, 59–80. London: Palgrave Mcmillan.

9. For more on State Pride see: Bilić, Bojan. 2016. "Europe ♥ Gays? Europeanisation and Pride Parades in Serbia." In *LGBT Activism and Europeanisation in the Post-Yugoslav Space: On the Rainbow Way to Europe*, edited by Bojan Bilić, 161–89. London: Palgrave Macmillan.

Chapter 8

The Grieving Dead

Haunting and the Haunted in the Spierig Brothers' Winchester *(2018)*

Racheal Harris

Although not widely embraced in contemporary society, there has long been an understanding among many cultural groups, along with religious and spiritual communities, that death is not an ending, but merely punctuation on the soul's continuing journey. Japanese culture, for instance, is rich with stories of the wandering and restless dead who can and do interact with the living. Here, veneration of the dead (especially of one's familial ancestors) holds a place of prominence. Similar views are held in many Indigenous cultures. In Australian aboriginal beliefs, the dead are not spoken of by name, lest it call their spirit back from The Dreaming. Likewise, the Maori tribes of Aotearoa (New Zealand) believe ancestral spirits watch over their living kin. Among Black cultures of Africa and the wider Caribbean diaspora, as well as in the United States, ancestral spirits remain in contact with the living and can be petitioned for help and guidance. Though ancient in origin, each remains a living culture, and thus is not immune to shifting societal attitudes and trends related to death and dying. Despite more "popular" opinions, often the product of globalization and secularism which perceive them as antiquated, communicative bonds which stretch beyond the realm of life and death continue to exist.

Though they may not discuss them in depth, the Abrahamic faiths each have connections to encounters between the living and spirit realm. Evidence of this can be located in Old and New Testament scriptures. An account in Samuel 1:28 is perhaps the most often quoted of these. This passage describes the spirit of the Prophet Samuel being raised from the dead by a female medium (described as a witch), at the behest of the beleaguered King Saul. This act reveals that the dead are aware of the living realm, and Samuel quickly confirms that Saul, having been witnessed by God in his indiscretions, will soon be called to answer for them. Somewhere within the various translations of this ancient account, a grim commandment arose, one which forbids calling upon the dead, to the point where it almost denies their existence. The New Testament, too, contains numerous accounts of spiritual contact, many of which involve Jesus. What was the coming of the Holy Spirit at Pentecost (Acts 2) if not an act of divine communication? And Jesus' transfiguration on the Mount (Matthew 17:1–8) was surely nothing if not a sign that life continues beyond the realm of the corporeal. Among many Spiritualists, the belief that Jesus was the ultimate medium remains popular and underscores his ability not only to commune with the dead, but to converse from beyond death. Nonetheless, superstition and damnation narratives which have appeared in scripture and popular culture, along with the general misconception that mediumship is a form of satanism or witchcraft, continue to complicate the perception of spirit communication today. In most Christian religions, spirit communication is frowned upon at best and dismissed at worst. Spiritualism is the exception to this rule. More so than any religion which draws some form of kinship from the Abrahamic faiths, Spiritualism embraces mediumship and the ability to commune with departed spirits, using the energy of living to do so.[1] Such explorations have been viewed with universal doubt, scorn, and disinterest. Yet they continue. In large part, the negative commentary seems to stem from academic circles and members of the religious community, as opposed to society at a grassroots level. And, though Spiritualism has commanded the attention of some high-profile people and celebrities, the bulk of its followers have always been laypeople who unite to offer support and service. One of the primary motivations of these functions is grief (Pearsall 1972, 10). More than a demonstration of theological radicalism, the purpose of Spiritualism and mediumistic communication has been to prove that life persists beyond the moment of mortal death. Few people are more interested in this cause than the recently bereaved, and it is grief which often generates interest in spirit communication. Even with the fear of sin and damnation, or shame born of public scorn or derision, grief, it seems, is a more powerful emotion.

In the contemporary world, film has become a popular medium to inspire discourse related to death, grief, and the afterlife. There is a litany of films which employ grief in their narratives of ghostly encounters and spiritual messages, but the focus of this chapter will be those which include Spiritualism. Using the Spierig Brothers' 2018 film *Winchester* (also known as *Winchester: The House that Spirits Built*) as a primary text, this chapter will consider how the dead not only communicate with the living, but how these communications are coded to speak not only to grief and the afterlife, but contemporary social issues. The motivation for the use of Spiritualism as a specific frame for this discussion is twofold.

Primarily, Spiritualism is and has always been concerned with proving that there is a life or energetic consciousness after death and the universal yearning for concrete proof of this fact is as present in the post-pandemic world of the 2020s as it has ever been. Perhaps more so. The proof Spiritualism offers, while rarely meeting the goalposts of scientific rigor or validity, is demonstrated through mediumship and the ability of the medium to transfer accurate messages between the living and the dead. Accuracy is reliant upon accounts, personality traits, or facts about the person (and sometimes about the "sitter") that are not widely known. Not all mediums would self-identify as Spiritualists in the religious sense, but all Spiritualists understand the importance of mediumship to their practice and use demonstrations of spiritual contact as proof of the continuance of the sentient soul after death. In a society in which secularism or New Age beliefs present a less constrictive or threatening atmosphere to consider our individual thoughts about mortality, Spiritualism provides an ideal platform for this discussion. Further, and as will be addressed, though *Winchester* might be set in 1906, the setting itself is as important to the message of the film as is the subject of Spiritualism.

The second motivation for the use of Spiritualism as a specific frame for this discussion, and one which is more relevant to the themes of this collection more broadly, is that the foundation of Spiritualism and the continued engagement of people with it, are rooted, perhaps more deeply than any other religious or spiritual practice, in grief. In 2021, Netflix released a series titled *Life After Death*, which examines the afterlife experiences and beliefs of various groups of people in the West. S1:E2 and S1:E3 of the series specifically focus on mediumship and, less overtly, Spiritualism. The enduring theme expressed in these episodes, from mediums, healers, and those who engaged their services, is that people turn to Spiritualism and mediums as a salve for their grief.[2] This grief is invariably linked to the loss of a loved one, though the purpose for proof and contact with a deceased spirit will vary. For some, it is a need for closure, for others it is a need for consolation. This consolation can only come from validation that there is an afterlife and that loved ones will be reunited again. *Winchester* draws on these historical themes in its narrative framework, but the subtle message, which is one concerned with grief, is timeless and universal. This makes the film a fitting narrative for both an analysis of grief in horror films, as well as how the expression of grief intersects with larger ideas of faith, love, and belief in the afterlife.

Films in which discarnate spirits commune with the living will usually employ either a possession narrative or use at least one character who possesses mediumistic abilities. In the last three decades, possession films have occupied the large share of these narratives. This might be attributed to the commercial success of earlier films such as William Friedkin's *The Exorcist* (1973). Compared to possession films, their mediumistic counterparts have either flown under the radar or camouflaged their content so that it is not always apparent. One example of this camouflaging is seen in M. Night Shyamalan's *The Sixth Sense* (1999), in which Cole (Haley Joel Osment) is clearly a clairvoyant and clairaudient medium, though this is never overtly stated. In more recent years, possession films have begun to incorporate elements of Spiritualism and mediumship into their plotlines more overtly, creating an almost hybrid genre. Examples here include the *Insidious* franchise (2010–present), Stiles White's *Ouija* (2014), Mike Flanagan's *Ouija: Origin of Evil* (2016), and James Wan's *The Conjuring* (2013). In each of these examples however, the narrative focus, and the source of fear, trends towards possession, with a particular focus on possession as a vehicle for diabolic spirits and entities as opposed to the general dead. Lorraine Warren, as she is portrayed in films from *The Conjuring* franchise, is a prime example of this trend. Although she features heavily in most of the films included within the franchise, and discusses the fact that she is a medium, her engagement with these skills is only a secondary plot device, with possession, and often exorcism, being the more primary focus. Similarly, Lorraine's mediumship assists her and her husband to help the afflicted, but only in the sense that it allows her to feel abnormal spirits and the presence of entities within the home. At no point does she offer readings or transmit messages to the living from the departed loved ones. In these films, the dead are almost exclusively malevolent, which is indicative of their strong ties to Catholicism and Catholic doctrine (which forbids spirit communication). At times, Lorraine also interacts with demonic entities in a mediumistic capacity, but this is not a discarnate spirit who once had a human form, rather it is a preternatural being. Again, this removes the possibility of or need for meaningful communication. The purpose of the offending entity is to bring grief, not to soothe it. The consequence of these depictions is a general misunderstanding of the larger cultural legacy of mediumship and the important role it has played in real-world scenarios.

Rather than addressing the "horror" aspect of these films, this chapter focuses on examples which draw on Spiritualism and Spiritualist practices as they are understood by the faith community who use mediumship to communicate with the spirits of lost loved ones. The aim is to dispel some elements of mediumship which are the highly problematic creations of Hollywood fantasy and, in doing so, to provide a historical context for the practice of mediumship as it pertains to the beliefs expressed in Spiritualism. Unlike possession narratives, the use of the Spiritualism and mediumship in film allows for meaningful communication between the living and the dead. The discussion that takes place in this liminal space expresses a wider range of emotions and, in the assessment of these accounts, what audiences encounter is the dead as sentient beings who, though they have departed their bodies, still retain memories and emotions deeply tied to the lives they left behind. Because the dialogue audiences see in Spiritualist narratives is reciprocal, it is also important for what it adds to a broader discussion around how grief is depicted in film and how this mirrors the grief experience in real life.

When Spiritualist themes are adapted to horror films, they are usually used interchangeably with other elements of occultism and witchcraft, and frequently, as mentioned above, draw on possession within the narrative. More accurate depictions of Spiritualism appear in Alejandro Amenábar's *The Others* (2001) and Peter Cornwell's *The Haunting in Connecticut* (2009), though these exist in the background of the primary plot. In another parallel to real life, both films also use grief as the primary emotion within their narrative. It is grief that opens the door between the living and the dead and grief that compels the characters to step through it. How they approach this end, however, does differ considerably between works.

In the case of *The Others*, it is not evident until the final moments of the film that, rather than being haunted, Grace (Nicole Kidman) and her children are the ones who have died and are now haunting their former family home. It is Grace's and the children's unwanted ghostly presence that prompts the family currently in residence to engage with a medium, who conducts a séance to establish contact with each of the deceased throughout the film. The scene in which Grace's daughter Anne (Alakina Mann) takes on the appearance of an old, blind woman is one of the most memorable scenes of the film, whilst also being one of the most prolonged examples of Spiritualism within the narrative. Nicholas (James Bentley), Grace's son, also interacts with a child named Victor (Alexander Vince) at various points in the film. Grace believes Victor to be an imaginary friend, and then a ghost. In fact, Victor is the living child, and it is his psychic abilities that are triggered by the presence of Grace and her children.

As the plot develops, it is inferred that perhaps both of Grace's children are aware that they are no longer living, yet they are both afraid to mention this to their devoutly religious mother and lack the communicative abilities to do so. This may be the reason why each engages with both Victor and the medium, particularly in the dénouement, in which they confront Grace with the truth behind the escalating situation within the home. The children's increasing sense of understanding, particularly after the mysterious return and subsequent disappearance of their father, a WWI soldier who was lost in battle, ties to the subplot, in which communication is happening between the living and the dead.

In this instance, the servants who come to assist with the running of the property have also been drawn in to assist Grace and her children in coming to the full recognition of their death. Having pre-deceased Grace by several decades, the servants are also aware of arrival of Victor and his family. In the final scene of the film, they tell Grace and her children that "others will come" and that sometimes the presence of the living will intrude on their afterlives and sometimes it will not. In this case, there is no suggestion that acceptance of death will be accompanied by a moving on or constitute an ascension into heaven: it is only the grief Grace feels for her actions (it was she who was responsible for the murder of her children and her own subsequent suicide) that is resolved. In keeping with Spiritualist themes, Grace's family is seen at the end of the film inhabiting a parallel dimension in which they continue to live in the home and conduct a form of life. This is not too far removed from the belief that the dead live in a parallel world in which they hold down jobs, marry, and mature. This parallel existence was often read as a "second chance" for those who had died young to live a full life (Morris 2014, 11, 59, 61).

Within the scope of the religious narrative that underpins *The Others*, the home also acts as a site of purgatory, where the dead (presumably) exist in atonement and contemplation (Ibáñez-Rosales and Altemir-Giral 2019, 49). The parallel lives narrative was particularly prominent among Spiritualist circles in relation to the death of small children, which will be discussed in more detail, and can be seen as a response to the acute grief and sense of loss that accompanies the death of an infant. In historical examples focused on spirit communication from children, detailed "proof" was offered, which outlined a continued existence, in a realm relatively consistent with the living world. Within this space, children were afforded care and education, giving them a type of second chance to grow up (Owen and Dallas 1920, 22). So, too, casualties from WWI often fell into a similar narrative category, and there is an abundance of accounts which mention deceased soldiers retaining their sense of identity in the spiritual realm. Here they were afforded the opportunity to continue the lives that war cut short. Such embellishments, while indicative of elements of the grief cycle, might also be understood as remnants of the Victorian preoccupation with romantic death, or as coping mechanisms for family members unable to process the grief of having lost a child so young and under such tragic circumstance.

Comparatively, *The Haunting in Connecticut* is based on the true story of a haunting which was made famous by the involvement of paranormal investigators Ed and Lorraine Warren. Both the cinematic account and the written account (*In a Dark Place*) on which the film is based have been accused of severely embellishing the facts, itself a phenomenon not uncommon to any kind of paranormal or parapsychological investigation. Unlike the written account, the film identifies the primary spirits who are trying to commune with the Campbell family as Spiritualists and uses flashback scenes of mediumship circles to convey this; however, it neither elaborates on the purpose of these circles nor on who the participants were. In this instance, the visions assist only in writing a narrative of the restless dead, bent on causing harm to the living. Increasing tensions within the home and the gradual possession of the eldest son, Matt (Kyle Gallner), lead to the discovery of bodies within the walls of home and the "freeing" of their attached spirits. While clearly being highlighted as conduits for communication, mediums and Spiritualism are coded as gatekeepers, with the ability to allow or to vanquish evil.

In this example, the grief portion of the narrative centers on anticipatory death and is related to Matt and his mother Sara (Virginia Madsen). Suffering from cancer, Matt is in the process of receiving experimental treatment which has compromised his immune system. As his illness escalates, so, too, do his mediumistic abilities and it is suggested that his approaching death allows him to become a conduit for the spirit communication he is receiving. In this instance, Sara's grief is relative to the impending death of her son. Though she has not officially lost Matt, his declining health amplifies her sense of helplessness and she enters phases of denial and anticipatory grief over his loss. Ultimately, Matt is able to leverage his relationship with Spirit to overcome his cancer diagnosis and, after freeing the souls trapped within the home, he undergoes a miraculous recovery. Rather than living his parallel life in another dimension, the updated narrative affords the more secular consolation of a second chance at life in this world.

Whereas *The Haunting in Connecticut* examines one of the real-life accounts of Ed and Lorraine Warren, the Spierig Brothers' *Winchester* draws on the historical legacy and mystery of Sarah Winchester. The film cites that its narrative is "inspired by true events" and presents a loosely based historical account of Sarah Winchester's later life, during the period in which she and her mysterious home were establishing an eccentric identity among San Francisco's elite. It suggests that after the death of both her daughter and husband, Sarah (Helen Mirren) is subsumed by grief. Her inability to resolve the pain of their loss leads her to become engaged with a medium, which triggers the beginning of what will become a life-long obsession with the spirit world.

Over time, Sarah's enduring grief and mental stability is called into question by members of the Winchester Repeating Arms Company's Board of Trustees, who seek to have her assessed by a psychiatrist. It is, of course, their intention that Sarah be found mentally unsound, in which case she will be forced to relinquish her majority ownership in the company. Dr. Eric Price (Jason Clarke) is engaged for this purpose. On sabbatical from practice after the suicide of his wife, Ruby (Laura Brent), Dr. Price is hesitant to take the position. However, his personal decline into alcohol and drug abuse have left him in a considerable amount of debt; therefore, he is ultimately persuaded by a substantial payment for his services. This payment is made under the assumption that Dr. Price will find in favor of the trustees and, as he sets out to the Winchester home, he seems happy to oblige.

Upon entering the home, Dr. Price meets Sarah's niece, Marion (Sarah Snook), who is seeking shelter, along with her son, Henry (Finn Scicluna-O'Prey), after the suicide death of her husband. Dr. Price is only in residence for a few hours before he notices strange occurrences within the home. These are discredited as being tricks of the imagination or the result of his laudanum addiction. As he then begins to assess Sarah, it becomes clear to him that she is completely dedicated to her beliefs, which are that she and her home are conduits for restless spirits who have been killed by the Winchester rifle. By her reasoning, she needs to atone for these deaths by assisting the spirits to find closure in their premature and violent deaths so they can move on. It is also revealed that Dr. Price has been summoned to the home at Sarah's insistence, as she believes that the events surrounding the death of his wife make him sensitive to the spirit world. Firmly entrenched in grief avoidance behaviors, Dr. Price is hostile to such suggestions, although the pair manage to form a mutually respectful accord.

In time, Dr. Price is called upon to confront the ghosts of his own past and, in doing so, has his eyes opened to the spirit world in which Sarah is active. Throughout the film, Dr. Price's own experience of loss (the suicide of his wife) is brought to the fore, with his own emotional processing of the event, and subsequent feelings about his role in it, being integral to assisting Sarah in her attempts to stop a malevolent force which threatens the life of her great-nephew. Sarah and Dr. Price not only reflect the ways in which gender influences the experience of the grief process but become examples of how grief is expressed as either an external or internal state.

In contrast to the film, the limited historical accounts of Sarah Winchester complicate any opportunity to engage with her in a meaningful way. Several authors have attempted to publish accounts of her life, but these are largely cobbled together from the recollections of neighbors, business records, and the occasional sensational newspaper article. Except for Mary Jo Ignoffo's *Captive of the Labyrinth: Sarah L. Winchester Heiress to the Rifle Fortune* (2010), most of these are viewed as fictional, with much of the same paranormal narrative that exists around the Winchester home but have become interchangeable with the story of her life. This issue is evidenced expertly in Joni Tevis's 2014 article, "What Looks Like Mad Disorder: The Sarah Winchester House," which uses the author's experience touring the home to demonstrate the difficulty in discussing Sarah Winchester with any sense of historical certainty. While there is evidence to suggest at least some kind of passing preoccupation with a belief in restless spirits, there are equally accounts which describe her merely as an eccentric widow, disinterested with the world outside of her home or the people dwelling within it (Ignoffo 2010, xix). There is no evidence to suggest that the historical Sarah Winchester felt any specific guilt over the loss of life related to the Winchester rifle and, considering that there were a range of other popular repeaters on the market at the time (Colt and Revolver being the main competition), it is unlikely that she felt any more of an obligation to the public than either of her business rivals (Argiro 2019, 73).

To atone for what it lacks in historical accuracy, the film takes a broad view of the trauma associated with historical, cultural, and national grief, and the how these elements continue to influence present-day society in America. This link between the film and a discourse on national grief (specific to gun violence) has been covered in detail by Thomas Robert Argiro in *Horror Comes Home* (2019) and so will only be mentioned here in passing. What has received less attention is the film's depiction of gender-specific grief, which is both a nuanced discussion on the different responses men and women exhibit relating to the death of a loved one. As such, this element of the plot, and its relationship to mediumship and Spiritualism, will be the focus of the rest of this chapter.

The connection between gender and grief is explored throughout the film in three different relationships. The first of these is the sibling relationship of the Block brothers which, rather than a meditation on familial grief, can be read as a meditation on the parallels between violence and the death of young men in the contemporary world. Even in the afterlife, Ben Block (the spiritual antagonist of the film) remains restless over the death of both his brothers during the Civil War. He seeks revenge on Sarah, whom he holds responsible. It is Ben's malevolent presence within the home that eventually brings Dr. Price and Sarah together as allies, with Ben functioning as their adversary. In this instance, the brothers are symbolic of a more general concept of masculinity, with their grief and rage being a comment on contemporary issues directly related to death among young men.

The parallel narrative addresses spousal grief, which both affects Dr. Price and provides his motivation for visiting the Winchester home. It is also responsible for his lapsed career and general decline into oblivion, as indicated through his alcohol and drug addiction. Unlike Marion, who is stoic and resigned to the death of her husband as well as her status as widow and single parent, Dr. Price's grief is profound and his expression of it is used as a mechanism through which the relationship between gender and spousal grief is discussed. Sarah is also a widow, but unlike Dr. Price or Marion, her grief is utilized differently within the film and represents that the final example of grief.

Sarah's story is illustrative of grief stemming from the loss of a child, which is the primary vehicle through which her motivations for spirit communication and atonement with the spirit world are categorized. It is Sarah's grief over the loss of her daughter that prompts her initial interest in Spiritualism. Of all the dialogues that take place during the film, however, Sarah's daughter is the only figure who does not actively speak with the living, nor is she seen in manifested form. This is intentional and, as will be discussed at the end of the chapter, in her absence, it is Sarah's daughter who speaks most profoundly about the lived experience of parental grief.

In the film, the Winchester mansion is haunted by a cavalcade of spirits, but the narrative focuses primarily on Ben Block (Eamon Farren), a Confederate soldier, bent on the destruction of Sarah, her family, and anyone else who should step into his path. A victim of suicide, Ben represents the idea that, far from being mournful, the deceased can be enraged, and it is this pent-up anger that prevents them from resting. Ben's rage is not directed as his own death, although that is part of it, but is more firmly linked to the death of his siblings. On the surface, emotions of disappointment and rage seem linked to their early deaths. With both Ben and his brothers deprived of the opportunity to live out their lives in any way that might have been fulfilling, one can also see some relationship between this and the death narratives present in the Spiritualist movement. From Sarah's perspective, if she can soothe Ben's anger, he and his brothers will find the opportunity to recommence their lives in the spirit world. Although this does little to detract from the fact that they are dead, to Sarah's logic, it is a form of atonement. When recounting the loss of the Block family to Dr. Price, Sarah makes a point of highlighting that the youngest sibling was only fourteen years old at the time of his death. By contemporary standards, this makes him little more than a child, and certainly someone who died too young and by senseless violence. This element of the Block story is where the film draws on the idea of sibling grief as a lens through which the larger idea of national grief might be explored. This is not only representative of a historical grief (represented in the war time narrative of the film), but rather a comment on contemporary society and the legacy of gun violence and death (particularly among young men) in American culture. Read another way, it offers a unique take on gender identity and the fractious relationship between toxic masculinity and feminism.

Argiro discusses the film as a meditation on gun violence and the national sense of mourning which America experiences annually in response to this aspect of its social identity. From this viewpoint, the expression of grief is a national and historical grief and shame, which encompasses the war dead as well as those killed as a result of various instances of domestic insurgence and daily societal violence. On the surface, this narrative is played out in the exchange between Ben Block, Dr. Price, and Sarah Winchester in their final confrontation in the gun room. On a deeper level, however, it is also a portrait of intimate grief and rage specific to the relationship between gun violence, death, and young men.

Statistically speaking, men are not only the primary perpetrators of gun violence, but they are also the primary victims. In all, 60 percent of male gun-related deaths in America are the result of suicide, compared to 37 percent which are related to murder (Pew 2019). Considering that Ben is the only one of the brothers to be given a comprehensive backstory and that his death is a death by suicide, it is important to consider what this implies about suicide and its relationship to gender and, more broadly, masculinity. One might interpret this as endemic of a culture in which masculinity and masculine norms have been ignored and allowed to fester into a crisis of identity, or as the inevitable consequence of a culture which has long lauded violence as an appropriate response to conflict. In this sense, the film is very much a product of the time of its production, even though it is reflecting an era long-since gone.

Masculinity becomes critical to assess in Ben's response to the death, both because it is framed in the emotion of rage but also because of the relationship of these elements to the larger discourse on Spiritualism. His rage is not merely directed towards the endemic social issues of the unchecked use and distribution of firearms, but one directed specifically at the character of Sarah Winchester. Although she has played no role in the development or distribution of the Winchester rifle, nor in any aspect of the military conflict during which his brothers were killed, in her engagement with mediumship, Sarah represents the rise of feminine influence and feminism on two important fronts. The first is relative to Spiritualism, which at the height of its popularity was one of the few public arenas in which women not only had control of proceedings but were viewed with a level of reverence and respect elevated from what they would encounter in any other area of life. Though male mediums did exist, they were far outnumbered by their female counterparts. Harkening back to the birth of the movement, spirit communication was first discussed by women (the Fox sisters) and for a long time, the mediumistic qualities of women were understood to be superior to those of men, specifically because of the female disposition towards emotional expression. The same emotions which had previously been determined to make women "the weaker sex," and intellectually inferior to men, had suddenly given them agency.

To tip the gender balance even further in the favor of women, Sarah is also the majority shareholder in her company, making her the CEO of operations and the sole person with fiscal decision-making powers. Within the historical narrative of the film, this status was uncommon, and is also at odds with the social expectations of gender at that time. Here, Sarah is read as a challenge to patriarchy and male dominance. Perhaps for these reasons, the Winchester

Repeating Rifle Company board members conveniently view her sensitivity to spirits as an opportunity to declare her incompetent to run the company. These themes can be also overlaid onto contemporary frictions around gender politics in the business world, which have provided fertile ground for extensive discussion on gender and power dynamics, as well as feminism and toxic masculinity.

Even outside of the professional world, the rise of feminism is cited as the main cause for the loss of masculine identities and the subsequent malaise of young men in the West (Whitehead 2019, 25; Harrington 2020, 5–6). Unlike gun violence, this is not a social problem limited to America. Britain, Australia, New Zealand, and several countries across Europe report young men of fifteen to twenty-five (the same age as Ben and his brothers in the film) as being the highest demographic to be victims of suicide (Whitehead 2019, 62–63; Chandler 2019, 1351). In the face of some staggering statistics, cultural discourse has been quick to turn its confusion and rage directly towards the feminist movement, blaming the emancipation of women from their traditional roles of domesticity and the fracturing of the family unit as primary factors in the loss of the masculine identity. This loss has, in turn, led to the fracturing of the male psyche, depression, frustration, and finally, higher suicide rates. Reading Ben's narrative in this way then, it is hardly surprising that Sarah is the target for his rage (which is really an expression of grief over a lost sense of male identity) or that he possesses her great-nephew in several of his attempts to torment and kill her. In Ben's final scene of the film, he is dispatched by the bullet which also killed Dr. Price for a short period of time (and was refurbished as a keepsake). Ironically, the bullet, originally fired by a woman, ultimately takes the life of two men.

The counter-narrative to Ben's rage, and another example of the male response to grief, is seen in Dr. Price and his battle over the loss of his wife.

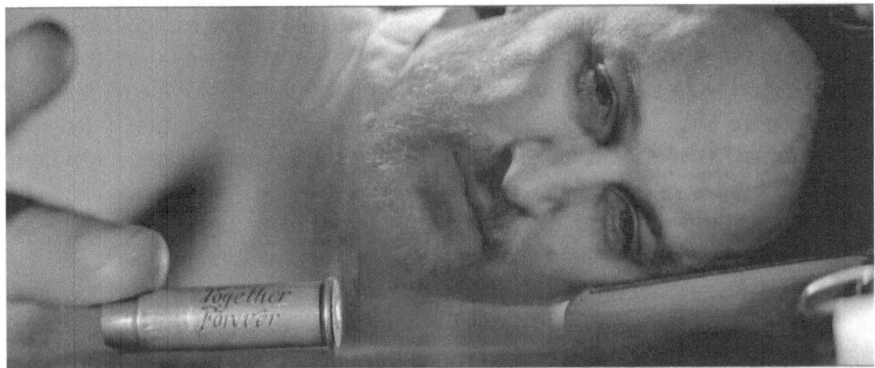

Figure 8.1 Dr. Eric Price (Jason Clarke) with the keepsake bullet.
Source: Winchester (2018)

In general, the expression of grief and the trajectory of mourning will vary greatly depending on the emotional disposition of the bereaved and their relationship to the deceased. Nonetheless, studies largely agree that men and women grieve quite differently. This is most evident when viewed from a social perspective and relates to expectations around gendered behaviors. Women are more inherently predisposed to sharing their grief, through public expression and the clear display of emotions. They tend to maintain close relationships (often with other women) outside of the home, giving them an alternative source of support and allowing a more varied support system throughout the grieving process.

In contrast, men have been encouraged to conceal their grief. This ties to the same ideas of masculinity that are responsible for the difficult dynamic of rage and grief discussed above. Repression of emotions can have a long-lasting psychological impact, and these are often channeled through relationships, particularly in a domestic setting. Historically, the attitude about men and emotion might best be illustrated in the "stiff upper lip" culture synonymous with the British Empire, or the "real mean don't cry" epithet that abounds throughout America and the Western world more broadly (Walter 1999, 134; Iwamoto et al. 2018, 1874). In these cultural settings, if it is discussed at all, grief discourse occurs fleetingly and out of the public eye. Many men do not openly express profound loss, and the shedding of tears is frowned upon at best and derided as weakness (signaling a lack of virility) at worst. As an almost ingrained or inherited response to this, men are more disposed to denying the grief experience entirely. Again, this reflects more enduring social ideas about maleness and masculinity. Curiously, and as Tony Walter highlights in his study of bereavement narratives and culture, the one relationship in which men are thought to grieve harder, more publicly, and for longer than women, is when they experience the death of a spouse (1999, 173). Even in social settings, spousal (where the man is the bereaved) grief is treated differently, and emotional responses tend to be treated with more compassion and understanding, if only by a small margin.

Walter's findings suggest that this response is directly linked to the fact that, in a spousal relationship, the wife generally becomes the emotional support system for her male partner, as well as the primary caregiver. Thus, the death of a wife is a more profoundly isolating experience for a husband, who already has fewer close, interpersonal relationships and, consequently, has difficulty in re-engaging with himself as a single man. Not only does he have to contend with the emotional weight of the loss, but as Walter suggests, resume responsibility for his domestic care, and the day-to-day scheduling of life. When children are an added element, the process is further complicated. Walter's research concludes that men battling with the loss of a wife are more likely to fall into depression, despondency, and self-harm (1999,

174). In some instances, the acute isolation will also prompt a relatively quick remarriage, which restores many of the emotional and physical needs left unattended but does not allow for an adequate grief period. Incidences where self-harm is present do not only refer to suicide and physical injury but include the abuse of alcohol and drugs or the ignoring of general health and well-being. Addictive behavior and a reliance on psychotropic drugs is where the audience finds Dr. Price when he is introduced in the narrative. As discussed above, this is the result of the recent loss of his wife. It is also important to add that Dr. Price was injured (and died for three minutes) during the event, having been mistakenly shot by his wife, who then turned the gun on herself. Nonetheless, Dr. Price was subsequential revived and recovered from the wound to his chest. Throughout the film, he is seen gesturing to the scar, which is above his heart, a gesture which also signals to his enduring guilt and grief over the event. This repeated gesture is also indicative of a grief which has been heavily internalized. Part of this internalization is relative to an inability to seek the adequate emotional support he requires to process the loss, but there is also a longing for conversation. Specifically, Dr. Price laments that he did not listen to his wife and consider an alternate treatment for her mental illness. In the wake of her death, he longs for the final opportunity to express the love he had for her but failed to show in his role as a husband, as well as a treating physician.

More than the other characters within the film, the relationship between Dr. Price and Ruby is one of specific, reciprocal conversation. Intermingled with their respective experience of grief is an almost overwhelming sense of guilt. While Sarah does interact with a range of spirits, taking direction and commencing construction on a physical room into which they can manifest, these are dialogues which are built around the death narrative rather than a pre-existing relationship. In the case of Ruby, however, the goal of her restless spirit is not simply to manifest into a room within the Winchester mansion, but to seek closure on her own grief about the incident surrounding her death and the near death of her husband. When she ultimately has the chance to replay the moment of her death, there is no suggestion that she had intended to injure her husband or commit a murder-suicide.

Although Ruby also died by suicide, unlike Ben Block, her torment is driven by a need for forgiveness and redemption. Not only does she need to forgive herself for her own actions, but for her husband to forgive himself, so that both are able to move on. Compared to Ben, Ruby's spirit is less intrusive, staying confined to the Garden Room until Dr. Price is prepared to engage with her in her spirit form. When she appears to Dr. Price, he is forced to accept the truth of his own mediumistic abilities. These are more pronounced than those which Sarah has displayed previously. Whereas Sarah has only been able to correspond through automatic writing, Dr. Price is both clairvoyant and clairaudient, meaning he can see and hear the dead. These abilities enhance the exchange between husband and wife and in doing so, encapsulate the very heart of the aims of mediumship. In their brief time together, the couple is provided a final opportunity to reconcile and forgive. As she reenacts the accidental "murder" of her husband, Ruby simultaneously releases them both from their grief, explaining that she needs him to forgive himself so that she can forgive herself and move on. Confirming that she will always love him while also affirming her continued presence (albeit in spirit form), Ruby provides Dr. Price with the knowledge he needs about the legitimacy of the spirit world, and thus substantiates Sarah's claims. Reaching this moment of truth assures that Dr. Price is able to drive Ben Block from the Winchester home; likewise, it releases Dr. Price from mourning and allows him to move forward. In the final scenes of the film, Dr. Price watches as the Garden Room, no longer of use, is disassembled. This is a fitting metaphor for his journey through to the other side of his grief. As he leaves the space, he confirms to Ruby that he will always miss her, and yet there is the sense that he is ready to return to the world of the living, to his previous career, and perhaps to another relationship.

Having lost her husband, Sarah Winchester is like Dr. Price but rather than focusing on her spouse, Sarah's grief narrative is primarily directed towards the loss of her infant daughter, Annie. In taking this approach, the film highlights another of the gender differences which exist between men and women when it comes to death, mourning, and the process of grief.

In the same study in which he concluded that the death of a spouse is most keenly felt by men, Tony Walter also concludes that for women, the death of a child is generally the most difficult loss to overcome (1999, 174–176). This does not suggest that fathers fail to love their children, or that they do not grieve for them for long and intense periods, any more than the previous findings suggest that wives do not suffer profound grief after the loss of a husband. Instead, Walter's study found that the narrative of child loss is different in the lives of mothers than it is in the lives of fathers. While part of this is tied to social ideas around femininity and the importance of motherhood as a rite of passage, this response is also likely related to the fact that it is women who carry a child through the gestational period, and give birth to it from their own bodies, so when it is lost, particularly when the child is an infant, the sorrow is felt on a physical as well as an emotional level. Much like the internalized experience of carrying the child, the burden of grief related to its death is also internalized by many women. In this film, a similar type of internalized loss is expressed through the physical and tangible absence of the child. In relation to mediumship, one must consider the fact that the core of the practice, the channeling of the message, also takes place internally. Bodies become the physical representation of the conduit between realms, with their internal energy accommodating the process of conversation (Gutierrez 2008, 310). When viewed in relation to Sara's grief, viewers see that as a means of negotiating her internal unrest she once again employs her body as a vessel, though in this case it is to provide care to restless spirits rather than her child.

Communication with children was one of the more common elements of mediumship during the era in which the film is set, and the same is true of historical records more broadly. Although neither the medium nor the sitter is ever able to dictate or guarantee who they bring through, an abundance of accounts exist that are focused on the reunion between parents and their children. Outside of séance notes and written accounts of children appearing in both demonstrations of physical mediumship and during platform readings, there was also a sub-section of literature published which focused explicitly on accounts of children who had passed on to the spirit world. G. Vale Owen's 1920 book *The Nurseries of Heaven* is one example and delivers a series of essays devoted to the topic. The intent of the text, which features accounts from both men and women, mediums and sitters, is to provide parents who are grieving the loss of a child some solace from accounts of others who have received messages and visitations from children who have crossed over. The enduring narrative expressed through the various essays, which cover both the philosophy and practice of Spiritualism and mediumship, is one that focuses on children "growing to maturity on the other side" (Owen 1920, 32). The book provides a clear image of children who are in the care of other deceased loved ones. They are raised and receive an education, much as they would in the living world, and although they frequently express sadness or confusion about the absence of a parent, they are unfailingly happy.

Although focused on the experience of mediumship more broadly, the account of Anne Manning Robbins in her book *Both Sides of the Veil* (1909) details a series of interactions in which the medium for whom she was transcribing sessions passed messages through to her which concerned the ongoing wellbeing of a deceased nephew. While Robbins does not detail how the child died or to which of her siblings her nephew belonged, she recounts the joy and peace attained by all members of her family upon hearing that the child was not only in the care of other departed loved ones but that he was aware of their enduring love for him. Unlike the accounts in *The Nurseries of Heaven*, Robbins presents a narrative of multiple contacts, during which the child ages and is able to demonstrate a more complete knowledge of his role in spirit. Relaying messages through the medium for Robbins to pass on to other members of the family, the child discussed aunts and uncles who have passed on, whilst also describing how happy he is to be in heaven. At several points, the child provides details about older family members, some of whom had died before his birth, which act as confirmation of the medium's validity.

Celebrity Spiritualists Sir Arthur Conan Doyle and Oliver Lodge also wrote extensively on encounters that they had with their own deceased children via the services of a medium. Both men were also mercilessly pilloried for sharing these accounts as much as they were for their beliefs in and involvement with the Spiritualist movement. Doyle lectured and wrote at length about the messages he received from his son, brother, and mother-in-law. Detailed accounts on all these experiences are present in his 1921 book *The Wanderings of a Spiritualist*, along with detailed accounts of the emotional response he had when communicating with his son. In contrast, Lodge penned *Raymond: Or Life After Death* (1916), which is an extensive account of several discussions he purported to have with his son, who died during WWI. While the book was a phenomenal success among Spiritualists, it was savaged by the press and literary critics, who called it "preposterous" (Wingett 2016, 51–52). That neither seemed particularly concerned about the criticism and scorn they faced, particularly in the immediate aftermath of both these publications, is indicative of the hold which spirit communication and the hope of confirmation of existence after death has on human emotions.

Unlike these examples, Sarah Winchester does not directly interact with her daughter during the film, nor does she confirm ever having received a spirit contact from her. During her first interview with Dr. Price however, it is made explicit that her initial interest in Spiritualism and mediumship was a consequence of the infant's death. Her actions thereafter are indicative of a profound and universal sense of grief, one that can only be completely understood by a parent who has suffered the loss of a child. In this sense, the visual absence of Annie from the narrative makes the clear statement that the loss of a child is a feeling ever present, one which pervades every aspect of a parent's life. This is as evident in Sarah's spiritual life as it is in her outward presentation. Throughout the film, she maintains full mourning regalia, indicating that she lives in a state of perpetual grief for the loss of her family, which is personified in her reminiscences of Annie. Through the eyes of Dr. Price, viewers also witness the physical mourning mementos which Sarah maintains as a link to the memory of her daughter. Spying on her one evening, Dr. Price observes Sarah remove a lock of hair and a photograph from a hidden safe in her private room. These she caresses gently, speaking to Annie as she is comforting herself. The interlude is used to bring together the various representations of grief within the film, as viewers witness Ben Block's rageful spirit enter the film, manifesting in front of Dr. Price's eyes and awakening him further to his own latent abilities. It is only after this moment that three different experiences of death and grief begin to merge, thus constructing the stage for the final reconciliation between the dead and the bereaved.

As an extension of Sarah and her beliefs, the Winchester home is also a primary, if understated, character within the film which will be touched upon briefly here as a physical representation of the internalized nature of parental grief. As Cleaver Patterson writes in the introduction to his study of the function and purpose of the home in horror films, "a house makes horror real" (2019, 3). While Patterson may be thinking of horror specifically in the terms of genre, the same can be true for metaphorical horror—such as that personified in the death of a child. In response to grief then, the home, with all its memories, smells, and familiarities stands to make the pain of loss very real. As one moves through the domestic space, memories of the deceased pervade every room. Constantly, one is reminded of what was but is no longer. This is the case in *Winchester*.

Although, the Winchester mansion is opulent and architecturally captivating from an aesthetic perspective, it is the function the house serves in a symbolic sense which is important to the relationship it has with the themes of the text and the audience. Specifically, the Winchester home is the physical conduit (whereas Sarah is the emotional tether) between realms. In her re-creation of rooms, the designs of which are dictated to her via her spiritual correspondence, Sarah provides a transit point, a liminal space where the dead can step back into the realm of the living. For viewers, this is the visual representation which would be absent in real life experiences of mental mediumship (which would be less compelling for a lay audience with no background on the realities of the practice). In most cases, the rooms are only a brief stopping ground, where the spirit is allowed a moment to express unresolved emotions and seek clarity about what has happened. After death has been accepted and Sarah has atoned for the role of the Winchester rifle within that death, the spirit is able to move on from the purgatorial existence it had been inhabiting to a more final state of energetic rest. Although this is at odds with the purpose of most mediumistic work, within this particular narrative, the rooms, like the home, are the tangible representation of an emotional and spiritual experience. In its almost labyrinthine layout and owing to its sheer scale, the home itself is also the physical representation of the internalized experience of the main characters' own experience of grief.

Grief, particularly when related to the loss of a loved one, is often described an isolating experience. Depending on the longevity and intensity with which one goes through the process, it can be easy to find oneself isolated and ostracized from the world. For this very reason, the family home becomes center stage for the grief and mourning rituals which are interacted as part of the coming to terms with the departure of a loved one. Home is a safe haven, in which raw emotions can be expressed, but can also be a prison, in the sense that the ever-present memory of the deceased within the home amplifies their absence. For the bereaved, there is always a risk that these familiar and once shared intimate spaces form the stage for a rumination narrative to take place, the constant reminders of the loss serving only to separate them further from those outside the home. In the case of the Winchester home, the physical structure acts very much as a mechanism which keeps people out, thus further isolating Sarah, and later Marion and her son, in a purgatorial state of loss.

Winchester is set in the days prior to the San Francisco earthquake of 1906, and a little more than a decade prior to WWI and the Spanish flu. In 2021, as the world emerges from another chapter of political instability and the aftermath of COVID-19, we are forced, once more, to consider the limitations of our own mortality on a global scale, and to confront the conflicting feelings which society and culture have conditioned us to have about death, dying, and spirituality. The urgency with which these themes are being revisited is evident not only in the rise of alternative spiritualities, but in the cultural mainstream where television documentaries like *Life After Death* (Netflix, 2021), and to some degree, reboots such as *Unsolved Mysteries* (2019–present) investigate the multiplicity of beliefs which exist around the dying and the afterlife. Rather than taking the same kind of tongue-in-cheek approach that would have been expected a decade ago, such investigations are again willing to entertain the possibility that the medical scientists of the present do not know all that there is to know about the continuance of the soul, or life after death. But then, perhaps a global pandemic has only amplified the fact that humans finally are emerging (through necessity) from a long denial of death and grief. Of course, horror films have been touching on these themes for decades. The inescapably tragedy of the phenomenally high death toll which greets us nightly on the news and social media reminds us of the fact that one day, we too will join the legions of the dead. In knowing this, we are no longer interpreting the dead through the self, but putting ourselves in the role of the dead. Unsurprisingly, this changes our concept of spiritual sentience. Although we are yet to return to a time where the discussion of afterlife consciousness is greeted with scientific, religious, or academic openness, what films like *Winchester* demonstrate is that there is an enduring fascination among the living with the idea of communing with the spirit world. In taking a historical approach, they also serve as a timely reminder that the past always informs the present.

BIBLIOGRAPHY

Argiro, Thomas Robert. 2019. "Ghost Karma: The Winchester House as Spiritual Reparation." In *Horror Comes Home: Essays on Hauntings, Possessions and Other Domestic Terror in Cinema*, edited by Cynthia J. Miller and A. Bowdoin Van Riper, 70–82. Jefferson, NC: McFarland.

Chandler, Amy. 2019. "Boys Don't Cry? Critical Phenomenology, Self-Harm and Suicide." *Sociological Review* 67 (6): 1350–66.

Doyle, Sir Arthur Conan. 1921. *The Wanderings of a Spiritualist*. London: Hodder and Stoughton.

Gramlich, John. 2019. "What the Data Says about Guns Deaths in the U.S." *Pew Research*. August 19, 2019. https://www.pewresearch.org/fact-tank/2019/08/16/what-the-data-says-about-gun-deaths-in-the-u-s/.

Gutierrez, Cathy. 2008. "Deadly Dates: Bodies and Sex in Spiritualist Heavens." In *Hidden Intercourse: Eros and Sexuality in the History of Western Esotericism*, edited by Wouter J. Hanegraaff and Jeffrey Krippal, 309–32. Leiden: Brill.

Harrington, Carol. 2020. "What is 'Toxic Masculinity' and Why Does It Matter?" *Men and Masculinities* (20) 10: 1–8.

Ibáñez-Rosales, Ismael, and Anabel Altemir-Giral. 2019. "This House is Ours: Haunting the Self in Alejandro Amenábar's *The Others*." In *Horror Comes Home: Essays on Hauntings, Possessions and Other Domestic Terror in Cinema*, edited by Cynthia J. Miller and A. Bowdoin Van Riper, 42–53. Jefferson, NC: McFarland.

Ignoffo, Mary Jo. 2010. *Captive of the Labyrinth: Sarah L. Winchester, Heiress to the Rifle Fortune*. Columbia, MO: University of Missouri Press.

Iwamoto, Derek K., Jennifer Brady, Aylin Kaya, and Athena Park. 2018. "Masculinity and Depression: A Longitudinal Investigation of Multidimensional Masculine Norms Among College Men." *American Journal of Men's Health* 12 (6): 1873–81.

Lodge, Oliver. 1916. *Raymond: or Life and Death*. New York: George H. Doran Company.

Morris, Dee. 2014. *Boston in the Golden Age of Spiritualism: Séances, Mediums, & Immortality*. Charleston, SC: The History Press.

Owen, G. Vale, and H. A. Dallas. 1920. *The Nurseries of Heaven: A Series of Essays by Various Writers Concerning the Future Life of Children, with Experiences of the Manifestation After Death*. London: Keegan & Paul, Trench, Trubner & Co., Ltd.

Patterson, Cleaver. 2020. *Don't Go Upstairs: A Room-by-Room Tour of the House in Horror Movies*. Jefferson, NC: McFarland.

Pearsall, Ronald. 1972. *The Table-Rappers*. London: Michael Joseph Ltd.

Reed, Carmen, Al Snedeker, and Ray Garton. 2014. *In A Dark Place*. New York: Graymalkin Media.

Robbins, Anne Manning. 1909. *Both Sides of the Veil: A Personal Experience*. Boston, MA: Sherman, French & Company.

Spierig, Michael and Peter Spierig. 2018. *Winchester*. DVD. United States: CBS Films/Blacklab Entertainment/ Imagine Design Networks.

Tevis, Joni. 2014. "What Looks Like Mad Disorder: The Sarah Winchester House." *Ecotone* 9 (2): 12–24.

Walter, Tony. 1999. *On Bereavement: The Culture of Grief*. Philadelphia, PA: Open University Press.

Whitehead, Stephen M. 2019. *Toxic Masculinity: Curing the Virus: Making Men, Smarter, Healthier, Safer*. London: AG Books.

Wingett, Matt. 2016. *Conan Doyle and the Mysterious World of Light 1887–1920*. Carlton, Victoria: Life Is Amazing.

NOTES

1. While not all Spiritualists would necessarily equate their beliefs with any form of Christianity or Judaism, the tenants of the Spiritualist doctrine still generally cite God as the omnipotent creator the universe. Among early Spiritualist groups it was also not uncommon to find members who were active members of the Christian faith community. This duality among members might be attributed to the adaptable framework under which Spiritualism operates.

2. Historically speaking, the same theme has always been a central part of the Spiritualist agenda. Although spirit communication was rising in prominence throughout the last few decades of the 1800s, Spiritualism has seen its most pronounced boom-times in the aftermath war (the Civil War in America and WWI globally) and global tragedy Perhaps the current pandemic is behind the public interest which impelled Netflix to release their documentary on the subject.

PART IV
Loss and the Known World
Grief and Annihilation

Chapter 9

"No One Will Miss It"

Lars Von Trier's Antichrist *(2009) and* Melancholia *(2011) and the World-Without-Us*

Michael Brown

ANTI-PHILOSOPHY AND THE "LOSS OF WORLD"

Lars von Trier's *Antichrist* (2009) and *Melancholia* (2011), the first two entries in his "Depression Trilogy," are in many ways complementary works that explore the complexity of grieving and loss through plot, performance styles, and carefully crafted aesthetic elements. In the former, a mother loses her infant son under tragic circumstances, prompting an overwhelming display of grief, guilt, and anxiety that becomes internalized and entwined with the trenchant mythology of the "evil" woman. As she and her psychoanalyst husband retreat to a cabin in the woods they call "Eden" to face their trauma, the film shifts into a horror narrative in which "nature" itself is revealed as a malevolent force. In the latter, a young bride's battle with depression seems to correspond with the imminent collision of the Earth with a rogue planet called Melancholia. In both films, the personal turmoil of their protagonists, their anxiety and depression respectively, is intimately bound to a confrontation with a "nature" or "world" that is seemingly hostile, or worse, indifferent to human concerns. Together, the films can be read as an extended argument against human exceptionalism. As such, both films are products of von Trier's continuing project of provocation in which his life and work is marked by an oppositional aesthetic aimed at the cultural, social, and political inheritance of humanist philosophies, most especially the post-Enlightenment privileging of reason and the individual subject. In this regard, the films share an affinity with contemporary philosopher Eugene Thacker's preoccupation with the "horror of philosophy" and its attendant motif of the "world-without-us." Taking a decidedly anti-anthropocentric view, Thacker's work challenges the capacity of human beings to ever comprehend the world, which he finds evidence for in supernatural horror's willingness to engage with and speculate on a "world" beyond our knowing. Shadowed by the growing concern over climate change, environmental collapse, and the fear of extinction, a radical rethinking of human-centric views is occasioned in both von Trier's films and contemporary philosophy. What emerges is the unsettling thought that the "world," whether conceived of as "nature" in *Antichrist* or "planet" in *Melancholia* is not "for us." As *Melancholia*'s title suggests, the film reflects an inability to perform the work of mourning, looking, as it does, toward a future loss in which all trace of the human is absent. By reading von Trier's *Antichrist* and *Melancholia* in concert with Thacker's speculative world-without-us, I will demonstrate how grief, mourning, and depression are vital constitutive elements of the films' horror and disaster narratives, confronting us with a powerful cinematic realization of our loss of "world."

Von Trier's mantle as *provocateur* in his formal experimentation (e.g., explicit subject matter, moral baiting, and controversial public statements) can be effectively understood as a sustained project of engagement with and interrogation of the intellectual and cultural inheritance of humanism. For Thomas Elsaesser, von Trier is a "thinker in cinema," using the language of cinema to conduct "thought experiments" (2016, 309). However, one must be mindful of the deep skepticism of von Trier's approach. Fellow Dane, Peter Schepelern, situates von Trier within a long, idiosyncratic Danish tradition of Cultural Liberalism which deploys mockery, sarcasm, and ridicule as "intellectual protest" against "conventional humanistic values" (2014). Consequently, Robert Sinnerbrink insists that von Trier's films be seen as "a series of experiments in 'anti-philosophy'" (2016, 95). He argues that:

> Anti-philosophy can be taken here in two senses, namely using philosophical ideas and themes "against" philosophy in its more traditional or received Enlightenment sense (philosophy as the highest expression of Enlightenment ideals of reason); and as a form of cinematic critique proceeding via negativistic means (by way of aesthetic expression and the evocation of negative or dissonant forms of cognitive experience). (2016, 101)

One way in which von Trier has implemented this oppositional tactic in his films is by having his characters personify a form of anti-Enlightenment through a metaphorical blindness. In his earliest films, which make up the

"Europa trilogy," it is his male protagonists, through their own naivety and idealism, who are ultimately responsible for destruction and mayhem. Hypnosis, a common metaphor in these films, encapsulates the characters' "lack of self-insight" (Bunch 2010). In his more recent films, especially the two I will be discussing, *Antichrist* and *Melancholia*, male characters continue to embody "blind" systems of rationalism or idealism; however, it is now female "seers" who bare the destruction and suffering. More generally, von Trier manipulates canonical film genres, such as melodrama, musicals, or *film noir*, with the intent of unmasking how "habitual forms of spectatorship" correspond with the "docile acceptance of social and historical reality" (Koutsourakis 2013, 29–30). This perceived docility is thrown into a state of rupture by von Trier's most identifiable trait as *provocateur*, his affective excess that circumvents measured response from audiences in much the same way that Antonin Artaud sought to do with his "theatre of cruelty" (1958, 79).

If the dangers of blind rationalism and the negativistic critique of the ideals of reason and humanism are emblematic of von Trier's work, then the same could be said of the horror genre. The contemporary American philosopher Eugene Thacker is equally skeptical of the self-aggrandizement of human reason. Throughout *In the Dust of This Planet* (2011), and the subsequent volumes, *Starry Speculative Corpse* (2015) and *Tentacles Longer Than Night* (2015), Thacker argues that the limits, perhaps even futility, of philosophy find their expression in the horror genre, a contention he emphasizes in the conceit of a "horror of philosophy," whereby the assumed privilege of philosophy is inverted. For Thacker, the horror of philosophy is "the isolation of those moments in which philosophy reveals its own limitations and constraints, moments in which thinking enigmatically confronts the horizon of its own possibility—the thought of the unthinkable" (2011, 2). The motif Thacker chooses to illustrate his point, the "unthinkable world," is directly borrowed from the horror genre with its fascination with the unknown, or *unknowable*. The world as both human and non-human has posed an irresolvable challenge for the tradition of Western thought, a concern which has dominated horror in a plethora of "monstrous" encounters with the unknown. In distilling the mythological, theological, and existential as the predominant forms by which we have sought to orientate ourselves within the world, Thacker concludes that "all of these interpretive lenses—mythological, theological, existential—have as their most basic presupposition a view of the world as a human-centric world, as a world 'for us' as human beings, living in human cultures, governed by human values" (2011, 4). In contrast, horror problematizes this anthropocentrism.

The suspicion that the world is not "for us" is explored, as I will show, through *Antichrist*'s "horror" of nature and *Melancholia*'s "disaster" of human finitude. Shadowing both films is contemporary ecological discourse and environmental anxiety. The "revenge-of-nature" trope has featured in both horror and disaster films for some time (e.g., Alfred Hitchcock's *The Birds* [1963], Colin Eggleston's *The Long Weekend* [1978], and Roland Emmerich's *The Day After Tomorrow* [2004]) (Wells 2000, 115). More recently, ecocriticism and debates around the "Anthropocene," the so-called "Age of Man" that recognizes the geological scale of the human impact on the environment, has informed a number of more nuanced theoretical frameworks within the field of horror such as "eco-horror," "ecoGothic," "monstrous nature," or "plant horror" (Foy 2010, 167–88; Smith and Hughes 2013; Murray and Heumann 2016; Keetley and Tenga 2016). Eco-horror films such as Carter Smith's *The Ruins* (2008) and M. Night Shyamalan's *The Happening* (2008) explicitly engage with ecological anxiety, whilst art-house films such as Alfonso Cuarón's *Gravity* (2013), Jeff Nichols' *Take Shelter* (2011), and Terrence Malick's *The Tree of Life* (2011) open themselves up to the cosmic. Perhaps not surprisingly, these anxieties are tinged with a sense of pathos occasioned by a psycho-ecological decentering of human primacy.

In both *Antichrist* and *Melancholia,* the battle of the central protagonists with anxiety and depression respectively, constitute a "loss of world." Whilst the lives of both characters are embroiled in personal emotional turmoil, for von Trier, characters function as more than individuals, they articulate a way of being in the world. In the field of trauma studies, trauma has been linked to the loss of what is referred to as the "assumptive world," that is the assumptions and beliefs that are foundational to a person's sense of reality. Following the introduction of this idea by C. M. Parkes, psychologist Ronnie Janoff-Bulman has suggested that traumatic events disrupt or shatter the assumptive world by challenging three basic human assumptions: the world is benevolent, the world is meaningful, and the self is worthy (1992, 6).[1] The collapse of these assumptions can be located within both *Antichrist* and *Melancholia,* whether it be in the encounter with a malevolent landscape, the collision with a rogue planet, the disintegration of humanist values, or the collapse into the personal hells of anxiety and depression. The conflation of the personal with the planetary in both films registers, rather than a simply psychological reading as some have presumed, a shift from the "human being" towards what Karl Marx once referred to as "species being" (Wartenberg 1982, 77–95).

The problem of the assumptive world posed in each film is really that of our concept of the "world" and the attendant belief that it exists "for us." For Thacker, the need for revision in our comprehension of "world" is aided by a new vocabulary. The human world, then, is the *world-for-us*, or simply *World*. The *world-in-itself*, conversely, is the elusive world around us, observable as physical phenomena, as climate, weather patterns, geology and so forth, the world as object, the *Earth*, which reveals itself to us only incompletely through the collation of scientific data and sense impressions. Inevitably, our contact with the *world-in-itself* cannot help but become the *world-for-us*, since it is we who are experiencing and interpreting it. Acknowledging this limit point, Thacker introduces the *world-without-us*, a "spectral and speculative world" defined by our inability to think it, that resides in the "very fissures, lapses and lacunae" between the *world-for-us* and the *world-in-itself*. The *world-without-us*, or *Planet*, implies a scale beyond the terrestrial, the *cosmological*, and can only exist as a "negative concept, simply that which remains 'after' the human [. . .] as impersonal and anonymous" (2011, 8, 7). The human and other-than-human entanglements that are the locus of much of the horror genre, then, can be understood as a "non-philosophical" exemplary of a radical non-anthropocentric move. It is these "fissures" that von Trier perhaps envisages when he declares that the true subject of his films is "the clash between nature and the mind" (Lumholdt 2003, 105). The encounter with the other-than-human world in von Trier's films is one that refuses the consoling fantasies of the world-for-us, producing horror as the "grief," "pain," and "despair" of *Antichrist*'s chapter titles (as well as the fictional constellation of the "Three Beggars") and the world-ending depression of *Melancholia*.

ANTICHRIST: "NATURE IS SATAN'S CHURCH"

Lars von Trier's *Antichrist* opens with a highly stylized reimagining of the Judeo-Christian allegory of "The Fall"—Adam and Eve's expulsion from the Garden of Eden after committing original sin. Here, an archetypal "He" (Willem Dafoe) and "She" (Charlotte Gainsbourg), as they are referred to in the credits, are in the midst of passionate lovemaking when, seemingly unbeknownst to them, their infant son Nic (Storm Acheche Sahlstrøm) escapes his cot and, drawn to an open window, falls to a tragic death in the winter snow below. Thus, the original sin becomes an originary trauma, infusing the primal scene with death and grief. She and He retreat to the seclusion of their cabin in the woods, which they call "Eden," to recover from the excruciating loss and trauma in the wake of this fatal accident. Before long, however, the return to the wilderness proves less than therapeutic when they confront a monstrous nature.

Initially, She is hospitalized with "atypical grief." Impatient with the progress of her recovery, He dismisses the advice of her doctor and takes over as therapist. As he is informing his wife of his intentions to withdraw her from hospital, the camera slowly zooms in on a bedside vase. As Amy Simmons points out, "[r]ather than capturing the cheerful blossoms, the camera closes in on the flower stems, submerged in their murky water, swirling with dead plant tissue and micro-organisms" (2015, 32). The soundtrack's indistinct noises gradually amplify, as if we too are about to be plunged into this stygian, hidden world. Retiring to their home, She's grief intensifies as she stops her medication and surrenders to the care of her husband. Becoming increasingly volatile, She is beset by episodes of panic, registered in bodily terms, through acts of self-violence, frantic sexual encounters, or a litany of physical symptoms—"dizzy spells, dry mouth, distorted hearing, trembling, heavy breathing, fast pulse, nausea"—ascribed to her anxiety by her husband. Intent on pinpointing the source of her fear, his psychotherapy exercises coax her into identifying "the woods," most especially those around their cabin "Eden." It was there that She had spent her final summer with Nic whilst writing her thesis on "gynocide," the violent persecution of women during the period of the witch-hunts.

The woods as a setting for unease and dread has a long history in human imagination. For Julian Hanich, the fear of the woods goes back "at least to the German fairy tales of the Brothers Grimm" (2011, 175). A recognizable trope throughout horror fiction and cinema, the forest as a landscape of fear is bound up with age-old, at least in Western thought, dualistic thinking that forever positions humans as outside and separate from nature, so that forests are the antithesis of civilization or the human-made world. Elizabeth Parker has posited that this divide is a direct consequence of the establishment of communities: "Human settlement has necessarily involved the clearing, taming, and cultivation of this landscape. The first thing that settlers do is to construct boundaries—we demarcate territory, we name and map the land, and we create firm distinctions between the 'inside' and the 'outside'" (2018, 277).

The transgression of boundaries and borders is habitually emphasized within horror's tropes, iconography, and settings to signal an ambivalence toward these conceptual categories (Langford 2005, 158). This is true of so-called cabin in the woods narratives which both spatialize and allegorize this anxiety over "nature," such that the "cabin and the surrounding wilderness gain a malevolent agency through their almost sentient role" (Grant 2014, 5). The intrusion of nature is often violently embodied within human characters via the ascendancy of "animalistic" traits. *Antichrist*'s strategy in this regard is to problematize the Cartesian dualisms manifest in the figure of She.

Tellingly, the imagined sovereignty over the woods is signaled in the naming of their cabin "Eden," reducing the forest to a "garden" for their use and enjoyment. As Magdalena Zolkos perceptibly notes, the Biblical "paradise" is etymologically derived from the Greek *paradeisos,* meaning "'the enclosure of nature,' or 'garden [park] surrounded by walls'" (2011, 182). Despite He's assurance in the "enclosure of nature," both physically and philosophically by human reason, *Antichrist* shows these boundaries as punctured and insupportable. Importantly, for Zolkos, this porousness "at the ontological level, suggests profound incongruities and 'contaminations' of the categories at hand, and, at the political level, problematizes any strict separation between the human and the other-than-human subjects" (2011, 183). Non-human subjects are afforded agency within the film, as will be seen, by means of a manipulation of cinematic language that disrupts the complacency of nature imagery.

Despite She's assertion that the woods are for her "the worst place," her husband insists that the solution to her grief and anxiety is a form of "exposure therapy," a cognitive therapy technique whereby patients are exposed incrementally to their worst fear in the hope of a psychological breakthrough. On the back of his assumed mastery of the natural order, He actively encourages She to identify with the woodlands. This injunction first occurs on the train journey to their cabin getaway. Initiating one of his "exercises," he prompts her to mentally transport herself to the woods. She's dreamlike sequence is captured in extreme slow motion and a bleached, blue-silvery palette, over which She whispers: "I'm at the bridge. It's evening. Almost no birds can be heard. The water is running without a sound. Darkness comes early down here." Notably, our entry to this space is presented through her eyes, an interior landscape represented by a transgression of boundaries. Part visualization but also part recollection, this exercise implies that the transgression has already happened. It also makes clear that the encounter to which they are headed is one not just with nature but also with the *thought* of nature, such that the world-in-itself, to which She ascribes a "strange kind of personality," interpenetrates the world-for-us [00:29:51].

This sequence also positions She as a "seer," one who "sees" beyond habitual ways of looking, a point accentuated by the non-naturalized cinematography. Her gaze unveils an apparently unseen aspect of the forest. Certain of the rational mind's dominion over nature, he explicitly encourages her to identify with the forest, asking her to imagine lying on the very grass that frightens her. Acting as her "guide," he instructs, "I want you to melt into the green. Don't fight it. Just . . . turn green" [00:31:34]. Through digital manipulation, we see her slowly dissolve into the greenery beneath her, compromising the epidermal and ontological safeguards of subjectivity. This act foreshadows the contentious triad of nature, evil, and the feminine that She will eventually personify. Conversely, his reductive assertion that "what the mind can conceive and believe, it can achieve" betrays an overzealous fealty to the powers of human cognition. His predominantly Jungian techniques misread her affective cues (pain, self-harm, etc.) as evidence of an inner imbalance and failure of emotion regulation. However, as Sinnerbrink maintains, *Antichrist*, through its privileging of the affective, can be read as "anti-cognitivist" in its approach, disrupting and refusing the intellectual stratagems of both He and audiences alike to account for the dissonance of the film, the irreconcilable encounter of the world-in-itself and the world-for-us (2011, 163).

Women have traditionally been more closely associated with nature than men, owing to physiological attributes like menstrual cycles, pregnancy, and child-rearing. This sentiment is reflected in the nomenclature of "Mother Nature" or "Mother Earth." However, as adherents to ecofeminism are quick to point out, there is a strong correlation between the "dualisms that link the subordination of women to the subordination of non-human nature" (Hay 2002, 75). This "nature-feminine principle," Peter Hay points out, is aligned with "the primitive rather than the civilized [. . .] with carnality rather than discipline, with associative, 'non-rigorous' thought rather than rationality, and so on" (2002, 75). In *Antichrist*, we witness several instances where He attempts to curb She's carnality and redirect her associative thought so as to placate her "atypical grief." Science, nonetheless, has been historically inclined to view the nature-feminine in terms of seduction. Kate Soper attests that nature is "the potential spouse of science, to be wooed, won, and, if necessary, forced to submit to intercourse" (2000, 141). The "battle of sexes" between She and He thus stages the radical misalignment of Western humanism's relationship to "nature." In this context, as Parker instructively notes, borrowing a term from Alanna F. Bondar, She in *Antichrist* is consistently depicted as a "'non-nurturing mother'" (2020, 127). This facet of She is evidenced from the outset as her carnality is tied to the neglect of her child's safety or later when it is revealed that She has been carelessly placing Nic's shoes on the wrong feet causing sustained injury. Throughout the film, the conjunction of the nature-feminine as aberrant and malevolent, as a "non-nurturing mother," inscribes nature not as an "Eden" but rather, as She pronounces later in the film, as "Satan's church"—a site of grief and horror.

Significantly, once at "Eden," it is He who undergoes "exposure therapy" with episodic encounters with monstrous nature. Prior to reaching the cabin, He chances upon the first of the "Three Beggars," a deer in the thicket, which, when startled, turns to run, exposing him, and us, to the stillborn foetus dangling from its womb. Later during the night, the cabin roof is pelted with a barrage of acorns and the following morning He awakens with his hand out an open window beset upon by blood-sucking ticks. Von Trier and his collaborators implement a number of cinematic devices to reproduce for the audience the disorientating effects that nature has on both He and She. Drawing inspiration from the painterly traditions of Hieronymus Bosch and Henri Rousseau, von Trier and his cinematographer, Don Mantle, create a landscape that warps and shifts, indeed at times appears ungrounded (Björkman 2009, 18). Through the use of zooming, close-ups, unusual angles, and irregular editing—such as the camera's emphasis on She's bare feet reluctantly trampling the forest substrata—the filmmakers constantly attend to the environment as active, the greenery incessantly vacillating and lurching, "showing nature as animated, vibrant, verdant, changing, pulsing, and breathing" (Marso 2015, 6).

This effect is further developed by the work of sound designer Kristian Eidnes Andersen, who employs several experimental sonic textures to defamiliarize the auditory responses of the audience to the environment. Andersen's range of drones and low-frequency sound was obtained through "numerous objects such as rocks, wood, grass and the human voice," so that "organic materials appear as unidentifiable noise in the ambient background of the film. Literally using the body as a sound effect, Andersen swallowed a small microphone to record bodily sounds from the inside, and then used these sounds in the mix . . . [along with] low rumbles, strange reverbs and distant droning sounds" (Simmons 2015, 24).

The distortion of the natural order signified by the manipulation of the sonic landscape conveys a sense of nature as invasive, breaching the demarcation between the inner and outer world of the human, gradually undermining our ability to safely separate them. In linking the droning sounds of *Antichrist*'s soundtrack to the visceral and corporeal violence of the "New Extremism," Lisa Coulthard has commented on how the various rumbles, vibrations, and organic collisions used in both *Antichrist* and *Melancholia* are experienced through the body as a "physiological, emotional, and psychological disturbance" (2013, 124). We could take this one step further and describe this disturbance as ontological.

At times, the discordance between auditory and visual signifiers in *Antichrist* explicitly disrupts the characters' ontological boundaries. This is most overt in the scene in which She recalls an incident from the previous summer in the woods. At her table in the cabin, sorting through material for her thesis, she hears a child crying. Suspecting Nic to be in distress, She rushes into the woods, which appear to warp and bend about her. After calling out to her son, she returns to the cabin to find him playing harmlessly with a block of wood, even as she continues to hear weeping. Baffled by the dislocated, uncanny voice, She re-enters the woods and this time the camera tracks abruptly upwards to reveal a wide-shot of the encompassing forest and hills from which the wailing appears to resonate. This voice without an object both anthropomorphizes nature and accentuates its "unnaturalness," transforming it from scenic, bucolic, and perhaps inert, to something agentive and capable of suffering, whilst proleptically connecting with her own loss to come. Later in evening, after recounting this experience, She attempts to explain to her husband her insights from this previous stay in Eden, sharing that: "The acorns fell on the roof vent. They kept falling and falling. And dying and dying. And I understood that everything that used to be beautiful about Eden was perhaps hideous. Now I could hear what I couldn't hear before: The cry of all the things that are to die" [00:49:54–00:50:35].

Despite the protests of her husband, that "thoughts distort reality" [00:50:59], her alertness to a nonhuman agency, again manifest as a "cry," explicitly links horror and grief as She announces that "nature is Satan's church" [00:51:14]. A number of commentators have acknowledged the recurring motif of falling within the film.[2] The falling acorns rhyme with the infant bird falling from its nest that they witness during one of his exercises. Both recall Nic's tragic fall in the opening scene and underscore the mythological "Fall" from Paradise. Yet *Antichrist* makes clear that the Fall *precedes* Eden, that nature is always already a site of suffering and decay, such that the other-than-human presences discoverable throughout the film are allowed to "speak" through a variety of grief, loss, pain, and chaos. She's grief in the film attains its "excessive" proportions precisely because it relates to a scale beyond the loss of her own child towards the knowledge that life may not be "for us," that life itself is indifferent to human concerns.

He's confrontation soon after with the second of the "Three Beggars" escalates these supernatural elements. Alone among some ferns, He becomes aware of a rustling. Upon investigating, both He and audience are startled by the sight of a self-devouring fox. When the fox speaks, declaring "chaos reigns," He is stupefied, stripped of the tools that would enable to him accommodate this experience into his pre-existing assumptive world [00:57:54]. The radical violation of the human episteme announced by the fox upends the order of things to be replaced by the "chaos" of an "unthinkable" world fundamentally outside human understanding. Positioned as a "man of science," He is frequently bewildered by his surroundings and rendered defenseless against the encroachment of nature, such as the aberrant form of the "Three Beggars." She's pointed reminder in the earlier hospital scene that He is "not a doctor" casts doubt over his apparently self-appointed authority [00:07:54]. Unlike the Biblical Adam who gets to name and, therefore, claim authority over all the animals, He in *Antichrist* is constantly undermined in his attempts to assert control over nature. Discussing He's interaction with the "Three Beggars," Rob White points out that "in each case he hears a rustle that prompts a studious look of curiosity which soon turns to horror when the creature is revealed. He wants nature to reward his curiosity, but he gets instead a bloody, messy, obscene revelation" (Power and White 2009). Whether is it the abortive deer, the self-cannibalizing fox or, finally, the crow that does not die, He finds himself paralyzed by "animal wrongness" (Power and White 2009). According to Zolkos, "[i]nsofar as the animals are 'messengers' that signify knowledge inaccessible to the masculine subject, they throw into question the epistemological privilege of the human. At the same time, they all contain a disturbing reminder of their un-nature-like-ness" (2011, 181).

Such encounters resemble what Thacker calls horror's "state of frozen thought," a "moment of absolute uncertainty—when both options seem equally plausible and implausible, when neither thought can be accepted or rejected, when everything can be explained and nothing can be explained—only in that moment do we really have this horror of philosophy, this questioning of the principle of sufficient reason" (2015, 133, 7).

In *Antichrist,* He's encounters with the deer and the talking fox, mimic this frozen thought; the camera's wide shot isolating him within an "unreasonable" landscape. His repeated attempts to part the greenery, to "penetrate" as it were the mysteries of a bucolic nature are consistently met with sights that repel his presumptive world. "Nature," as philosopher Graham Harman warns us, "is not natural and can never be naturalized" (2011, 251). "Nature," in other words, is not simply an inert object but an *intellectual* project that construes the world-in-itself through a plethora of historically contingent interpretive practices that have at their center the world-for-us.

Compelled to remain in the cabin because of a downpour, He locates She's neglected dissertation research in the attic. When the pages of her notes regress into incoherent scrawls, his mounting suspicion that her emotional instability existed prior to Nic's death seems unmistakably confirmed. With this in mind, He devises a final exercise for her. Asked to role-play "rational thought" to his "nature," She probes:

She: Okay Mr. Nature, what do you want?

He: To hurt you as much as I can.

She: How?

. . .

He: By killing you.

She: Nature can't hurt me. You're just the whole greenery outside.

He: No, I'm more than that. I'm outside, but also . . . within. The nature of all human beings.

She: Oh, that kind of nature. The kind of nature that causes people to do evil things against women.

He: That's exactly who I am. [01:02:40–01:03:57]

The qualifying "outside, but also within" makes explicit what until now in the film had only been implied by a series of boundary crossings. The unfathomable Otherness of a "nature" that does not behave as we think it should is personified by an animistic She. Her assertion that "women do not control their own bodies—Nature does" [01:04:42], leaves us in little doubt that She acknowledges the "contamination" by the "other-than-human," whereas He struggles to maintain the fantasy of human primacy (Zolkos 2011, 183). Throughout the film, we realize, She has already foreseen, and internalized, nature's indifference to human concerns, prompting her warning to He: "This may not last. Have you ever thought of that?"

In Eugene Thacker's *Tentacles Longer Than Night,* he describes a similar erasure of the subject-object divide, between self and world. If we accept human beings as a continuation of, and thus identical with, the natural world, then we must recognize nature as pre-existent, immanent, and unconcerned with the desires of the individual or species. For Thacker this "nature" is:

> one that courses through self and world, but that does so without aim or end, indifferent to the self's possessive individualism and the species' sense of superiority. What thinks in me is what is outside me. Is this not also a description of 'nature' as invasive, contagious, over-running the human [. . .] Would this not [be] a *naturhorror*? (2015, 144–45)

The nature-feminine of She, the aberrant "Three Beggars," and the malevolent woods materialize the *naturhorror* of *Antichrist.* A "nature" that is indifferent to human concerns whilst "coursing through" the human can only be, for us, horrific, and in terms of the mythological and theological, or the iconography of cinematic horror, "evil." The consummation of this evil is announced by the arrival of the "Three Beggars," an unholy trilogy of pain, grief, and despair.

She in *Antichrist* is constructed as a "monstrous" mother, who has internalized her research into the witch-hunts to a degree where She herself perhaps begins to inhabit the malignant character of a "witch," as when She insists that "If human nature is evil, then that goes as well for . . . the nature of all the sisters" [01:04:23]. As She is making these claims in the film, the shot transfers to the attic, lingering again on the medieval depictions of witches. In the dappled light, the camera lingers on an image of a woman cast as demonic and monstrous. Her judgment and identification with the "witches," along with the film's graphic genital mutilation scene, where She cuts off her own clitoris with a pair of scissors, has spurred numerous accusations of misogyny and a wave of disapproval and outrage from a proportion of critics.[3] It is more helpful, I would suggest, to view von Trier's abject and wounded bodies as the unwilling objects of rationalism's deforming and distorting power. Lori J. Marso perceptively notes that "[von Trier's] refusal to look away from or remediate such feelings, his commitment to record and explore them, is mistakable for a patriarchal pleasure rather than as a critique of patriarchy's effects" (2015, 5). Similarly, a more recent film that chronicles Judeo-Christian patriarchal violence on a personified Mother Nature is Darren Aronofsky's *mother!* (2017), albeit in a way that preserves nature's "purity" as a nurturing mother. In this way, while *Antichrist*'s depiction of aberrant nature is indeed gendered female, the locus of criticism is an epistemological order codified as male, rational, and authoritative, fictionalized as "He," whom von Trier insists is intended as a "caricature," one in a long line of self-deluding, "blind" male protagonists (Björkman 2009, 18). The propensity to subjugate the natural world and exploit it as a resource for the benefit of "mankind" is echoed in the domination of women. Indeed, in the words of Patsy Hallen, "Is it an accident that modern science was born during 'the burning times' when 8–11 million women were killed on charges of witchcraft?" (Hay 2002, 76). The extraordinary violence in the film is a structural violence that has been perpetuated by an anthropocentric refusal to see the world-in-itself as anything other than a world-for-us, the figure of blind rationalism inexhaustibly "explaining" the world to itself. In *Antichrist*, the attempt to "wall" in nature through the discourses of rationalism correlates to the "therapeutic" control of the body, as in He's attempt to name and tame She's anxious body earlier in the film. The accompanying visuals, which almost medically illustrate her symptoms, are repeated by von Trier toward the end of the film, when He strangles her to death. With the recurrence of these images during the film's climax, the absence of the proprietary power of language reduces the close-ups of the body's panicked flesh to the irrational. In the act of strangulation, He participates in a long history of gynocide, relegating her body to a pyre constructed from forest branches, once again unifying the destruction of the feminine with nature whilst replicating the burning of witches.

"Nature" in *Antichrist* is aberrant and grotesque because it is presented as radically not-for-us. It overruns through the human and negates the recuperative processes of philosophy and rationalist thought, leaving behind an Eden that is "malformed" (Power and White 2009). The film attends to the mutual entanglements of human and non-human worlds, yet whether it is the "cry" of the forest, the speaking fox, or the female figuration of nature, von Trier's concession to the mythological and theological retains the anthropomorphic. That is, these images betray the inexorable difficulty of human conceptualizations of nature, even as their interpenetration is acknowledged. Whilst overdetermined by myth and religious allegory, *Antichrist*'s privileging of monstrous nature discloses the fallacy of a world-for-us. Nor does it, like many "revenge-of-nature" narratives, romanticize nature as a place of balance if not for the interventions of humans. Rather it presents nature as a site of disorder and "chaos" despite our judicial attempts to impose harmony upon it. The "cosmic misalign[ment]" that Nina Power identifies in *Antichrist* between the categories of a humanist epistemology, manifest in the horror produced by an "unthinking acceptance of modern rationality," is made even more explicit in von Trier's follow up feature in which cosmic bodies literally collide (2009). In *Melancholia*, an end-of-the-world disaster film, von Trier imagines the paradoxical event of mourning the end of the human. Such a conceit further decenters the human, opening up a space for the discussion of the speculative world-without-us, which perhaps permits us a *cosmological* view, one mediated by cinema.

"THE EARTH IS EVIL": MOURNING, MELANCHOLIA, AND THE WORLD-WITHOUT-US

As *Antichrist* made clear, the human and nonhuman world are inseparable concepts, the world-in-itself revealed to us most clearly in moments of horror. In *Melancholia*, however, the disaster narrative of a planetary collision affords an exploration of the "unknowable" or "unthinkable" by projecting a literal world without us. By attending to the privileging of sight in the narrative, in collaboration with von Trier's deviations from genre convention, the state of melancholia in the film proleptically performs a radical anti-anthropocentrism and approximates a cosmological perspective.

The film opens with a series of tableaux, a mesmerizing succession of sixteen slow-motion shots drawing on several artistic and intertextual references, including Pieter Bruegel the Elder's *Hunters in the Snow* and an allusion to John Everett Millais's *Ophelia*, as well as foreshadowing moments from the story to come, such as the interplanetary "dance of death" between "Melancholia" and the Earth. Accompanied by the Prelude from Wagner's *Tristan und Isolde,* a musical refrain repeated several times throughout the film that traps us in a "state of stasis," the overall impression suggests a decidedly Romantic sensibility (Nicolini n.d.). Moreover, "[t]he effect is of predestination: we know from the beginning that the characters are trapped and that the planet will be destroyed" (Gordon 2012). The decision to play out the narrative trajectory up-front, to sign-post the film's ending, can be read as a sly acknowledgment on von Trier's part of the predictability of disaster and apocalyptic narratives; we know from genre conventions that the disaster will eventuate. However, the "predestination" afforded by these *tableaux vivant* connotes a particular, but powerful, subtext to the film's arc which allows us to consolidate a number of concepts under discussion, such as the thought of the unthinkable and the threat of extinction, whilst aligning it with the state of melancholia, all of which is intimated by the very first shot of the film, as Justine (Kirsten Dunst) slowly opens her eyes in a bedraggled, heavy-lidded, straight-to-camera gaze. This attention to her unflinching stare, as birds appear to fall from the sky around her like some doomsday omen, I would argue, privileges her "sight" within the world of the film and positions her as a figure for whom, and for the audience who share in these images with her, the end had already happened. The suggestion of prophecy in the character of Justine effectively forecloses any prospect of futurity in the narrative. This foreclosure recalls Jean-François Lyotard's "solar catastrophism," in which the scientific knowledge of the sun's eventual demise pre-emptively marks the futility of human philosophy so that "[w]ith the disappearance of earth, thought will have stopped—leaving the disappearance absolutely unthought of" (1991, 24). The state of melancholia, whilst coupled with this "visionary" trope, remains unfixed and is not limited solely to Justine, but in fact permeates the filmic text and problematizes, I argue, humanity's uneasy "planetary attachments," to borrow a term from Nicole Merola (2014, 249).

As with von Trier's other films, *Melancholia* is divided into chapters. The first, "Justine," follows the ill-fated wedding reception of Justine and Michael (Alexander Skarsgård). Kim Nicolini's insight that the film "contains multiple disaster narratives—the wedding disaster, the emotional disaster, and the apocalypse disaster," opens the way for us to consider how once again von Trier scrambles genre elements (n.d., 1). The opening chapter's black comedy of errors and touches of melodrama, those features that make the film, in von Trier's mock provocateur assessment, "a woman's film!" once again delivers up his female protagonist to a hostile world, a world set within the Old World manor and vast estate of the privileged few: Justine's brother-in-law, John (Kiefer Sutherland), and sister, Claire (Charlotte Gainsbourg), and those who have gathered to celebrate her marriage, including her advertising boss, the arch-capitalist Jack (Stellan Skarsgård) (von Trier n.d.). Over the duration of her wedding night, Justine will find herself deprived of it all: her husband, her lucrative job, even the comfort of her fractured family—her unsympathetic mother, Gaby (Charlotte Rampling), and her oafish father, Dexter (John Hurt). Like her namesake from the Marquis de Sade tale, Justine attracts her own litany of "misfortunes." The resultant deep depression into which she descends constitutes "a 'loss of world' that finds its objective correlative in a cinematic fantasy of world annihilation" (Sinnerbrink 2014, 111). However, Justine's melancholia exceeds the thematic value of personal trauma or disaster and resists readings that consign her condition to metaphor or allegory.

The form that melancholia takes in the film is that of a lost future, and it is by examining how the film literalizes the "loss of world" in play with the conventions of disaster movies, apocalyptic narratives, and the trope of the visionary woman "touched" by "madness" that we will arrive in the vicinity of the nebulous world-without-us. The attribution of "sight" to Justine has been remarked upon by a number of commentators, but only Joshua Foa Dienstag has located this characterization within the broader practice of von Trier (Brown 2012; Doyle 2013, 19–37; Cruz 2015). For Dienstag, von Trier's female leads "see more clearly what is not apparent to others, or to the audience," such that "the power of perceiving ... makes them into something other-than-human, into witches, seers," as we have seen in *Antichrist*, for example (2015, 1, 9). Most often, this device is generally present as a "blind man/visionary woman dyad" (8). In *Melancholia*, Justine's ability to see what others cannot has her gaze drawn to the sky repeatedly, discerning what others are always late to acknowledge. An early example occurs as Justine finally arrives, two hours late, to her wedding reception, but stops short to observe an irregular star in the heavens, to which the amateur astronomer, John, replies, "I'm amazed that you can see that" [00:12:17], before proceeding to misidentify it as Antares from the constellation Scorpio (Cruz 2015). Reference is made more explicitly later in the film to Justine's ability to "know things" in the scene in which she reveals the results of a bean lottery from earlier during the wedding.

That it is a melancholic who is afforded the burden of foresight is a trope with a long literary and cinematic heritage, going as far back as the classical period's association of madness, with prophecy. Rather than reproduce the correlation between emotional "excess," madness and unreason, the function of melancholia in von Trier's film is more akin to a repudiation of society's governing structures and rituals that serve only to indulge illusions of a world-for-us and obscure certain ecological and planetary certainties (Doyle 2013, 30). That von Trier chooses the romantic and more resonant "melancholia" over the more clinical "depression" in his references in the film is telling in this respect and continues his skepticism of post-Enlightenment rationalism. Justine's melancholia is not reduced to unreason, nor can it be limited to an individual pathology. Von Trier's presentation of melancholia is demonstrably more than the familiar, but reductionist "moral or intellectual failure, a kind of unseemly self-indulgence," which is how Justine's brother-in-law, John, seems to view it (Shaviro 2012, 20). Nor can it be expunged or alleviated by Claire's well-meaning, but misdirected inducements, "simple pleasures" like a nice bath or a home-cooked meal (Dienstag 2015, 6). Rather, Justine's melancholia has its own "ontological consistency" (2015, 20). In this way, melancholia is not solely limited to Justine, but relates to what Steven Shaviro calls the "cosmic drama" in the film, the vulnerability of human concerns to the cosmological (2012, 6).

In "Mourning and Melancholia," Freud distinguishes melancholia from the similar processes of mourning by observing that in the former the subject "internalizes" an "unknown loss," a lost object that eludes conscious identification but which nevertheless facilitated a relationship to the external world (1957, 245). The Ego, according to Freud, absorbs this loss to a degree that the self exhibits "an overcoming of the instinct which compels every living thing to cling to life" (1957, 246). More complexly in melancholia, "countless separate struggles are carried on over the object, in which hate and love contend with each other; the one seeks to detach the libido from the object, the other to maintain this position of the libido" (1957, 256). The lost object of the melancholic, then, is "kept alive as a non-being" and takes the form of what Tim Matts and Aidan Tynan term an "ungrievable loss" (2012). The loss that Justine experiences in *Melancholia* cannot be mourned satisfactorily, I propose, because it has *yet* to happen and is in fact *deferred* for the time being. The loss of the Earth that is yet to come cannot be other than "unthinkable" and "ungrievable" for everyone on Earth, including Justine.

While Justine struggles to make her melancholia understood by those around her, she retreats away from those social and ritualistic structures that shore up a view of the world as a world-for-us, and seeks out a more authentic "world," towards nature, even if, as is the case when she takes leave of her wedding and drives across John's beloved eighteen-hole golf course, it is to piss on it. Rather than the chthonic, unruly nature shown in *Antichrist*, the carefully manicured grounds of the estate in *Melancholia* leave us no doubt of human interference in the "world," such that a world outside our own, a world-in-itself, cannot be reached, nor the world-for-us escaped—this is made literal in a number of thwarted attempts to leave the boundaries of the estate, either by Justine while riding her horse, or later Claire, as she attempts vainly to evade the impending planetary collision. Although nature in the film has been "tamed" and symmetrically arranged according to the "civilizing" tastes of the wealthy, Justine intuitively transfers her energy to it, as when she again abandons her own wedding and fucks a near-stranger in a sand bunker, which, coincidentally, looks suspiciously like an impact crater. It must be said, however, that these attempts convey frustration and fail to revive Justine in any satisfactory way. The "organised garden of delights" imagined by human hubris blocks Justine's identification with the lost object of her desire and reveals obliquely the "mutual entanglements" of human and nonhuman worlds (Lord 2013, 186). Struggling to articulate her inner turmoil to her sister at one point during the wedding, Justine describes an image, familiar from the prologue, of herself walking through a woods, dragging along tendril-like materials that seem to fix her to the Earth. "I'm trudging through a grey woolly yarn," she tells Claire, "It's clinging to my legs. It's really heavy to drag along" [00:28:30–00:28:58]. Rather than the anxiety-inducing *naturhorror* of *Antichrist*, nature in *Melancholia* is, for Justine, a site of ambivalence, "in which hate and love contend with each other" (Freud 1957, 256).

It is in the second chapter, "Claire" that the "fly-by," the rogue planet Melancholia, emerges from behind the sun and begins its approach toward Earth. We are informed, care of John's "trust [in] the scientists," that the planet will pass safely by the Earth, with only minimal effect. But for Justine,

Figure 9.1 "I'm trudging through a grey woolly yarn. It's clinging to my legs. It's really heavy to drag along." Kirsten Dunst (as Justine).
Source: Melancholia (2011)

the Earth is already a half-dead thing. This is most clear in the scene where, having failed to entice Justine to take a bath, Claire prepares her favorite meal. Gathered somewhat furtively around the family dinner table, Claire, John, and their young son, Leo (Cameron Spurr), look on as Justine takes a mouthful of meatloaf. Spitting it out onto a napkin, she begins to sob dejectedly, informing the table that, "it tastes like ashes." Dominic Fox, discussing what he calls "militant dysphoria," suggests that in the extreme state of depression "the distinction between living and dead matter collapses. The world *is dead*, and life appears within it as an irrational persistence, an insupportable excrescence" (Shaviro 2012, 20). "Militant" may not be an accurate measure of Justine's state; however, it is apparent from her remarks that the life-giving sustenance of Earth, the meat that despite being dead provides fuel for life, is already beyond life. As Catherine Lord points out, "ash is the material left after bodies are burned. It is the final detritus or 'left-over' from life . . . its ultimate death state" (2013, 191). Tracing the roots of the word "melancholia" itself, Dienstag reminds us that its origins lie with the ancient Greeks, who associated the condition with "an excess of the black bile," one of four "humors" connected to the four elements—water, air, earth, and fire. Significantly, black bile's corresponding element was earth, such that "a melancholic could be said to be someone too full of the earth" (Dienstag 2015, 6). The lost object, then, after which Justine cannot fully mourn is the Earth itself, which, owing to her prophetic sight, is, for her, already dead.

The loss of world carried by Justine defies a sufficient accounting precisely because it registers an impossibility. Responding to Lyotard's reflections on the death of the sun, Ray Brassier, in *Nihil Unbound: Enlightenment and Extinction*, insists that: "*everything is dead already* . . . far from lying in wait in for us in the far distant future, on the other side of the terrestrial horizon, the solar catastrophe needs to be grasped as something that *has already happened*; as the aboriginal trauma driving the history of terrestrial life as an elaborately circuitous detour from stellar death" (2007, 223).

The cognition of this limit-thought, like human extinction, is an ontological problem infecting the present, reminding us that Thacker's world-without-us "is not to be found in a 'great beyond' that is exterior to the World (the world-for-us) or the Earth (the world-in-itself); rather, it is in the very fissures, lapses, or lacunae in the World and the Earth" (2011, 7–8). Through the cinematic conceit of an interplanetary disaster narrative and a prophetic protagonist, von Trier conjures up a simulated instance of this loss of world. "Prophecy reverses the temporality of melancholia," perceives Nathan Brown, "the melancholic prophet proleptically interiorises the future loss ... a loss which, in prophetic time, has *already happened*, so that it can happen to her, now" (2012). The temporal deferment of the moment of death, which is nonetheless felt in the now, can only lead to a being-in-the-world that is "split, torn, divided, torqued," and an ontological position performed as an act of negation of self and world (2012).

Crucially for Justine, the approach of Melancholia confers legitimacy on her state of being and marks a shift in her relationship to the world. In Freudian terms, her libido is displaced onto this new "love-object," this secondary planet which offers to fulfil the promise of her visions and a release from her "dead" attachments. Her inertia slowly lessens its grip. Exiting the house in middle of the night, witnessed by her sister Claire, Justine makes her way to the edges of a stream, lying naked under the blue light of Melancholia, participating in a cosmic seduction. Kirsten Dunst, in the DVD commentary, reflects that "Justine comes from this planet, maybe, it's her Mother Earth coming to take her" (Gordon 2012). Christopher Peterson connects this image to an earlier moment in the film where Justine is peering through a telescope at some lanterns released into the sky during her wedding ceremony. As she closes her eyes, we see several magnificent shots of supernovae as if we share her inner vision. Peterson proposes that "her attraction to the lanterns and other celestial objects implies an affinity with their rootlessness and errancy," an "interplanetary gaze" (2015, 11). The scaling up of Justine's vision affords her a perspective that is *cosmological*. Shedding the "mutual entanglements" of the World and the Earth, so violently enmeshed in *Antichrist*, Justine glimpses the Planetary in all its cold indifference to the human.

As the planet Melancholia shifts closer to Earth, those around Justine find themselves confronted with the thought of extinction. Despite the assurances of the "scientists," for whose authority and acumen the figure of John is a stand-in, Melancholia's slingshot orbit defies their expectations and begins its unstoppable collision course with Earth. John's telescope, despite its symbolic reminder of the discovery that Earth is not at the center of things, "the instrument central to the Copernican revolution and the emergence of humanism itself," fails to "see" what Justine now "knows" (DeFazio 2013, 45). The film, as Rob White points out, "shrinks Science to the pitiful little wire ring-on-a-stick that Claire uses to falsely reassure herself that the planet is veering away" (Power and White 2012). When the scientists' miscalculations become clear to John, he retreats to the horse stables and summarily kills himself. With his removal from the narrative, the structures that sustained him and which he represented—economic rationalism, science, optimism, gender politics—collapse and simply cease to matter. The systems which seemed so oppressive in previous von Trier films, including *Antichrist*, fade into insignificance (Shaviro 2012, 36).

Claire, on the other hand, fumbles desperately in the wake of these old conventions, clinging to those forms of etiquette and displays of civility that make this world a world-for-us. She incessantly acts out the humanist illusion of "the individual meaningfully engaging with the world" (O'Brien 2015, 103). Claire is anything but "clear," as her name seems to imply (Dienstag 2015, 8). In her uncertainty, she clings to her family, turning to her sister, ironically, for comfort. Justine refuses to spare her sister's self-deceptions, stating plainly that "The earth is evil. We don't need to grieve for it" [01:31:08]. Claire is stupefied, but Justine insists that "Nobody will miss it" [01:31:18]. Justine's "nobody will miss it" holds literally true and teeters on the edge of philosophy's limit-thought and the cultural moment of extinction anxiety as we have been following it. From Lyotard's realization that there be "no sublation or deferral" in the end of thought and the question of human finitude endemic to Anthropocene, speculative realist and ecological discourse to Thacker's world-without-us, Justine's simple phrase exemplifies what Ray Brassier calls the "truth of extinction" (2007, 205). "But where would Leo grow up?" Claire implores [01:31:27]. Claire's denial exhibits what Thacker calls the "attempt to put things in human terms, in the terms of the world-for-us" (2011, 4–5). Her thoughts can only reprise the anthropocentric concerns of life and continuation. Her words are devoted solely to a "reinscription of herself at the center of a world that would no longer exist" (Peterson 2015, 10). "All I know is, life on earth is evil," Justine answers [01:31:34]. Claire, however, is undeterred:

Claire: There may be life somewhere else.

Justine: But there isn't.

Claire: How do you know?

Justine: Because I know things.

Claire: Oh, yes, you always imagine, you did.

[...]

Justine: I know things. And when I say we're alone ... we're alone. Life is only on Earth. And not for long [01:31:41–01:32:53].

Though Justine offers no hope for the possibility of life or planet surviving the collision, Claire is unable to surrender her humanist ideals. Faced with the impending cataclysm, Claire's attempts to escape seem evermore foolhardy, her trying to flee the estate, despite John's admission to Leo that Melancholia's return would mean there would be "nothing to do and nowhere to hide" [01:58:27].

If *Melancholia* is a film of "multiple disasters," then it is equally true that there are multiple collisions. "Systems collide and explode," Kim Nicolini informs us, "cinematic aesthetics clash; expectations from characters are in conflict throughout, and nothing is stable" (n.d., 6). Once again, von Trier destabilizes cinematic forms and their structures of cultural-historical meaning by upending genre conventions. Contrary to what we have come to expect from apocalyptic cinema, *Melancholia* retracts one of the primary responsibilities of disaster or sci-fi end-of-the-world films—the fantasy of survival. As Susan Sontag has noted, films of this kind permit viewers to "participate in the fantasy of living through one's own death and more, the death of cities, the destruction of humanity itself" (1965, 44). *Melancholia* withholds such effects-laden displays of world-collapse and human endurance, resolute in its refusal of consolation. There is no "sublime spectacle of destruction ... hyperbolic devastation, and frenetically edited chaos" (Shaviro 2012, 6). There can be no "last man" to rue the loss of humanity and there will be no "revelation," suggested by the term "apocalypse." Extinction, as Ray Brassier points out, must be understood as not just a biological event, but also "as that which levels the transcendence ascribed to the human" (2007, 224).

Emerging out of discussions around the Anthropocene, species extinction and planet-wide climate change, philosophical, and cultural "speculations" are inclined to preserve, to extend the disembodied gaze of the human beyond finitude and to indulge in a process of memorialization in which the future ruins of our cities and monuments and our anthropogenic imprint *at least* mark our absence (Matt and Tynan 2012). The pathos of non-fiction best-sellers like *The World Without Us*, by Alan Weisman, or the anthropomorphic machines of Pixar animation, *WALL-E* (2008), open up a space, paradoxically, for a collective nostalgia for the passing of the human and an appetite for elegy and memory. Recent films, such as Terrence Malick's *The Tree of Life* (2011), Béla Tarr's *The Turin Horse* (2011), Jeff Nichols's *Take Shelter* (2011), Christopher Nolan's *Interstellar* (2014), and Alfonso

Cuarón's *Gravity* (2013), each thematize nature, the environment, or the cosmic, revealing human beings as being acted *upon* by the world rather than the other way around, offering up a restaging of origins, endings, and rebirths. In contrast, *Melancholia* denies the fantasy of survival, with the attendant promise of renewal and rebirth, as well as the solace of elegy or witness. The film's ending cannot be recuperated, which is why we as viewers should take care not to reduce the end-of-the-world to just metaphor, or what Christopher Peterson, alluding to the film's final sequence, calls the "magic cave of allegory," whereby the catastrophe becomes a stand-in for depression, domestic drama, or the end of the "worlds" of capitalism, gender or cinema itself (2013, 400–422).[4]

In the final moments of the film, Justine gathers sticks with her nephew, Leo. They are constructing a "magic cave," a makeshift tepee out of fallen branches, that Justine hopes will comfort the frightened child. During this moment, the camera tilts down to Justine's footfall amid the grassy clearing. All manner of writhing worms and insects are seen disturbed in a close-up shot that recalls *Antichrist's* seething woods. But the illusion of Eden's "walled garden" is replaced by the transparent fiction of a "magic cave." In spite of von Trier's declaration that "we melancholiacs [sic] don't value rituals . . . It seems so phony," and Justine's continuous aversion to the rituals of family, marriage, and society throughout the narrative, she relents for the benefit of Leo and the by now inconsolable Claire (Thorsen 2011). Wagner's music swells one final time as Leo closes his eyes and Justine turns her back on the incoming planet. Claire, however, cannot but help steal a terrified glance toward the intrusion of the absolute, non-human Melancholia, "'trying to see beyond seeing,' peering over a horizon that cannot ultimately be crossed" (Peterson 2013, 419). Claire's glance is our collective, speculative glance, a side-long glimpse at the "unthinkable," Thacker's spectral world-without-us, "the subtraction of the human from the world" (2011, 5).

Of course, the interplanetary collision in the final scene of *Melancholia* cannot give us access to the world-without-us. Justine's melancholia, in its excess of feeling and prophetic sight, delivers a distressing and subjectively embodied experience of the loss of world. Regardless of Justine's ability to "know things," like any of us, she cannot "know" extinction or the end-of-the-world because "humans are only an instance of the concept species as indeed would be any other life form. But one never experiences being a concept" (Chakrabarty 2009, 220). As Peggy Kamuf acknowledges:

> the end of all life . . . is precisely what we cannot think except in a mode and as a vestige of survival beyond the annihilation that will therefore not have been total . . . the loss of everything as not-quite everything; there remains a

Figure 9.2 Peering over the horizon of extinction. Left: Cameron Spurr (as Leo). Center: Kirsten Dunst (as Justine). Right: Charlotte Gainsbourg (as Claire).
Source: *Melancholia (2011)*

> remainder for the speculative imagination, which can project the end of everything only by surviving to mourn it. (Peterson 2013, 411)

At the moment of impact, the screen goes black, the music cuts out. We hear an earth-shaking rumble and finally silence, as the credits begin. The film ends as the world ends, yet the film and the audience are the remainder, the exception, the trace that suspends the world-without-us. The film performs a slingshot orbit, the "circuitous detour" of an end that had already taken place in the opening tableau. "The earth is destroyed," Nathan Brown reminds us, "what had already happened has happened" (2012). *Melancholia*, regardless of its apparent nihilism, does not leave us to mourn. For some, it "leaves the viewer in a state of ecstasy" (Schwarzbaum 2011). Perhaps, like Justine, "we don't need to grieve for it." Or perhaps without the fantasy, and burden, of survival, the film offers a vicarious, if momentary, truth that otherwise will remain "unthinkable." As with all his films, however, von Trier frustrates any reductive meaning, and while *Melancholia* offers a decisive end, it does not, and cannot, give us closure.

CONCLUSION

The protagonists in both *Antichrist* and *Melancholia* are consumed by grief, sadness, and melancholia. It is through their positions as "seers" that we, too, as audience, are afforded a glimpse into the horror of a world beyond our knowing, a world that is not "for us." As human beings engaged in presumptive schema, whether it be mythological, theological, or post-Enlightenment rationalism, we are in danger of inexorable "blindness." Von Trier's cinematic provocations and Thacker's "horror of philosophy" draw on anti-philosophical stratagems to decenter human primacy, affording attention to the torsion between human and non-human "worlds." In the midst of current ecological uncertainty and looming environmental collapse due to human-induced climate change—the dark legacy of the so-called Anthropocene—we are poised perilously at the limit of human thought, Ray Brassier's "truth of extinction" or Thacker's world-without-us. Whether conceived as an aberrant, overrunning nature or collision with an indifferent blue planet, von Trier's films ask us to speculate on not just a planet but a universe in which all traces of the human is absent. In this cosmological perspective, we may discern horror and grief in the loss of our world. These speculations have their limit, however. After all, no one will miss it.

BIBLIOGRAPHY

Artaud, Antonin. 1958. *The Theatre and Its Double*. New York: Grove Press.
Badley, Linda. 2011. *Lars von Trier*. Chicago: University of Illinois Press.
Björkman, Stig. 2009. "Making the Waves." *Sight & Sound* 19 (8): 16–19.
Brassier, Ray. 2007. *Nihil Unbound: Enlightenment and Extinction*. Hampshire: Palgrave Macmillan.
Brown, Nathan. 2012. "Origin and Extinction, Mourning and Melancholia." *Mute*, September 9, 2012. https://www.metamute.org/editorial/articles/origin-and-extinction-mourning-and-melancholia.
Bunch, Mads. 2010. "Behind Idealism: The Discrepancy between Philosophy and Reality in the Cinema of Lars von Trier." *Scandinavian-Canadian Journal / Études Scandinaves Au Canada* 19: 144–63. https://scancan.net/bunch_1_19.htm.
Chakrabarty, Dipesh. 2009. "The Climate of History: Four Theses." *Critical Inquiry* 35 (2): 197–222.
Coulthard, Lisa. 2013. "Dirty Sound: Haptic Noise in New Extremism." In *The Oxford Handbook of Sound and Image in Digital Media*, edited by Carol Vernallis, Amy Herzog, and John Richardson, 115–26. Oxford: Oxford University Press.
Cruz, Cynthia. 2015. "Justine, a Prophet: Blindness and Vision in Lars von Trier's *Melancholia*." *Hyperallergic*. Last modified September 5, 2015. https://hyperallergic.com/233564/justine-a-prophet-blindness-and-vision-in-lars-von-triers-melancholia/.
DeFazio, Kimberly. 2013. "Melancholia and Posthumanist Metaphysics." In *Stories in Post-Human Cultures*, edited by Adam L. Brackin and Natacha Guyot, 39–49. Oxford: Brill.
Dienstag, Joshua Foa. 2015. "Evils of Representation: Werewolves, Pessimism, and Realism in *Europa* and *Melancholia*." *Theory & Event* 18 (2). https://www.muse.jhu.edu/article/578630.
Doyle, Briohny. 2013. "Prognosis End-Time: Madness and Prophecy in *Melancholia* and *Take Shelter*." *Altre Modernità* 9: 19–37.

Elsaesser, Thomas. 2016. "Black Suns and a Bright Planet: Melancholia as Thought Experiment." In *Politics, Theory, and Film: Critical Encounters with Lars von Trier*, edited by Bonnie Honig and Lori J. Marso, 305–55. Oxford: Oxford Univerity Press.

Foy, Joseph J. 2010. "It Came from Planet Earth: Eco-Horror and the Politics of Postenvironmentalism in *The Happening*." In *Homer Simpson Marches on Washington: Dissent through American Popular Culture*, edited by Timothy M. Dale and Joseph J. Foy, 167–88. Lexington: University Press of Kentucky.

Freud, Sigmund. 1957. "Mourning and Melancholia." In *The Standard Edition of the Complete Psychological Works of Sigmund Freud, Volume XIV (1914–1916): On the History of the Psycho-Analytic Movement, Papers on Metapsychology and Other Works*, 237–58. London: Random House.

Gordon, Andrew. 2012. "The Bride of *Melancholia*." *PYSART: A Hyperlink Journal for the Psychological Study of the Arts*. Last Modified September 7, 2012. http://psyartjournal.com/article/show/gordon-the_bride_of_melancholia.

Grant, Matthew. 2014. "The Cabin on the Screen: Defining the 'Cabin Horror' Film." *Film Matters* 5 (1): 5–12.

Hanich, Julian. 2011. *Cinematic Emotion in Horror Films and Thrillers: The Aesthetic Paradox of Pleasurable Fear*. New York: Routledge.

Harman, Graham. 2011. *Guerrilla Metaphysics: Phenomenology and the Carpentry of Things*. Peru: Open Court Publishing.

Hay, Peter Robert. 2002. *Main Currents in Western Environmental Thought*. Bloomington: Indiana University Press.

Janoff-Bulman, Ronnie. 1992. *Shattered Assumptions*. New York: Free Press.

Keetley, Dawn, and Angela Tenga. 2016. *Plant Horror: Approaches to the Monstrous Vegetal in Fiction and Film*. London: Palgrave Macmillan.

Koutsourakis, Angelos. 2013. *Politics as Form in Lars Von Trier a Post-Brechtian Reading*. New York: Bloomsbury.

Langford, Barry. 2005. *Film Genre: Hollywood and Beyond*. Edinburgh: Edinburgh University Press.

Lord, Catherine. 2013. "Her Green Materials: Mourning, 'Melancholia,' and Not-so-Vital Materialisms." *Necsus: European Journal of Media Studies* 2 (1): 179–96.

Lumholdt, Jan. 2003. *Lars von Trie: Interviews*. Jackson: University Press of Mississippi.

Lyotard, Jean-François. 1991. *The Inhuman: Reflections on Time*. Cambridge: Polity Press.

Marso, Lori J. 2015. "Must We Burn Lars von Trier? Simone de Beauvoir's Body Politics in *Antichrist*." *Theory and Event* 18 (2): 1–14.

Matts, Tim, and Aidan Tynan. 2012. "The Melancholy of Extinction: Lars von Trier's *Melancholia* as an Environmental Film." *M/C Journal* 15 (3). https://journal.media-culture.org.au/index.php/mcjournal/article/view/491.

Merola, Nicole. 2014. "Mediating Anthropocene Planetary Attachments: Lars von Trier's *Melancholia*." In *Design, Mediation, and the Posthuman*, edited by Dennis

M. Weiss, Amy D. Propen, and Colbey Emerson Reid, 249–68. Lanham, MD: Lexington Books.
Murray, Robin L., and Joseph K. Heumann. 2016. *Monstrous Nature: Environment and Horror on the Big Screen*. Lincoln: Univeristy of Nebraska Press.
Nicolini, Kim. n.d. "Freedom in Oblivion: Post-Feminist Possibilities in Lars Von Trier's *Melancholia.*" Accessed May 16, 2016. https://www.kimnicolini.com/wp-content/uploads/2012/04/Melancholia_KN-4-5-12.pdf.
O'Brien, Gabrielle. 2015. "Planetary Provocations: Lars von Trier's' *Melancholia*." *Screen Education* 77: 102–9.
Parker, Elizabeth. 2020. *The Forest and the EcoGothic: The Deep Dark Woods in the Popular Imagination*. Palgrave Gothic. Cham: Palgrave Macmillan.
———. 2018. "Who's Afraid of the Big Bad Woods?: Deep Dark Forests and Literary Horror." In *The Palgrave Handbook to Horror Literature*, edited by Kevin Corstorphine and Laura R. Kremmel, 275–90. Cham: Palgrave Macmillan.
Peterson, Christopher. 2015. "The *Gravity* of *Melancholia*: A Critique of Speculative Realism." *Theory and Event* 18 (2): 1–15.
———. 2013. "The Magic Cave of Allegory: Lars von Trier's *Melancholia*." *Discourse: Journal for Theoretical Studies in Media and Culture* 35 (3): 400–422.
Power, Nina, and Rob White. 2009. "*Antichrist*: A Discussion." *Film Quarterly*, December 1, 2009. https://filmquarterly.org/2009/12/01/antichrist-a-discussion/.
———. 2012. "Lars von Trier's *Melancholia*: A Discussion." *Film Quarterly*, January 10, 2012. https://filmquarterly.org/2012/01/10/lars-von-triers-melancholia-a-discussion/.
Schepelern, Peter. 2014. "Lars von Trier and Cultural Liberalism." *Danish Film Institute*, Last modified January 30, 2014. https://www.dfi.dk/en/english/lars-von-trier-and-cultural-liberalism.
Schwarzbaum, Lisa. 2011. "Cannes Film Festival: Lars von Trier's Stunning *Melancholia*—The End of the World (And a Challenge to *The Tree of Life*)." *Entertainment Weekly*. May 18, 2011. https://ew.com/article/2011/05/18/cannes-film-festival-lars-von-trier-melancholia-terrence-malick/.
Shaviro, Steven. 2012. "MELANCHOLIA, or the Romantic Anti-Sublime." *Sequence: Serial Studies in Media, Film, and Music Sequence* 1. https://reframe.sussex.ac.uk/sequence/files/2012/12/MELANCHOLIA-or-The-Romantic-Anti-Sublime-SEQUENCE-1.1-2012-Steven-Shaviro.pdf.
Simmons, Amy. 2015. *Antichrist (Devil's Advocates)*. Leighton Buzzard: Auteur.
Sinnerbrink, Robert. 2014. "Anatomy of *Melancholia*." *Angelaki* 19 (4): 111–26.
———. 2011. *New Philosophies of Film: Thinking Images*. London & New York: Continuum.
———. 2016. "Provocation and Perversity: Lars von Trier's Cinematic Anti-Philosophy." In *The Global Auteur*, edited by Seung-hoon Jeong and Jeremi Szaniawski, 95–114. New York: Bloomsbury.
Smith, Andrew, and William Hughes. 2013. *EcoGothic*. Manchester: Manchester University Press.
Sontag, Susan. 1965. "The Imagination of Disaster." *Commentary* 40 (4): 42–48.

Soper, Kate. 2000. "Naturalized Woman and Feminized Nature." In *The Green Studies Reader: From Romanticism to Ecocriticism*, edited by Laurence Coupe, 139–43. London: Routledge.

Thacker, Eugene. 2011. *In the Dust of This Planet: Horror of Philosophy, Volume 1*. Winchester and Washington: Zero Books.

———. 2015. *Tentacles Longer Than Night: Horror of Philosophy, Volume 3*. Winchester and Washington: Zero Books.

Thorsen, Nils. 2011. "Longing for the End of It All: An Interview with Lars von Trier." *Melancholia Press Kit for Cannes Film Festival*. https://www.festival-cannes.com/en/films/melancholia.

Trier, Lars von. 2009. *Antichrist*. DVD. Pyrmont, NSW: Paramount Home Entertainment.

———. n.d. "A Beautiful Movie About the End of the World (Director's Statement)." Last Modified 2011. http://www.melancholiathemovie.com/#_directorsstatement.

———. 2011. *Melancholia*. DVD. Melbourne: Madman Entertainment.

Wartenberg, Thomas E. 1982. "'Species-Being' and 'Human Nature' in Marx." *Human Studies* 5 (2): 77–95.

Wells, Paul. 2000. *The Horror Genre: From Beelzebub to Blair Witch*. London: Wallflower.

Zolkos, Magdalena. 2011. "Violent Affects: Nature and the Feminine in Lars von Trier's Antichrist." *Parrhesia* 13: 177–89.

NOTES

1. See also: Kauffman, Jeffrey ed. 2003. *Loss of the Assumptive World: A Theory of Traumatic Loss*. New York: Brunner-Routledge.

2. See also: Parker, Elizabeth. 2020. *The Forest and the EcoGothic: The Deep Dark Woods in the Popular Imagination*. Palgrave Gothic. Cham, Switzerland: Palgrave Macmillan,128.

3. See also: Badley, Linda. 2011. *Lars von Trier*. Chicago: University of Illinois Press,143.

4. See also: LeBeau, Richard. 2011. "Hauntingly Accurate Portrayals of Severe Mental Illness at a Theater Near You." *Psychology in Action*, December 12, 2011. https://www.psychologyinaction.org/psychology-in-action-1/2011/12/12/hauntingly-accurate-portrayals-of-severe-mental-illness-at-a-theater-near-you.

Index

Page references for figures are italicized

A24, xiv, 49–67
Abrahamson, Lenny, 51
accident, xv, xvii, 35, 54, 63, 84, 159, 173
Aćimović, Ana, 131
acorn, 176, 177, 178
AIDS, 133, 140
airplane, 92
Aja, Alexandre, 19
Aksentijević, Nataša, 131
alcohol, 131, 151, 153, 158
Alfredson, Tomas, xiii, 48n7
Aliens, 110
ambulance, 63, 119
Amenábar, Alejandro, xiii, 149
American Civil War, 153, 165n2
Amityville 2: The Possession, 62, 86n7
Andersen, Kristian Eidnes, 177
Anderson, John, 20
Ansen, David, 21
Antares, 184
anthropophagi, 121
Antichrist, xvii, 103n2, 169–82, 191–2
anti-Enlightenment, 170
anxiety, 78, 81, 90, 95, 97, 98, 99, 102, 121, 169, 172, 174, 175, 185
apocalypse, 59, 183, 189

apocalyptic narrative, 182, 183
Aranđelović, Mariana, 131
Aranjuez, Adolfo, 72, 86n2
Arens, William, 121
Argiro, Thomas Robert, 153, 154
Arkadija, 136
Armstrong, Richard, xi
Aronofsky, Darren, 181
Artaud, Antonin, 171
Association Rainbow, 136
Aster, Ari, xii, xiv–xv, 49–67, 87–103
Åström, Anna, 97
astronomer, 184
attic, 63, 179, 180
automatic writing, 158

Babadook, The, xii, xv, 20, 71–104
Backer, Ron, 27
backpacking, 96
Badley, Linda, 195n3
Balanzategui, Jessica, 6–7, 12
banquet, 14
Baquero, Ivana, 3, *9*
Barber, Nicholas, 53
Barely Lethal, 51
barn, 99, 134
Barreiro, Francisco, 107

basement, 26–30, 35, 47n3, 83, 84
bath, 115, 184, 186
bathroom, 92, 115, 117
Bayona, Juan Antonio, xiii, xiv, 19–48
beach, 21, 26, 32, 47n3
Beato, Carmen, 107
Becker, Ernest, 56, 59, 60, 61, 62–3
Beckford, William, 126n4
bed, 13, 22, 34, 43, 47n1, 63, 76, 80, 82, 117
bedroom, 22, 30, 35, 80, 89, 119
bedsheet ghost, 22
Beetlejuice, 22
Belchite, 8
Belgrade, 130, 134, 136
Benshoff, Harry, 109, 126n4
Bentley, James, 149
Bergman, Ingmar, 50
Bernardoni, James, 27
Bicentennial Projects, 123
bile, 83, 111, 175, 178, 186
bird, 26, 42, 178, 182
Birds, The, 117, 172
Blackcoat's Daughter, The, 52
black market, 132
blanket, 27, 28, 29, 30, 99
blind, 149
blind rationalism, 171, 181
blizzard, 90
Blomgren, Mats, 97
Blomgren, Vilhelm, 89
blood, xiii, 4, 13, 15, 19, 113
Blumhouse Productions, 53
Bojàri, Zsolt, 88
Bondar, Alanna F., 176
bone, 8, 94, 100
Book of Crossroads, 4, 5, 13
Bosch, Hieronymus, 176
Bosnia, 133, 135, 140
Both Sides of the Veil, 160
Bradley, Laura, 53
Bradshaw, Peter, 86n2
Braham, Persephone, 121
Brassier, Ray, 186, 188, 189, 192

breath, 4, 25, 37, 38, 42, 84, 92, 94, 95, 97–8, 174, 177
Brent, Laura, 151
bride, 169
Brothers Grimm, 174
Brown, Jennifer, 114, 120, 121
Brown, Karin, 16
Brown, Nathan, 187, 191
Bruegel, Pieter, 182
Buerger, Shelley, 77
bullet, 156, *156*
burlesque, xvi
Burns, Marilyn, 102
Burr, Ty, 21
Burton, Tim, 22
bus, 117, 134
Byrne, Gabriel, 54

cabin, xvii, 98, 112, 169, 173, 174, 175, 176, 177, 179
Campbell, Neve, 109
cancer, 133, 151
candle, 97, 114
cannibal, 102, 107–26, 178
Cannibal Ferox, 113
Cannibal Holocaust, 113
cape, 23
capitalism, 109, 122, 129, 130, 190
Captive of the Labyrinth: Sarah L. Winchester Heiress to the Rifle Fortune, 152
car, xv, 7, 9, 42, 43, 63, 80, 89, 93, 107, 112, 133, 134
Caribbean, 120–1, 145
carnivalesque, 42, 88, 92, 101
Carpenter, John, 101, 197
Carrie, 27, 110, 117
Carulla, Montserrat, 24
Castillo, Debra A., 111
castration anxiety, 59, 63
catharsis, xi, xiii, 96, 99,
Catholicism, 64, 148
Cat People, 50
Cavell, Stanley, 95
Cayo, Fernando, 22

ceremony, 98, 187
chainsaw, 20, 44, 102
Chandor, J. C., 51
Character Analysis, 59
Chávez, Alan, 107, 126n5
C.H.U.D., 112
Church, David, 50
Civilization and Its Discontents, 62, 63
clairaudience, 148, 159
clairvoyance, 148, 159
Clark, Roger, 5
Clarke, Jason, 151, *156*
Climax, 52
clock, 113, 114
closet, *75*
cloud, 100
Clover, Carol, 86n1, 109, 120
Collette, Toni, 53, 110
colonialism, xvi, 120, 121, 123
Columbus, Christopher, 120–1
coming-of-age, 113–4
Common Sense Media, 20
Conjuring, The, 86n7, 148
Cornwell, Peter, 149
corpse, 29, 31, 111, 113
"cosmic drama," 184
Coulthard, Lisa, 177
COVID-19, 147, 163
Creed, Barbara, 47n4, 74, 117
Croatia, 133, 135, 140
crow, 178
crown, 92, 98, 99, *101*
Cruz, Lenika, xii
cry, 116, 118, 119, 157, 177, 178, 181
Csànyi, Klaudia, 88, *96*
Cuarón, Alfonso, 172, 189
cult, 97, 99, 100
Cultural Liberalism, 170
Curtis, Jamie Lee, 101

Dafoe, Willem, 103n2, 173
Damiani, Damiano, 62
Damnjanović, Predrag, 132
Davies, Ann, 30, 47n4
Davis, Essie, 72, 75, *75*, *82*

Dawn of the Dead, 111
Day After Tomorrow, The, 172
death drive, 42
de Beauvoir, Simone, 88, 92–3, 99–100
decapitate, 54, 55, 63
deer, 26, 176, 178, 179
Delgado, Maria, 32, 34
Deleuze, Gilles, 129–30, 134–5, 137, 138
del Toro, Guillermo, xiii–xiv, 3–18, 20, 34–5, 38, 48n7, 114
demon, xii, 54, 55, 56, 57, 58, 59, 62, 72, 83, 122, 148, 180
Denial of Death, The, 56, 60
Denis, Claire, 52
DePalma, Brian, 27, 47n5
depression, 54, 75, 78, 80, 83, 116, 156, 157, 169, 170, 172, 173, 183, 184, 186, 190
Derry, Charles, 14
de Sade, Marquis, 183
detritus, 186
Devil's Rejects, The, 19
DeVito, Danny, 52
Dienstag, Joshua Foa, 183–4, 186
dinner table, 13, 63, 186
disaster movies, 183
disaster narrative, 182, 187
dissociative identity disorder, 54
doll, 35, 54, 58
dollhouse, 54, 58
Donner, Richard, 74
doppelgänger, 34
Đorđević, Ivan, 132
Đorđević, Mladen, xiii, xvi, 127–43
Dowd, Ann, 54
Doyle, Sir Arthur Conan, 161
Dracula (novel), 114
dread, xiv, 20, 21, 26, 53, 64, 174
dream, 35, 76, 83, 96
drug abuse, 151, 153, 158
dual ending, 15, 16
Dunst, Kirsten, 182, *186*, 187, *191*

Eating Raoul, 112

Ebert, Roger, 20
"ecoGothic," 172
"eco-horror," 172
Edelstein, David, 19
Eggers, Robert, xi, 52
Eggleston, Colin, 172
Ehrlich, David, 51, 52
elevated horror, xiv, 49–67
Eljaiek-Rodríguez, Gabriel, 115, 122, 123
Elsaesser, Thomas, 170
England, 22, 126n4
Enlightenment, 90, 170
Epte River, 100
E.T., 22
eulogy, 53
European Union, 127
evil, 58, 59, 108, 109, 116, 151, 175, 179, 180, 182, 188
Ex Machina, 51
exorcism, 148
Exorcist, The, 62, 71, 72, 74, 82, 86n7, 148
extinction event, xvii

face pareidolia, 100
fairy, 8–9, 10, 15
fairy tale, 3–18, 28, 31, 48, 57, 99, 174
Family Guy, 47n6
Farren, Eamon, 154
fascism, 4, 5, 8, 14, 15
Father Ted, 22
femininity, 65, 90, 110, 119, 159
feminism, 154, 155, 156, 176
femme fatale, 109, 119
Fenkel, David, 51
fertility, 98
film noir, 171
Final Girl, 47n4, 109, 120
fish, 26
Flanagan, Mike, 148
flower, 7, 11, 14, 84, 93, 96, 98, 99, 173–4. *See also* rose
flute, 96
Focus Features, 52

Fon, Gabi, 88
Forest and the EcoGothic: The Deep Dark Woods in the Popular Imagination, The, 195n2
fox, 178, 179, 181
Fox, Dominic, 186
Frakes, Kevin, 53
Freud, Sigmund, 10, 11, 59, 61, 62, 63, 72, 86n2, 137, 184–5, 187
Friedkin, William, 62, 71, 86n7, 148
frown, 92, 99
fruit, 14
Fuller, Matthew, 137–8, 139
funeral, 53
Future of an Illusion and *Civilization and Its Discontents, The*, 62

Gainsbourg, Charlotte, 103n2, 173, 183, *191*
Gallner, Kyle, 151
Garden of Eden, 173
Gardner, Kate, 53
Garland, Alex, 51
gas mask, 89, 95, 100
Gayten, 136
gender, xv, xvi, xvii, 55, 69–103, 107–26, 145–65, 181, 188, 190
Gender and the Nuclear Family in Twenty-First Century Horror, 110
genital mutilation, 180
ghost, 8, 22, 26, 27, 28, 37, 40, 96, 149, 152
Ghost Story, A, xiii, 51, 52
Gibson, Mel, 19
Gil, Ariadna, 4
Glazer, Jonathan, 51
Gleiberman, Owen, 51
Gligorić, Aleksandar, 131
goggles, 23
golf course, 185
gore, xiii, 53, 60, 61, 87, 113
Goriunova, Olga, 137–8, 139
gothic, 21, 24, 29, 30, 31, 38, 43, 114, 125n3, 126, 172, 195n2
Grant, Barry Keith, 109

grass, 94, 175, 177, 190
Grau, Michel, xvi, 107–26
Gravity, 172, 189
Green Inferno, The, 113
Green Room, 52
Griffin, Peter, 47n6
Grill, Isabelle, 98
Guattari, Félix, 129–30, 134–5, 137, 138, 139
gun, 119, 153, 154, 155, 156, 158
gun violence, xvi–xvii, 154–5, 156
gynocide, 174, 181

Hallen, Patsy, 181
Halloween, 101
Hamlet, 4, 8
hand, 5, 23, 25, 27, 32, 33, *35*, 35, 36, 37, 38, 39, 42, 53, 62, 83, 94, 97, 98, 115, 116, 117, 119, 127, 132, 135, 176
Hanich, Julian, 174
Happening, The, 172
happy ending, 16, 31
Hårga, xv, 87, 97
Harman, Graham, 179
Harper, William Jackson, 89
Haunting in Connecticut, The, 149, 150–1
Haute Tension, 19
Hay, Peter, 176
heaven, 93, 150, 160
Henshaw, Daniel, 80
Hereditary, xii, xiii, xiv, 49–67, 112
heroin, 131, 134
High Life, 52
Hills Have Eyes, The, 112
Hills Have Eyes Part II, The, 112
Hitchcock, Alfred, 30, 74, 172
HIV, 24, 25, 29, 131, 134
Hodges, John, 51
Hogan, Erin K., 31
Hollywood, 57, 148
Holmes, Alex, 82
homophobia, 116
Hooper, Tobe, 101–2

Horror Comes Home, 153
horse, 185
horse stable, 188
hospital, 54, 109, 173, 178
hospital gown, 120
Hostel, 19
Hour of the Wolf, 50
hug, 77, 97
human sacrifice, 94–5, 98–9, 102
Hunters in the Snow, 182
Hurt, John, 183

Ibarra, Enrique Ajuria, 121
icebox trade, 30–1
ice cream, 80
Ichi the Killer, 19
idealism, 171
Ignatius, Jeff, 34
Ignoffo, Mary Jo, 152
imaginary friend, 37, 149
incest, 114–5, 116
In Fabric, 52
Insidious, 148
instrumental grief, 34, 36, 43
International Self-Care Foundation, 78, 79
Interstellar, 189
In the Dust of This Planet, 171
intuitive grief, 34, 36, 38, 43
Irréversible, 19
isolation, xv, 10, 35, 38, 39, 76, 79, 81, 98, 131, 132, 134, 135, 141, 158, 171
It Chapter One, xiii
It Chapter Two, xiii
It Comes at Night, xi, 51, 52
I Walked with a Zombie, 50

Jackson, Kimberley, 110
Jacob's Ladder (2019), xiii
Janghwa, Hongryeon, 48n7
Janoff-Bulman, Ronnie, 172
Jáuregui, Carlos, 120
Jenkins, Barry, 51
Jersey 2nd Ave, 52–3
Jesus, 59, 146

Jew of Malta, The, 58
Jones, Darryl, 87
Jones, Doug, 6
Jovanović, Mihajlo, 130
Jovanović, Srđan, 131
Jung, Carl, 175

Kamuf, Peggy, 190
Katz, Daniel, 51
Keen, Sam, 60
Kenny, Glenn, 74
Kent, Jennifer, xii, xv, 20, 71–103
Kerr, John, 44
key, 14
Khan, Genghis, 121
Kidman, Nicole, 149
Kierkegaard, Søren Aabye, 56
Killing of a Sacred Deer, The, xi, 20, 52
Kim, Jee-woon, 48n7
King Paimon, 55, 57, 64
King Saul, 146
kiss, 42. 80, 117–8
Klass, Dennis, 11
Knežević, Radivoj, 131
Knight, Jacob, 53
Knudsen, Lars, 53
Kolsch, Kevin, xii
Konkle, Amanda, 72–3, 74, 86n2
Korine, Harmony, 51
Kosovo War, 134, 135, 136, 141
Krlic, Bobby, 103n3
Kroenert, Tim, 31
Kübler-Ross, Elizabeth, 55–7
Kubrick, Stanley, 27, 50, 57, 71

Labris, 136
Lacan, Jacques Marie Émile, 137
Laggies, 51
Lambda, 136
lantern, 187
Lanthimos, Yorgos, xi, 20, 52
lapot, 134
laptop, 36, 38, 88
Lars von Trier, 195n3

Låt den rätte komma. See *Let the Right One In*
laudanum, 152
Leatherface, 44, 102
Lee, Sohyun, 39–40
Lema-Hincapié, Andrés, 111
Let the Right One In, xiii, 48n7
Lewis, Matthew, 126n4
Lewis, Vek, 111
Lewton, Val, 50
LGBTQIA+, xvi, 108, 109, 111, 112, 114, 116, 117–8, 120, 125n4, 127–43
Life After Death (television series), 147, 163
Life and Death of the Porno Gang, The, 127–43
lighthouse, 26, 30
Lighthouse, The, 52
Lodge, Oliver, 161
lonely, 10, 42, 88, 98, 102
Long Weekend, The, 172
López, Sergi, 4
Lord, Catherine, 186
Loss of the Assumptive World: A Theory of Traumatic Loss, 195n1
lottery, 184
Lowery, David, xiii, 51, 52
lullaby, xiv, 4, 17
Lyotard, Jean-François, 183, 186, 188

MacFarlane, Seth, 47n6
Machiavelli, Niccolò di Bernardo dei, 58, 62
machismo, xvi, 110–1, 116, 118, 119
madness, 35, 73, 74, 183, 184
Madsen, Virginia, 151
Magnus, 136, 143n8
Malick, Terrence, 172, 189
mall, 80, 111, 123
mandrake root, 13
Man-Eating Myth, The, 121
Mann, Alakina, 149
mansion, xvii, 21, 24, 29, 30, 31, 38, 43, 154, 158, 162
Mantle, Don, 176

Maori, 145
map, 34, 35, 38, 120
marijuana, 131
Marlowe, Christopher, 58
marriage, 8, 13, 33–44, 95, 109, 111, 114, 158, 183, 190
Marso, Lori J., 180
Marx, Karl, 172
masculinity, 110, 118, 119, 153, 155–7
mask, 28
Massumi, Brian, 138–9
maternal ambivalence, 74
Matts, Tim, 185
May Queen, xv, 92, 97, 98, 100, *101*
McCort, Jessica, 12
McDonald, Keith, 5
McElhinney, Hayley, 77
meatloaf, 186
medium, xvii, 40, 145–65
Melancholia, xiii, xvii, 169–73
melodrama, 95, 113, 114, 125n2–3, 171, 183
Men, Women, and Chainsaws: Gender in the Modern Horror Film, 86n1
Merin, Jennifer, 48n7
Merola, Nicole, 183
Mexico City, xvi, 107–26
Midsommar, xii, xv, 52, 87–103
Miike, Takashi, 19
Miletić, Srđan, 131
Milin, Srbolijub, 132
"militant dysphoria," 186
Millais, John Everett, 182
Milošević, Slobodan, 127, 130, 131, 132, 134, 135, 136, 140, 142n5
minotaur, 121
Mirren, Helen, 151
mirror, 89, 91, 95, *96*, 103n1, 114
Mitchell, Paul, 73
Mizoguchi, Kenji, 67n4
Monet, Claude, 100
"monstrous nature," 172, 173, 176, 181
Moonlight, 51
Moran, Tony, 101
Most Violent Year, A, 51

mother!, 181
Mother Earth, 100, 176, 187
motherhood, xv, 47n4, 71–103, 159
Mother Nature, 176, 180–1
mouse, 26
Munchausen, 52
murder, 58, 109, 114, 150, 155, 159
murder-suicide, xv, 89, 158
Muschietti, Andrés, xiii
mysticism, 55

naked, 187
NATO, 127, 130, 134, 135, 141
nature, 8, 87–103, 169–95
naturhorror, 180, 185
Netflix, 147, 165n2
Newman, Kyle, 51
newspaper, xiii, 35, 36, 152
Ng, Andrew Hock Soon, 42
Nichols, Jeff, 172, 189
Nicolini, Kim, 183, 189
Nightingale, The, 86n5
Nihil Unbound: Enlightenment and Extinction, 186–7
Niš, 136
Noble, Fiona, 5
Noé, Gaspar, 19, 52
Nolan, Christopher, 189
nonlinear, 15, 16
Novi Sad, 136
nuclear family, xvi, 59, 61, 108, 109, 113, 114, 115, 116, 119
Nurseries of Heaven, The, 160

oboe, 24
occult, 65, 113, 149
Omen, The, 74
Onibaba, 67n4
Open Society Foundation, 131
Ophelia, 182
orange juice, 23, 25, 39
Orbey, Eren, xii
Orfanato, El. See *Orphanage, The*
Orphanage, The, xiii, xiv, 19–48, 112
Osment, Haley Joel, 148

Others, The, xiii, 112, 149–50
Ouija, 148
Ouija: Origin of Evil, 148
overdose, 134, 138
Owen, G. Vale, 160

pagan, 55, 59, 64, 92, 93, 94, 97, 102
panic attack, 88, *96*
Pan's Labyrinth, xiii, xiv, 3–18
paranormal, 41, 150–1, 152
Park, Gene, 91
Parker, Elizabeth, 174, 176, 195n2
Parker, Rozsika, 74
Parkes, C. M., 172
party, 81, 91,
Passion of the Christ, The, 19
pathetic fallacy, 24
patriarchy, 64, 107–26, 128, 132, 135, 137, 139, 141, 155
Patterson, Cleaver, 162
peephole, 98
Perkins, Oz, 52
Perlich, John, 6
Peter Pan, 32, 43
Peterson, Christopher, 187, 190
Pet Sematary (2019), xii
photograph, 39, 154, 161. *See also* Polaroid
piano, 22–3, 24, 32, 33, 35, 39
Picture of Dorian Gray, The, 114
pill, 23, 25, 29, 40
pizzeria, 89
phone, 34, 35, 88, 89, 102
physician, xvii, 25, 158
Pixar, 189
planetary collision, 182, 185
"plant horror," 172
Polanski, Roman, 110
Polaroid, 38
police, 34, 38, 63, 78, 108, 113, 119, 126n5, 132, 134, 135, 136
Polo, Marco, 121
Poltergeist, 40
Poplars on the Epte, 100

possession, xiv, 62, 64, 71, 72, 74, 75, 81, 82–3, 86n7, 147–8, 149, 151
post-Enlightenment, 64, 170, 184, 191
Poulter, Will, 89
Power, Nina, 181–2
Prado, Ignacio M. Sánchez, 122
Pride Parade, 128, 136–7, 143n9
Príncep, Roger, 21, *24*
prostitute, 107, 116, 117, 119
Protestantism, 59
psilocybin mushrooms, 94–5, 133
psychiatrist, 151
psychic, 149
Psycho, 30, 74, 117
Pugh, Florence, 87, *96*, *101*
Puig, Claudia, 21
purgatory, 150
pyromania, 55, 58

Quigley, Karen, 22
Quigley, Paula, 76, 86n2

radio, 35, 38
rain, 38, 84
rainbow-washing, 137
Rampling, Charlotte, 183
Rank, Otto, 56
rape, 86n5, 113
Raymond: Or Life After Death, 161
rebirth, 15, 59, 120, 190
Reich, Wilhelm, 59
repression, 56, 59, 62, 72, 80, 82, 83, 84, 112, 116, 157
return of the repressed, 72, 75, 122
"revenge-of-nature," 172, 181
Reynor, Jack, 89
ritual, 92, 94, 95, 102, 107, 108–9, 112, 113, 116, 117, 119, 120, 121, 122, 123, 134, 162, 184, 185, 190
Robbins, Anne Manning, 160
Romero, George, 111
Room, 51
rose, 42, 43
Rose, Steve, 53
Rosemary's Baby, 110, 113

Rosenblatt, Paul C., 15–6
Rosenthal, David M., xiii
Roth, Eli, 113
Rousseau, Henri, 176
Ruda, Belén, 21
Ruins, The, 172
Rusnak, Stacy, 115, 123
Russell, Lorena, 113

Šabac, 136
Sabbadini, Andrea, 3
Sacco, Noah, 53
Sahlstrøm, Storm Acheche, 173
Saint Anthony, 30, 31
Sami, 93
Sánchez, Sergio G., 21, 47–8nn7–8
San Francisco, 151, 163
satanism, 146
Saulnier, Jeremy, 52
Saw, 19
Scandinavia, 88, 90, 91, 92, 93
scar, 133, 158
Schepelern, Peter, 170
schizophrenia, 54, 55, 58, 61, 62
school, 63, 74, 77
Schopenhauer, Arthur, 56
Schubart, Rikke, 6, 12, 16
Scorpio (constellation), 184
Scream, 109, 110
Screen Gems, 52
Scrubs, 22
séance, 32, 40, 54, 149, 160
Searchlight, Pictures, 52
Second Sex, The, 88
Sedgwick, Eve Kosofsky, 126n4
self-care, xv, 71–103
self-harm, 133, 157, 158, 175
self-violence, 174
Serbia, xvi, 127–43
Serbian Orthodox Church, 136
Shapiro, Milly, 54
Sharrett, Christopher, 50
Shaviro, Steven, 135, 184
Shelton, Lynn, 51
Shindo, Kaneto, 67n4

Shining, The, 50, 57, 71
Shults, Trey Edward, xi, 51, 52
Shyamalan, M. Night, 72, 148, 172
silence, 26, 91, 132, 191
Silverman, Phyllis R., 11
Sinnerbrink, Robert, 170, 175–6
Sixth Sense, The, 72, 110, 148
Skarsgård, Alexander, 183
Skarsgård, Stellan, 183
slasher, 20, 60
sleep, 21, 22, 26, 30, 43, 47n1, 74, 76, 78, 79, 80, 90, 96
sleepwalking, 58, 61
smile, 33, 37, 91, 92, 96, 99
Smith, Carter, 172
Smith, Paul Julian, 114
Snook, Sarah, 152
snow, 89, 90, 102, 173
Sobchack, Vivian, 113
Socialist Federal Republic of Yugoslavia, 127, 132, 134, 135, 140
social media, 52, 163
social worker, 24, 78, 84
soldier, 10, 133, 149, 150, 154
Somos lo que hay. See *We Are What We Are*
Soper, Kate, 176
Spanish Civil War, 3–18
Spanish Flu, 163
Spierig, Michael, xiii, xvi–xvii, 145–65
Spierig, Peter, xiii, xvi–xvii, 145–65
Spinoza, Baruch, 138
Spiritualism, 146–65
Spring Breakers, 51
Spurr, Cameron, 186, *191*
Stalker, 50
Starry Speculative Corpse, 171
Stefansky, Emma, xii
St-Georges, Charles, 25
Stoker, Bram, 114
Strange Thing about the Johnsons, The, 52
strangle, 83, 181
Strickland, Peter, 52
Subero, Gustavo, 110, 118, 122, 125n3

sublimation, 62, 88, 92, 99
suicide, xiv, xv, 29, 31, 89, 132, 134, 138, 140, 152, 150, 151, 152, 154, 155, 156, 158
Superman (character), 23
Superman logo, 47n2
supernovae, 187
Sutherland, Kiefer, 183
sweater, 40, 43, 88
Sweden, xv, 87–103
sympathy, 28, 41, 89, 118, 119, 120, 123

taboo, 12, 44, 114, 116
Take Shelter, 172, 189
Tammi, Emma, 20
Tarkovsky, Andrei, 50
Tarr, Béla, 189
taxi, 108, 111
telescope, 187–8
television, 35, 36, 38, 52, 80, 135, 163
Tenochtitlan, 113
Tentacles Longer Than Night, 171, 180
Terrible Child, 74
Tevis, Joni, 152
Texas Chain Saw Massacre, The, 101–2, 112
Texas Chain Saw Massacre 2, The, 112
Thacker, Eugene, xvii, 169–195
Thousand Plateaus: Capitalism and Schizophrenia, A, 129–30
thunder, 24
tianguis, 123
title sequence, 21
toad, 13
tombstone, 8
torture porn, 19, 20
toxic masculinity, 154, 156
train, 103n2, 118, 133, 175
Travels of Sir John Mandeville, The, 121
tree, 11, 13, 14, 84, 94, 95, 100, *101*, 133
treehouse, 55, 59, 64, 74
Tree of Life, The, 172, 189
Tristan und Isolde, 182
Turin Horse, The, 189

Tynan, Aidan, 185

Ugetsu, 67n4
Ulrich, Skeet, 109
uncanny, 13, 26, 88, 177
Underground Realm, xiv, 3, 4, 7, 8, 11, 13, 15, 16
Under the Skin, 51
United Nations, 78
Unsolved Mysteries, 163

Vargas, Carlos Gerardo Zermeño, 111
Varsamopoulou, Evy, 12
vaudeville, 127, 133
vault, 24
Verdú, Maribel, 6
Vespucci, Amerigo, 121
vibrator, 80
Victorian Era, 126, 150
Vince, Alexander, 149
violin, xi, 89, 98
virgin, 109
voiceover, 4, 7
vomit, 82, 83, 111
von Trier, Lars, xiii, xvii, 103n2, 169–95

Wagner, Wilhelm Richard, 182
Walden, Jennifer, 91
Walker, Michael, 42
WALL-E, 189
Walpole, Horace, 126n4
Walter, Tony, 157, 159
Wan, James, 148
Wanderings of a Spiritualist, The, 161
Warren, Ed, 150–1
Warren, Lorraine, 148, 150–1
watch, 15, 111, 116, 117, 118
We Are What We Are, xvi, 107–26
wedding, 183, 184, 185, 187
wedding band/ring, 33, *33*, 35, 36, 39
Weisman, Alan, 189
West, Alexandra, 8, 13
West, Barbara, 77
wheelchair, 6, 35, 99
White, Rob, 188

White, Stiles, 148
Widmyer, Dennis, xii
widow, 71, 153
Wilde, Oscar, 114
Williams, Tony, 111
Willis, Bruce, 110
Winchester, xiii, xvi–xvii, 145–65
Winchester, Sarah (real-life person), 145–65
Winchester mansion, xvii, 145–65
Winchester Repeating Arms, xvi, 145–65
Wind, The, 20,
Winspear, Ben, 72
Wiseman, Noah, 72, *75*
witch, 146, 174, 180, 181, 184
Witch, The, xi, 52, 53
witchcraft, 146, 149, 181
Wolff, Alex, 54
womanhood, 87–103
Wood, Robin, 122

woods, 8, *9*, 9, 96, 102, 103n2, 112, 133, 169, 173, 174, 175, 177, 180, 185, 190
World Health Organization, 78
World War I, 149, 150, 161, 163, 165n2
"world-without-us," xvii, 169–95
World Without Us, The, 189
worm, 84, 190
Wright, Bob, 4, 8, 9–10, 11, 12–3, 14–5, 16

yarn, 185, *186*

Zinoman, Jason, xi, 112
Život i smrt porno bande. See *Life and Death of the Porno Gang, The*

Žižek, Slavoj, 114
Zogović, Bojan, 131
Zolkos, Magdalena, 174–5, 178–9
Zombie, Rob, 19

About the Contributors

Erica Joan Dymond is an assistant professor of English at East Stroudsburg University, with a PhD in English from Lehigh University. She has been a consulting editor for the peer-reviewed, academic journal *The Explicator* since 2011. She has also acted as a manuscript reviewer for the Amazon Breakthrough Novel Award as well as a peer-reviewer for Focal Press, Routledge, and Columbia University Press. Her work has been published in academic journals such as *The Journal of Popular Culture* and *The Explicator*. Likewise, her work appears in academic texts such as *A Cuban Cinema Companion* and *The Encyclopedia of Japanese Horror Films*. She is co-editor of *The Encyclopedia of Sexism in American Films* (Rowman & Littlefield 2019) and the forthcoming *The Encyclopedia of LGBTQIA+ Portrayals in American Films* (Rowman & Littlefield 2022) as well as *Reclaiming the Tomboy: The Body, Identity, and Representation* (Lexington 2022).

Aspen Taylor Ballas holds a master's in the Humanities with a concentration in visual studies from the University of Colorado at Denver. She works as an instructor in the Humanities and Social Sciences at Northern New Mexico College. While cinema serves as her primary area of research, her work in visual studies extends to fine art and popular media. Her work is largely influenced by critical theory, decolonial thought, race studies, Marxism, and existentialism.

Michael Brown is a film and media scholar and early-career researcher based in Brisbane, Australia. Recent publications include "The Thing in the Ice: The Weird in John Carpenter's *The Thing*" for the Irish *Journal of Gothic and Horror Studies* and "The Demon Pazuzu as Noise in *The Exorcist*" for *Revenant Journal*. His area of interest includes sound studies, the weird, pessimism, horror, and the gothic. His chapter entitled "Sonic Arcanum: Sound, Ritual and Magic in Contemporary Horror" will appear in *The Routledge*

Companion to Horror and Media Studies. He is currently researching archive horror.

Megan DeVirgilis is a Cuban American scholar and educator. She received her PhD in Spanish from Temple University and is now an assistant professor of Spanish in the Department of World Languages & International Studies at Morgan State University. Her research focuses on the relationship between ideology and cultural production, with a special focus on gothic aesthetics in Latin American literature and film. Her current book project on female vampires in Latin American and Spanish gothic-inspired tales of the early twentieth century is funded by the National Endowment for the Humanities.

Andrija Filipović is associate professor of Philosophy and Art & Media Theory at the Faculty of Media and Communications, Singidunum University in Belgrade, Serbia. They are the author of *Arsahumana: Anthropocene ontographies in the 21st century art and culture* (2022), *Conditio ahumana: Immanence and the ahuman in the Anthropocene* (2019), and monographs on Brian Massumi (2016) and Gilles Deleuze (2015). Their articles appeared in *Sexualities, The Comparatist, Contemporary Social Science, Journal of Homosexuality, NORMA*, and a number of edited volumes. Their research interests include environmental humanities, queer theory, and contemporary continental philosophy and aesthetics. They are executive editor of *AM: Journal of Art and Media Studies*.

Andrew Grossman is the editor of the anthology *Queer Asian Cinema: Shadows in the Shade*, an editor of *Bright Lights Film Journal*, and a columnist for *Popmatters*. He has contributed book chapters to numerous anthologies, including *New Korean Cinema* (University of Edinburgh Press), *Asexualities: Feminist and Queer Perspectives* (Routledge), *Chinese Connections* (Temple University Press), *Hong Kong Horror Cinema* (University of Edinburgh Press), *Trumping Truth* (MacFarland), *Alice in Wonderland in Film and Popular Culture* (Palgrave), and *East Asian Film Remakes* (forthcoming from University of Edinburgh Press). He also directed a feature documentary, *Not That Kind of Christian!!*, which appeared at the 2007 Montreal World Film Festival.

Racheal Harris is a PhD candidate in sociology at Deakin University, Australia. Her doctoral thesis examines spiritual experiences and afterlife beliefs as they relate to the continued bonds between women and their companion animals. More broadly, her research interests relate to any topic which explores religious belief and spirituality, both historically and in contemporary society. She has published widely on these subjects.

Todd K. Platts is professor of sociology at Piedmont Virginia Community College. He published extensively on horror cinema. He recently co-edited *Blumhouse Productions: The New House of Horror* (University of Wales Press 2022). He is currently editing an anthology on *The Conjuring* Universe and writing a monograph on zombie cinema.

Lindsey Scott is lecturer in English Literature at the University of Suffolk, UK, where she teaches adaptation studies, children's literature, and gothic horror in young adult fiction. She is the co-editor of *Investigating Stranger Things: Upside Down in the World of Mainstream Cult Entertainment* (Palgrave 2021), and her work has appeared in edited collections and academic journals including *Literature/Film Quarterly*, *Cinephile*, and *Shakespeare Survey*.

Rebecca L. Willoughby earned her PhD in English and Film Studies from Lehigh University and is an assistant professor in Student Success at Bloomsburg University in Pennsylvania, where she teaches courses in writing, literature, and film. Her research focuses on gender and sexuality in horror cinema, particularly in the slasher film.

www.ingramcontent.com/pod-product-compliance
Lightning Source LLC
Chambersburg PA
CBHW021353300426
44114CB00012B/1213